Managing the Business Environment

Linda Bennett

INTERNATIONAL THOMSON BUSINESS PRESS
I T P® An International Thomson Publishing Company

London • Bonn • Boston • Johannesburg • Madrid • Melbourne • Mexico City • New York • Paris
Singapore • Tokyo • Toronto • Albany, NY • Belmont, CA • Cincinnati, OH • Detroit, MI

Managing the Business Environment

Copyright ©1977 Linda Bennett

First published by International Thomson Business Press

I(T)P® A division of International Thomson Publishing Inc.
The ITP logo is a trademark under licence

British Library Cataloguing-in-Publication Data
A catalogue record for this book is available from the British Library

First edition 1997

Typeset by Photoprint Typesetters, Devon
Printed in the UK by Clays Ltd, Bungay, Suffolk

ISBN 1861521766

International Thomson Business Press
Berkshire House
168–173 High Holborn
London WC1V 7AA
UK

International Thomson Business Press
20 Park Plaza
13th Floor
Boston MA 02116
USA

http://www.itbp.com

Contents

Introduction

Managing the Business Environment combines an exploration of the four major facets – Political, Economic, Social and Technological. These underpin the business environment and interlink to form the complex set of circmstances within which all organizations perform, with an attempt to generate an awareness in the reader of how these elements can be managed so that suitable strategies to accommodate them are developed. It is therefore essential reading for any student or business practitioner who is embarking on a study of business strategy. While not a short book, it is not intended to be exhaustive in its approach; it attempts to furnish readers with a sound and stimulating framework, from which they can go on to pursue the concepts further on their own. It therefore supports and encourages the methodology of 'Student-Centred Learning'. It is specifically intended to act as a preparatory text before the student progresses to a specialized book on strategic management.

The text is aimed at students and readers from a wide range of cultural backgrounds, and examples are taken from businesses and not-for-profit organizations operating in all parts of the world. The main thread of the text is enhanced throughout with 'key concepts', which enlarge upon, reinforce or summarize important ideas as they are introduced, 'boxes' which provide further elucidation or explanation, and 'mini-case studies' which offer practical examples to illustrate conditions, problems or opportunities as they are being discussed. Some of these mini-cases will be expanded into full-length case studies in the Lecturer's Resource Manual that accompanies this book.

The book therefore has a very broad subject-matter, but there is one linking theme throughout the text: the idea that organizations (of whatever type) continue to exist, to justify themselves, and to develop with the ever-changing world only if they succeed in adding value for the customer at a price which he or she is willing to pay. **Adding value** is the continuous sub-text of this book. Within each chapter, the notion of adding value is discussed as it relates to the particular area of the environment that is being studied. The author believes that this is the key business management theme of the 1990s, a period in which managers, 'specialists' and entrepreneurs in all types of organization have been obliged to consolidate their resources, to shave away costs, and generally become more creative and ingenious at making more out of less.

The book therefore provides an invaluable text for lecturers and students seeking a truly relevant approach to the current business environment. It can act as a key linking text for today's modular courses, and although it is primarily intended for business studies degree students and non-specialist business students – for instance, those 'majoring' in accountancy, computing, hospitality management, etc. – who are required or have chosen to take one or more business modules as part of their degree, it is also a suitable foundation text for MBA and DMS students, particularly those with no previous management or business education background.

THE ARRANGEMENT AND USE OF THE TEXT

Chapter One explains in detail what is meant by the 'adding value' theme, what the main elements of the business environment are, with examples of the relevance of each, and how addressing them involves knowledge of the various strategic options available. Some modern approaches to strategy are also briefly explained and illustrated. It is essential that all students therefore read this chapter, so that they are thoroughly conversant with the concepts of **adding value** and **strategy**.

The five chapters which follow can be taken as separate entities, and used to provide information and generate debate for business environment modules. Alternatively, they can be read consecutively or out of sequence to form an entire business environment course in their own right (the original intention when the book was conceived), with a continuing emphasis on adding value. Some MBA and DMS courses have now developed a 'link' module on 'adding value', and the text is clearly particularly apposite for these. There is some occasional overlap in the information contained within the chapters, as the author strongly believes that this is preferable to a complicated system of cross-referencing, which would not lend itself to reading out of sequence.

Chapters Two and Three. It was necessary to divide what began life as one chapter on **politics** into two, not only because the original chapter grew increasingly long and unwieldy, but also because it became evident that there were two major themes to address. These are the broader aspects of political theory and ideology, which lead to government policies that shape the ways that organizations behave, and a more practical consideration of the major political organizations and alliances that exist in the world today, and how they influence the economic environment. (Because it is important for the student to understand why the modern world economic environment exists as it does, reference has been made to some now obsolete organizations – notably, COMECON – since their influence is still being felt in the geographical areas where they were powerful, and, indirectly, in the world as a whole.) Clearly, the power balances within the organizations discussed in Chapter Three shift and change all the time; however, it is more important for the student's understanding of world economic issues to be furnished with enough examples illustrating **how** national and international political groups gather and wield power, rather than to have a snapshot picture of the particular power balance which prevails at the time of study (if, indeed, this is possible). It is therefore the chief aim of these two chapters to give the student a competent insight into the theory and practice of national and world politics as they affect the organization seeking to add value. He or she can then make informed inferences about new situations as they occur.

Chapter Four arises naturally out of Chapters Two and Three, since the economic measures which governments take are directly related to their ideological beliefs, and the particular power structure that they are trying to create. This chapter on the **economic** aspects of the business environment does not pretend to be a substitute for the study of economic theory, which all mainstream business students (whatever their level of study) will address in greater depth elsewhere. The chapter does, however, offer a basic grounding in economics within the context of adding value, not only to demonstrate the relevance of economic theory in the wider business environment (a point that students sometimes lose sight of when they become enmeshed in the graphs and calculations of some of the more nitty-gritty economics exercises), but also to introduce the subject of economic theory in as straightforward a way as possible to non-specialist students and the business practitioner. The emphasis throughout is therefore on economic theory as it contributes to or hinders the notion of adding value.

Chapter Five looks at the changing **social** context within which organizations operate. Continuing with the 'making more out of less' theme that forms one of the main strands of the philosophy of adding value in the 1990s, it looks at 'flat' organizational structures, new ways of arranging and managing the workforce, new relevances to modern working life (in particular, the management of the 'knowledge worker', or highly-educated specialist) and at the motivational and economic issues that need to be addressed if the changing organization is to be able to reinvent itself successfully in the twenty-first century. 'People issues', having enjoyed a renaissance in the 1960s, have too often since been dismissed as 'soft', 'woolly' or 'irrelevant' in the tougher economic climate of the 1970s and 1980s. This chapter argues that the business managers and leaders of tomorrow need to take them seriously (not sentimentally) if they are to build successful organizations capable of adding value to meet the sophisticated demands of the next century. In some ways, this is the most important chapter in the whole book, and should be read carefully in conjunction with any of the other chapters used.

Chapter Six provides an introduction to the vast range of **techno-logical** issues that confront the manager of today. It makes the point that technology as the route to adding value takes many guises, from the simple to the complex, but that the use of information technology (IT) holds the most wide-reaching implications for the manager of the future. The chapter looks at IT not simply as the provider of tools to be used to add value more efficiently, but also as an agent to radically reshape the way in which the organization thinks about and builds itself. Thus, drawing both on the 'social' chapter which precedes it, and looking forward to the chapter 'Strategies for adding value' that follows it, the concept of 'business re-engineering' is discussed. This chapter introduces mainstream management students to a radically creative and integral approach to the use of IT. It also provides an invaluable insight into the broader environment for information technology and computing students, who may eventually be involved in designing some of the computer systems and software for the styles of organization described.

Chapter Seven. The final chapter, 'Strategies for adding value', begins by examining in closer detail the traditional functions of the organization itself. The marketing, finance, operations, IT and personnel functions, and the role of the strategic leader, are discussed, each within the context of adding value and the wider context of issues arising in the previous chapters. The relevance of strategy to structure is then explored, and the work of some of the key strategic thinkers of the past 20 years introduced. The chapter attempts to draw together the threads of all the preceding chapters, not by alluding to their subject-matter in any detail, but by emphasizing the need for a strategic approach, underpinned by a suitable structure and organizational philosophy. This is in order to create a resolution of (or strategic 'fit' for) the issues raised by an all-round awareness of the external environment. It therefore picks up on some of the strategic approaches raised in Chapter One: there is more cross-referencing between Chapters One and Seven than between other areas of the text, and they can profitably be used as preliminary reading to a more specialized text on strategy (e.g., John L. Thompson's *Strategic Management: Awareness and Change*). This is a logical progression for the student to make when he or she has reached the end of this book.

EXERCISES AND REVISION TOOLS

There are some suggestions for exercises and further topics for research scattered throughout the text, but the main vehicle for applied learning is intended to rest with the mini-cases. These are meant to be used as starting-points for class discussion or individual study. Careful reading of them will illustrate the relevance of the models, theories and approaches to management described in the main text to the 'real-life' situations described in the cases. They update the student with regard to the particular organizations or industries to which they refer, which in turn obliges the student to become familiar with the financial press, on-line business information services, and other contemporary sources of information.

What is adding value? 1

LEARNING OBJECTIVES

- To define the concept of adding value, and explain what it implies for for-profit and not-for-profit, servicing and manufacturing organizations.
- To grasp the idea of the value chain and the value system, and demonstrate a clear understanding of the associated issues of objectives and stakeholders, and the concepts of core competencies, culture, systems and synergy. This will follow on from an understanding of Michael Porter's exposition of the value chain as it is applied to specific examples of individual industries.
- To give a brief account of what is meant by 'performance measurement'.
- To gain an insight into the key concepts of competitive advantage and competition within industries, referring to the work of Michael Porter, John Kay and others.
- To decipher the acronym PEST, and understand the elements which make it up, and how they may together be used to analyze turbulent and changing external environments.
- To understand the significance of the structure and values of the internal organization in the successful carrying out of the added-value process.

This chapter gives you a rudimentary knowledge of a range of strategies for adding value.

INTRODUCTION

Why do organizations **exist**? What are humans busy **doing** when they go to work? If you were the hypothetical Martian, looking down from your alien planet, how would you explain the flurry of human activity which humans call 'work', and which involves the expenditure of resources, both tangible (e.g., raw materials, energy, buildings) and intangible (e.g., skill, know-how, commitment)? What is it all **about**?

If you took one perspective, you might conclude that work is about making money. Fine; but what about the vast number of 'not-for-profit' organizations in the world? All right, then, you might refine your original idea of profit by stating that organizations in which people work provide something, and in return receive a reward – financial or non-financial – depending on their nature. This, too, is true as far as it goes, but it doesn't succeed in capturing the economic realities of the situation. Can a reward of any size be demanded? How small a reward is acceptable? By what criteria is it, or should it be, determined that the reward will be paid?

By pondering on this, you are likely to reach a very important conclusion: that all resources, natural, man-made or human, are in limited supply. Those that are not finite will replenish themselves only if they are utilized in a sustainable way. For reasons we examine in detail later, organizations are likely to continue to have access to those resources only if their outputs are **effective** and **efficient**, as well as **economical**. Therefore, it is necessary for organizations to **target** and to **measure** as precisely as possible what they do. How can they do this? In order to arrive at an answer, let us return to the original question: **what** do they do?

Now the answer may be clearer. Organizations have to **add value** for the customer. As we shall see later in this chapter, in order to achieve long-term success, they have to add value for a range of stakeholders. Satisfying the needs of the customer is the lynch-pin of all of their activities, because it is the customer who pays and therefore generates the wealth which keeps the organization going. They add value by offering the customer what he or she wants at a price that he or she is willing to pay; but this cannot be any price. The price must be set at a level that will ensure that the organization can flourish in the present and develop for the future.

Thus, adding value is a complex process: complex, because determining what activities will prove valuable enough to the customer is both an art (in the sense that a creative approach is needed) and a science (because some careful measuring of inputs and outputs is called for); complex also because the value-adding activities take place within a series of intra- and inter-organizational configurations. What is meant by this will emerge as the book progresses, but a starting point is the understanding and acceptance of the idea that no organization can exist or operate within a vacuum: it affects and is affected by its wider environment. Let us take the case of this book. Figure 1.1 shows in diagrammatic form the main value-adding activities which enabled you to gain access to your copy. Let us examine them in detail.

ADDING VALUE: AN EXAMPLE

In the first place, the book was conceived of and written by the author. This particular book is intended for management education. The

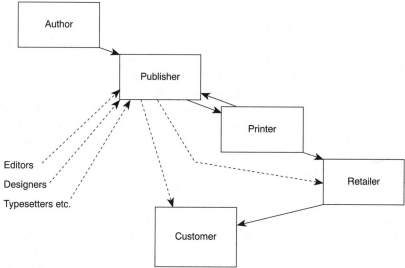

Figure 1.1 The notion of added value: the book.

author added value by presenting management ideas with up-to-date examples in a way which the customer – the student – would (hopefully!) find understandable, relevant and enjoyable.

The text was then submitted to the publisher, who added value again by deploying a range of skilled staff to make the text as clear and pleasant to use as possible. This staff will typically have included editors to rearrange the text, perhaps to give it a 'house style'; designers to make it look attractive on the page, and typesetters, who have the technological skills to carry out their instructions.

When the publisher was satisfied that they had added the maximum possible value to the author's original script, it was submitted to the printer, who brought a new range of value-adding skills to make the manuscript into a commercial product. The printer may or may not have employed a separate agent to bind the resulting volumes. He or she will certainly have submitted an example of the finished product to the publisher for comment and approval before embarking on the complete print run.

The next and perhaps most significant question of all in the value-adding process will have been how to reach the customer. This necessitated two sets of value-adding activities: the first set, traditionally conducted by the marketing department, will have been intended to make both the retailer and the ultimate customer aware of the book. This awareness-raising may have been carried out by advertising, by making sure the book was included on bibliographical databases, and by employing a sales force to promote it. Usually, all these methods will have been employed. The second series of activities, which may have been undertaken by the publisher or a subcontracted agent, will have consisted of storing and distributing the book so that it reached the retailers (scattered throughout the country, perhaps through many countries) at the right time.

The final value-adding activity before the book reached you, the customer, will have been its classification, display and promotion by either a bookseller or a librarian. The value that they will have added, as well as making you aware of the book, will have been associated with their professional expertise, and your confidence in the body of acquired knowledge on which they will have drawn to select this book, as opposed to another. In the case of the textbook, this knowledge will probably have been gained through contact with the academic staff likely to refer you to the book.

This is not the end of the process, for in order that the author can continue to produce books that are relevant to your needs, and perhaps enable the later updating of this book, your reaction as a customer is needed. This, in fact, is where the publishing industry experiences more problems than some other industries. Good feedback mechanisms from the customer are difficult to put in place, but publishers do gain some information – from sales figures, obviously; from, in this case, feedback from lecturers and librarians; and (sometimes, but not as frequently as in other industries) from market surveys.

KEY CONCEPT 1.1: THE VALUE CHAIN

'In competitive terms, value is the amount buyers are willing to pay for what a firm provides them.'

'The value chain disaggregates a firm into its strategically relevant activities in order to understand the behaviour of costs and the existing and potential sources of differentiation'.

(Porter, Michael, 1985)

Companies gain competitive advantage by performing all the activities described by the value chain either at a lower cost or better than their competitors (the two variables are not necessarily mutually exclusive).

Figure 1.3 provides an illustration of the activities embraced by the value chain and their relationships to each other.

The following text offers brief descriptions of the nature of these nine value chain activities as identified by Porter (1985).

Primary activities

● **Inbound logistics**
Connected with receiving, storing and redistributing raw materials, 'inbound logistics' therefore includes warehousing, inventory control and arrangements with suppliers.

- **Operations**
  What many people would identify as the 'main activity' of the company – the transformation of inputs into the final product form. This includes production, assembly, packaging, testing, etc.
- **Outbound logistics**
  Concerned with storing the product and distributing it to buyers. Therefore involves all distribution activities, order processing and scheduling.
- **Marketing and sales**
  Porter defines this area of activity as 'associated with providing a means by which buyers can purchase the product and inducing them to do so'; later writers might add that this is a two-way process, and that working closely with the buyer determines the form that all other activities take. There may in many industries be a seamless continuation between marketing and sales and service.
- **Service**
  See above. In Porter's terms, this includes providing service to enhance or maintain the value of the product (or, it might be added, the customer's perception of this), for example, with regard to installation, repair, training, etc.

  Clearly, the relative importance of each of these activities depends on the type of organization being analyzed and the nature of the industry within which it functions; almost all organizations will, however, carry out each of these kinds of activity to some degree.

Support activities

- **Procurement**
  Porter emphasizes that this refers to the purchasing *function*, not to the purchased inputs *per se*. Therefore, what is being described is the procurement 'technology' – whom should be dealt with and how, channels of communication, etc. Procurement in its true sense is spread throughout the firm, and includes the acquisition of intangibles such as expertise. Although the cost of the actual procurement activities may be relatively insignificant, **what** is purchased and **how** has a profound effect, not only on the organization's costs, but also on **how it adds value and pursues excellence** (in the form of differentiation or low cost – i.e., what the customer wants).
- **Technology development**
  This is not synonymous with Research & Development, Information Technology Development, or the application of

scientific subtechnologies. Rather, it includes all of these things. It is concerned with any of the practical (scientific or artistic) skills related to producing the organization's output. This may include activities relevant to individual primary or support activities. In some industries, it may hold the key to competitive advantage.

● **Human resource management**
This is a crucial and sentitive part of the value chain. It includes all the activities involved in the recruitment, training and deployment of personnel. It also includes tasks related to individual primary and support activities (e.g., the recruitment of technicians, secretaries and so on), and the development of policies and decisions that affect the value chain (union negotiations, company codes of practice). Inconsistencies, which may cause frictions, are almost inevitable, and it is likely that variables – such as costs of training vs. employee turnover – are imperfectly understood. Clearly, effective human resource management is the linch-pin of all value-adding activities.

● **Firm infrastructure**
According to Porter, writing in 1985, firm infrastructure consists of:

> 'A number of activities, including general management, planning, finance, accounting, legal government affairs and quality management'.

Therefore, it is driven by a blend of structural and cultural imperatives. Porter also says that in some organizations it is merely viewed as 'overhead', but that it can be a powerful source of competitive advantage. Up-to-date thinking might take these points further, and claim that the infrastructure of the organization is what determines its ability to build intra- and inter-organizational linkages successfully. It is both the philosophy and the enabling mechanism that powers the adding-value strategy.

Activity types

Porter adds that within each category of primary and support activities, three activity types can be separated out:

1 *Direct* – e.g., assembly, parts machining.
2 *Indirect* – e.g., maintenance, scheduling.
2 *Quality assurance* – e.g., monitoring, reworking.

Finally, Porter stresses the interdependence and interconnectedness of the value chain:

'Although value activities are the building blocks of competitive advantage, the value chain is not a collection of independent activities, but a system of interdependent activities. **Value activities are related by linkages within the value chain'**.

MERCHANDIZING THE BOOK: HOW NEW CHANNELS OF DISTRIBUTION MAY RECONFIGURE THE VALUE SYSTEM IN THE PUBLISHING INDUSTRY

In 1992, Proctor and Gamble decided to bring the merchandizing of its Cover Girl cosmetics range inhouse, leaving two sophisicated merchandizing – or rack jobbing – companies, Thomas Cork, SML and Aspern Field Marketing, looking for a new line to put into supermarkets. Simultaneously, they decided on books.

The retail grocery sector is very competitive: every square inch of retail space is minutely monitored, and products moved and removed to maximize profits. The supermarket chains are ruthless on margins, taking ever larger volumes, shaving the suppliers' profitability on orders to the bone. Many suppliers have foundered, partly because the supermarkets expect very high levels of service from their merchandizers, and partly because it is hard to be profitable if you are putting only a single line of product into a chain of stores.

Aspern and Cork had the advantage of diversity: Aspern's clients include Vodafone and Rowntree's; Cork is a subsidiary of the largest pet accessories company in the world. Aspern and Cork believed that they could give a better quality of service than existing book merchandizers, and therefore Cork took over Calder, and Aspern took over Foreword, the two leading suppliers. The mergers created a flood of returns to publishers, as the new owners introduced new disciplines.

Andy Mitchell, the Aspern sales director, said: 'We asked them which of their accounts had plannogrammes (a plan which shows exactly how much space should be given to each title in each store; how many face-out displays each title should take up, which shelf it should be displayed on and how many copies of each title should be there. Both Aspern and Cork adhere to these strictly). They said "none, the reps have total autonomy to do what they want."

'The rep would go in and say: "You need some top titles there. What have we got in the van?" It would not be targeted to the outlet.

'What we have been trying to do is to ensure that the product is matched to the customer walking through the door. We can have the right product for the right store; we can measure the results immediately so that we know what does and does not sell.'

The ability of Cork and Aspern to provide top revenues per foot of shelf space has convinced the supermarkets that they can make money out of books; but the level of 'returns' to publishers associated with the new generation of merchandizers is higher (since titles which don't 'perform' are not tolerated), and the publishers have felt it. There has been talk about putting an end to sale-or-return agreements with supermarkets to solve the problem; but in all probability that would deter supermarkets from stocking books at all.

The more intelligent answer may lie in publishers accepting the need to work more closely with wholesalers. One of the wholesalers' executives said:

> 'What we would like to see is all publishers working closely with us, asking us where product is going and wanting to know what other product they produce can find a market .... . When they commission product, on what basis do they commission that product?'

For some publishers, looking at books in this way may come as something of a shock; if they can get over the shock, they may discover that forging new partnerships will add more value for the customer; it will also change the shape of the publishing industry itself.

Source: Gasson, Christopher (1994) 'Putting publishers on the rack', *The Bookseller*, June 3rd.

Themes arising from the value-adding process

A number of themes emerge from this simplified account of the genesis of a book:

- A **chain of activities** is involved, which requires co-ordination and co-operation from a large number of people working in many different but complementary organizations.
- Each part of the chain, whether represented by an individual or a group of people, is motivated by a set of **objectives**, or purpose. These form a subset of the overall objective of producing the book that the customer requires at a price that he/she will pay. Thus, the designers want the book to look beautiful, but know that they must not charge for more of their time than the market will bear; the printer wants his/her work to bear the hallmark of quality, but must choose paper which the customer will like, yet which will not tip the price beyond what is felt to be affordable. Each of these operators within the value chain is a **stakeholder** of the final production. Their objectives are likely to differ, but it is important that the differences can be resolved sufficiently for the maximum of added value to have been achieved at every stage. This is often not easy, and frequently involves accommodating or manoeuvring round internal (and sometimes external) politics. There are other stakeholders besides those

involved in the creating process, including customers and competitors of the organization. (Key Concept 1.2 explains **objectives** and **stakeholders** in more detail; Case 1.2 examines the concepts within the context of the British Coal Corporation in 1993.)

KEY CONCEPT 1.2: OBJECTIVES AND STAKEHOLDERS

Objectives can be set at two levels: they can define the broad purpose of a company, and they can also provide specific and measurable milestones indicating progress towards an overall objective, purpose or 'mission'. Additionally, they may act as constraints. Objectives may usefully be arranged in a hierarchy, graduating from the general to the very specific, detailed and quantifiable.

What influences objectives?

Objectives may be 'official' and planned; but they are also influenced and determined by the personal, cultural, political and ethical drives and perspectives of **stakeholders**. Drucker says that an organization's objectives should address eight main areas: market standing, innovation, productivity, physical/financial resources, profitability, manager performance/development, worker performance/attitude and public responsibility. Jauch and Glueck propose that objectives are influenced by:

- forces in the environment and external power relationships
- internal resources and power relationships
- the value system of top executives
- awareness of management of the past development of the firm.

These influencing factors lead directly to questions about the stakeholders:

- Who are the stakeholders (generic groups/specific individuals or groups?)
- What is the nature of the perceived stake?
- Do individual stakeholders play more than one role?
- Are groups of stakeholders interconnected?

Stakeholder theory

Freeman defines stakeholders as any group or individual who can affect, or is affected by, the accomplishment of organizational purpose. This concept can be represented diagrammatically as a stakeholder map. In a stakeholder map, '+' relationships are positive, or likely to have a beneficial influence on the fulfillment of the organization's objectives; '−' relationships are negative, or likely to have an adverse influence; and ' = ' relationships are neutral, or not likely to have an influence.

Case 1.2 gives a stakeholder map, with explanatory text, for British Coal.

CASE 1.2

THE STAKEHOLDERS OF BRITISH COAL IN THE SUMMER OF 1993

In 1993, the British Government published a White Paper entitled 'The Prospects for Coal'. This fuelled the controversy concerning decisions about the future of the British Coal industry, including numerous questions about UK energy policy, government competence, the nature of supply and demand for coal, and the objectives of the decision-makers, the British Coal Corporation (BCC) and the British government.

Figure 1.2 offers a stakeholder map describing all those who took part in this controversy. It will be seen that the framework is a useful shorthand device for capturing the complexity of their interrelationships. The **objectives** that preoccupied the major **stakeholders** are summarized below:

BCC's board objectives

BCC aimed to reduce capacity while increasing productivity at its 'best' pits in order to minimize costs and maximize short-term profit. Nineteen pits fell into this category. BCC regarded the remainder of its pits to be a drain on the profitability of the rest, and therefore wanted to close them immediately. BCC's decision to close mines was probably at least partly motivated by the need to prove that mines were profitable in the short term, in the run-up to privatization.

BCC wanted to modify its working practices, which had been constrained by the law for 80 years, and particularly to put in place a more flexible workforce. Since this would be fiercely opposed by the unions, BCC's stated objective of minimizing costs in order to be more competitive would also fulfil the unstated 'political' objective of reducing the impact of union opposition by demoralizing the workforce.

Multiple objective conflict

On the one hand, as we have seen, the board of BCC had the objective of maximizing short-term profits by selling off uneconomic mines; on

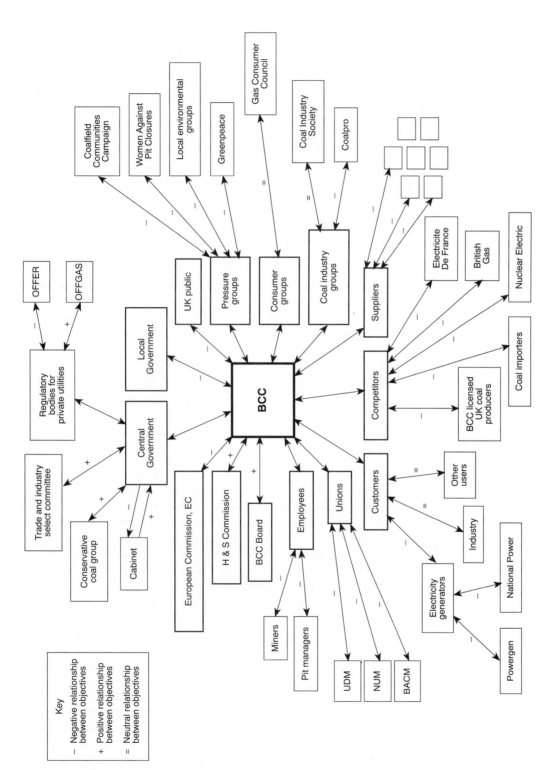

Figure 1.2 BCC stakeholder map.

the other hand, they had the objective of maximizing market share by reducing possible sources of competition. Therefore, by making it clear that private mining contractors would be rigourously examined before they would be granted mining licences, and that any operations licensed would be policed, the board hoped that some potential applicants would be deterred.

Central Government objectives

'Competitive markets provide the best means of ensuring that the nation has access to secure, diverse and sustainable supplies of energy in the forms that people and businesses want, and at competitive prices'. (White Paper, 1993).

The highest-priority objective of the government was therefore to privatize BCC at the earliest opportunity; in order to do this, they were prepared to undertake commitments that did not make economic sense, such as subsidizing the power generating companies who were British Coal's largest customers. Therefore, another complicating political factor emerged: that the government may have been more concerned with the political ideology of privatization, and possibly with the extra revenue that it might eventually bring to the Treasury, than with their avowed belief in competitive markets. There was a yet more 'unofficial' possible hidden agenda: that the government was influenced by a desire to turn the tables on the miners after the prolonged strike of 1984.

Multiple objective conflict

The government was the owner of BCC and a major shareholder in the two generating companies, which were the principal customers of BCC. The dual role could have been used by the government to aid BCC by redressing the power balance – i.e., by not giving extra help to the power generators, who, as customers, were in the strong position. However, the government chose not to do this, and also set in motion plans to sell its stake in the power generators, thus eventually intending to remove its influence upon the latter.

As owner of BCC, the government was responsible for appointing the BCC board, and could therefore directly influence the range of views expressed by that board. This accounted for the extent of congruence between the objectives of BCC and the government.

Conservative Coal Group objectives

The Conservative Coal Group was formed by 30 Conservative backbenchers who strongly disagreed with the proposal to close 31 mines. Their predominant fear was that, in future years, Britain might lose its capacity for domestic coal production, exhaust all supplies of natural gas and oil, and then be held captive to the prices of imported fuel.

The objectives of the Group were therefore to advocate the measures outlined by the Select Committee to enable BCC to compete in a fairer market. In this sense, they supported the objectives of BCC (hence '+' in the stakeholder map).

Multiple objective conflict

The Group members obviously had loyalty to the government, which enjoyed only a small majority. Although they could have turned the latter point to their advantage, by threatening withdrawal of their support, in practice no party member wants his or her party to be defeated in the Commons. Therefore political expediency was likely to become an overriding objective.

Unions

The main objectives of all the unions involved were to gain security of employment and safe working practices. They were sceptical about BCC's aims on both counts, and therefore implacably opposed to proposed changes in work organization. A further objective was that of securing a British coal industry for future generations. The unions felt that BCC and the government had set too high a priority on short-term profits. Therefore, as the stakeholder map indicates, there was considerable conflict in the (perceived) objectives of the two groups.

Multiple objective conflict and associations with other stakeholders

Members of unions were also employees, members of pressure groups, and members of the UK public at large. Some conflict might have arisen between these roles, though it was likely to have been on points of detail rather than major shifts in attitude.

The British public objectives

The British public is by definition a very broad-based group, embracing many different views. The prevailing opinion that seemed to emerge from the debate in 1993 was that the country required from BCC a secure, efficient and environmentally sensitive contribution to an effective overall national energy strategy. Given the situation in 1993, this would conflict with BCC's profit objective.

A brief assessment of the stakeholder approach to BCC

The stakeholder map offers a framework within which the complex analysis of BCC's objectives, its stakeholders and their objectives could be examined meaningfully and clearly. It helps to explain that there was considerable conflict even at the broader levels in the hierarchy of objectives. It also helps by indicating that there were other strategic options that BCC could pursue, based on the alternative views of what its objectives should have been. Finally, it emphasizes the fact that the power to pursue any of these options lay mainly in the hands of the government at that time.

Source: adapted from work undertaken by Marie Kerr, The University of Huddersfield, 1993.

DETERMINANTS OF THE VALUE-ADDING PROFILE

The idea of core competencies

- It will have become evident from the processes described in producing a book that at each stage the publisher has to decide whether it is more appropriate to use in-house expertise, or to 'outsource' the skill or function required. This decision has to be made in all types and sizes of organization, and is commonly known as the '**make or buy**' decision.

In the 1990s, writers on management have emphasized the need for organizations to focus on what they are good at – in the words of Peters and Waterman, to 'stick to the knitting'. This may indicate the desirability of outsourcing activities that are not part of the organization's central areas of expertise – such as distribution, in the case of publishing – so that the organization can focus better on its key areas of expertise. The key capabilities and areas of expertise within a company have been called its '**core competencies**' by Prahalad and Hamel (1990). It is, however, most important – and by no means always a simple task – to identify with accuracy what those core competencies are; an organization which decides to stop developing activities which may contribute to its future competiveness is clearly making itself very vulnerable.

Therefore, when it is making the 'make or buy' decision, the organization is also making a **strategic** decision: it is identifying the nature of its core activities, and thus deciding which skills it should invest in in order to pursue these, and which are peripheral and can therefore be both safely and effectively outsourced. Outsourcing, however, does not mean that the organization can wash its hands of the particular activity concerned; it means developing a close relationship with the organization whose expertise it is tapping into. Most organizations need to develop a series of these relationships; in some the resulting inter-relationships grow into **networks** of great complexity.

An introduction to the concepts of culture, systems and synergy

- Respect and understanding is needed between all parties contributing towards the final product. This requires, not only an understanding of each other's objectives and expertise, but an appreciation of the **culture** of the organizations involved. Key Concept 1.3 offers some approaches towards appreciating the idea of 'culture'.

- Following on from this, it will be evident that the group of activities required to produce the book form a **system**, which may be broken up into a series of **sub-systems**. In order for value to be added with the maximum of effectiveness and efficiency, it is imperative that there are both strong communications channels and enabling good will (shared values) informing these sub-systems.

KEY CONCEPT 1.3: CULTURE

In organizational terms, what is culture? Schein offers the following definition:

> '[Culture is] the deeper level of assumptions and beliefs that are shared by members of an organisation, that operate unconsciously, and that define, in a basic taken-for-granted situation, an organisation's view of itself and its environment'.

Simply – and yet complicatedly – it is the **way** that people in an organization do things, and the way in which the organization itself goes about performing its tasks. It therefore consists of a set of **beliefs**, widely shared, about how people should behave at work, and a set of **values** that order goals and tasks in terms of their importance.

Some of the behavioural patterns of an organization have been deliberately formulated, but many of them are unconscious. Induction into an organization for a newcomer can be a lengthy and painful process. The message, partly overt, but probably more inferential, is 'This is the way we do things here'.

Some organizations are very keen on creating the right image, and promoting what they believe they are 'about' – e.g., clean workspace, fast attention to customers. As long as this is not overdone, it does not intrude upon the consciousness – but it is **there**. It is not noticed in the same way as places that are untidy or inadequate – e.g., shops with empty dispensers, receptionists who are rude or who fail to answer telephones immediately.

Positive attributes like these – even though, individually, they might be quite minor – contribute to the adding-value process. Even though people may not be able to put their finger on the reason why they like dealing with the organization, the feeling is still there, and it can be very important. It can also help the organization to iron things out when mistakes are made.

The great and consistently successful organizations of the west (e.g., Royal Dutch Shell, Proctor and Gamble, Marks & Spencer) became great because they developed strong cultures. However, there is one caveat: it is important to get the culture right as well as strong. A culture that is strong and wrong for its environment will send the organization heading for decline.

From the many studies of corporate culture, three main types can be identified:

1 Power culture.
2 Role culture, or bureaucracy.
3 Task, or organic culture.

The generic culture type which has gained most favour in recent years is the task (organic) culture, championed by writers such as Rosabeth Moss Kanter and Peters and Waterman. The other types have lost ground because, with the exception of the entrepreneurial start-up venture (which needs the drive), organizations based on the exercise of power are becoming less acceptable to educated, thinking employees; while bureaucracies cannot cope with rapidly changing conditions, and do not provide enough career challenges.

Can corporate cultures be changed?

Both theory and practical experience suggest that this is possible, but crisis which **demands** a response may be needed before a real change can occur. The role of the organization's leader is fundamental to successful cultural change.

Pumpin suggests the following parameters be used to establish the nature of an organization's culture:

Attitude to customers	How marketing-oriented is the company?
Attitude to staff	How do they communicate with superiors? How much are they encouraged to participate?
Attitude to results and performance	How target-oriented are the staff?
Attitude to innovation	Does the organization encourage it? Is it accepted that people have to learn, to some degree, through failure? (The people who fail in big things, through negligence or ineptitude, are fundamentally different from people who 'have a go' and fail)

Attitude to costs	Are costs reduced without sacrificing quality? (Remember, low cost doesn't mean 'cheap')
Attitude to the organization	Loyalty and commitment?
Attitudes to technology	How important is technology and progress with technology to the organization?

Note: It is important to remember that there is no one right way of doing things, nor one right set of attitudes to have: the 'best way' can only be what is appropriate for the organization.

We consider the importance of systems later in the book. For the moment, it is necessary to emphasize that if each of the value-adding activities identified makes the maximum possible contribution to the final product, the set of interdependent linkages that have been achieved themselves produce a final factor – a quality resulting from the network of relationships that cannot be accounted for by the simple 1+1+1 effect of building activity upon activity. This quality is known as **synergy**, which can be defined as 'more than the sum of its parts'. It is also sometimes expressed as the 2+2 = 5 factor.

It is worth spending a little time considering the concept of synergy. Synergy defines how a company is going to succeed in its present and future ventures by identifying the match between its **capabilities** and the **opportunities** that are available to it. Igor Ansoff (1988) says that synergy is derived from both the economic benefits of economies of scale, and from what he terms 'managerial synergy'. Simply explained, managerial synergy is the application of experience and knowledge gained in one business to a new area of activity, with resulting benefits. The opposite, or 'negative synergy', occurs when managers enter unfamiliar businesses, or try to apply inappropriate solutions. The potential for a particular organization to achieve synergies depends on its own capabilities in each of the areas in which it operates. Hiroyuki Itami (1987) views synergy as the process of making better use of resources. He identifies two types of resource:

- physical assets, such as manufacturing facilities
- invisible assets, or 'intangible resources' such as brand names, knowledge of customers, expertise in a technology.

The latter he considers to be more valuable to the organization, because they are difficult for competitors to copy. They also have the advantage of benefiting from, rather than being depleted by, frequent use. Therefore, according to Itami, achieving synergy means gaining a 'free ride', since there is no cost attached to exploiting this type of asset. Such a free ride might be gained by a publisher who was able to achieve substantial advance sales of a new book because of the reputation the author had already achieved with his or her previous work.

Itami points out, however, that while many companies overlook the possibilities of synergies altogether, some are tempted to overestimate the benefits that they are likely to gain, and therefore try to justify the development of unprofitable products.

THE VALUE CHAIN

The elements which have been described so far are incorporated within what has been called the '**value chain**'. The value chain concept has been explained in detail by Michael Porter (Key Concept 1.1.).

Example 1: The publishing industry

Now that you have studied the idea of the value chain, you may find it useful to examine our example of the book more specifically within its context. Figure 1.3 represents the value-chain of producing the book in diagrammatic form.

Let us begin with the **primary activities**. The primary activities are the sequence of physical actions which result in the organization's end product – in this case, the book.

Inbound Logistics

There are two parallel sets of raw materials which need to have value added to them in order to result in the net product of the book: the book as the intellectual creation of its author, and the book as artefact (that is, either a collection of paper, boards, illustrations, glue and ink; or an assembly of electronic components). Different types of resources (involving human skills and technological investment) need to be commissioned or deployed by the publisher in order to arrive at the end product. Despite the fact that they may be committed by financial advances and binding contracts, authors may not produce the goods on time, or, sometimes, not at all. Therefore, the publisher takes on an element of risk even at this stage. A good relationship between the author and publisher (usually personified by the editor) is essential.

In order to remain competitive in the essential arena of providing value for money, the publishing house is obliged to encourage and promote innovations in typesetting, printing, paper and ink, or, alternatively, electronic developments. Some of these may be 'outsourced', in which case monitoring the suppliers' quality and prices becomes part of the publisher's value-adding activities.

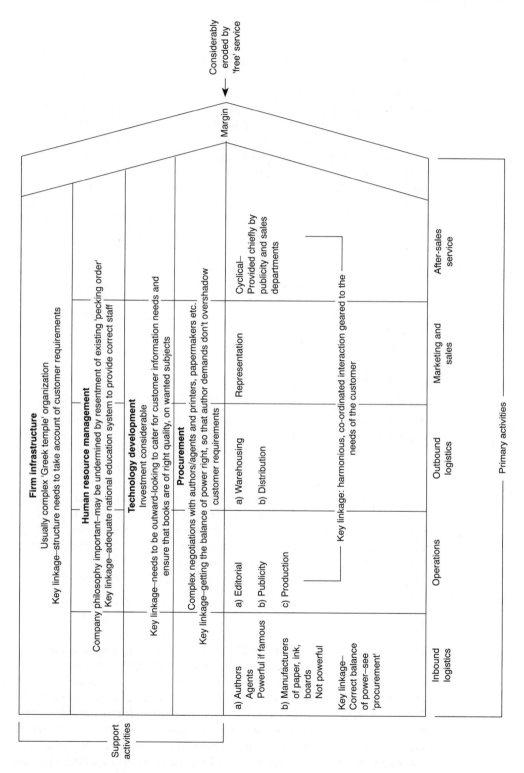

Figure 1.3 Value chain diagram of the production of the book.

Operations

When the typescript has been edited, the 'operations' stage is reached, at which the book requires further intellectual skills expending upon it in order to promote it. Advance information about its forthcoming publication is needed by key customers, especially the large retailing chains, academic bookshops and library booksellers. Details about the author, his or her track record, opportunities to meet him or her, and other information and incentives designed to make the new book as interesting as possible (thus adding 'intangible' value) have to be disseminated by the publicity department. Between them, the editorial and publicity departments are also responsible for keeping a checklist of the whole of the publisher's output, including what material is currently available. This may be stored in a printed catalogue or electronic format, and also needs to be passed on and kept accurately up to date with data-holding bodies such as Whitaker's *Books in Print*, the national book cataloguing agency. Contributing to data banks adds value in another oblique way, by providing the customer with access to a comprehensive range of products from which he or she may choose.

Outbound logistics

Distribution in the book industry demands a further complex infrastructure of warehousing, order sending and receiving, and delivery activities. Once more, these may or may not be performed 'in-house', and whether they are or not, these activities need monitoring, since it is the publisher's responsibility to ensure that their wares may be accessed easily by each of the remaining customers (wholesalers, booksellers, librarians, individual book-buyers) in the value chain. There is a danger that some publishing houses, because they do not perform these activities themselves, or perform them at a distance, fail to understand this responsibility, because they perceive that their primary task is to produce the book, not to distribute it. The vital imperative of 'keeping close to the customer' is clearly significant here.

Marketing and sales

In publishing, marketing and sales are typically performed by a specific department. This department has to liaise with the editorial and publicity departments, who are principally involved in 'operations'; and, as typically, is often made to feel or is considered to be 'inferior' to them. There may be a clash of objectives, since editorial and publicity staff are mainly concerned with authors' needs and requirements, while marketing and sales staff are principally concerned with those of the customers. Marketing and sales staff may feel further aggrieved by the fact that sometimes 'key' accounts are serviced by Head Office – not always a wise decision, since it is the task of the representative also to deal with complaints and carry requests to 'return' unsold stock (an unusual provision both widespread in and peculiar to the book trade). Clearly, for the value-adding process to gain the maximum of impetus, any points of conflict need to be resolved by referring to the only logical criterion – namely, how best to serve the customer. (The book industry is atypical here, however, because the author can also be regarded as a 'customer' of the services which the publisher provides.)

After-sales service

Whether the publisher is dealing with wholesalers, booksellers or librarians, the after-sales service is the link in a continuous cycle, in which the publisher's representative tries to create new opportunities for a new sales cycle while dealing with the problems of previous sales cycles on the same visit. This is where all the value-adding activities are tied together, including 'intangibles' – for representatives also try to make sure that the booksellers and so on are getting the right information in the right quantities at the right time from the editorial and sales departments, and act as messengers for complaints about warehousing and deliveries.

Next we approach the **secondary activities**, that is, the set of norms and values which dictates how the organization is governed and the cultural 'rules' which it observes.

Firm infrastructure

The formal and informal structures of the publishing house, and its 'culture', all of which are implied by this term, necessarily vary in complexity according to its size and scope, but, except in the smallest companies, are generally intricate. Because of the range of skills needed to enable the company to function, it tends to have what Handy terms a 'Greek Temple' management style – that is, power is diffused through the 'pillars' of the organization, but is also considerable at the top. The latter may be felt to the extent that it militates against the added value philosophy: some publishing companies seem 'top heavy' under scrutiny, with decisions sometimes made by senior executives (often drawing high salaries, given the profit margins) without sufficient reference to the grass roots staff and customers.

Human resource management

An acceptance of the company philosophy at all levels is important. Porter remarks on inequalities of staff treatment almost inevitably taking place in all types of organization, and publishing is not an exception. In all except the youngest and most informal publishing houses, a 'pecking order' among and within departments can be observed, with the editorial department traditionally taking precedence (though their right to prime place is increasingly being challenged by sales). Sometimes, the resulting dissent may be healthy, and contribute to the value-adding process by helping everyone within the company to keep their focus on the customer; at others, obvious rifts may appear, which are damaging to the company once they become observed by those with an interest in it, but standing outside its immediate boundary (that is, customers, suppliers, and so on.)

Technological development

All publishers are obliged to invest in technology, and are dependent on computers for almost every aspect of their operations. In order to remain competitive, they also have to be prepared either to invest in, or to seek out and monitor suppliers of, continually improved book-producing techniques, such as new methods of reproducing photographic illustrations, cheaper 'inserts', and so on, which add value. A shortcoming of some publishers is that they do not always choose to support the wider technological developments of the book-disseminating **value system** in which they operate – for example, tele-ordering, the electronic ordering system available by subscription to all booksellers and publishers. Those who don't support technological refinements of this kind are detracting from the value-added process for the industry as a whole.

Procurement

Refer both to what Porter says about 'procurement' in Key Concept 1.1, and to 'inbound logistics' at the beginning of this section. Not only is procurement complex and diverse, but it is usually carried out on an international basis, regardless of the nationality of the publishing house or the language in which it is publishing. It involves, on the one hand, negotiating with authors and their agents (where the balance of power is determined by the author's prestige), and, on the other hand, with suppliers of ink, paper, board, etc., and possibly 'book-packagers' or assemblers. Competition tends to be cut-throat in these fields, which means the publisher is normally at an advantage.

The Margin

The primary activities, buttressed by the support activities, lead to the creation of the 'margin' which produces the profit. For the publisher, as for any other business organization, this is achieved by performing a juggling act with the resources, involving elements of luck and calculated risk as well as demanding a highly-developed perception of the potential for synergy; if this synthesis is successful, value is added at every stage for which the customer is prepared to pay. In common with other organizations, the margin is partially created by the provision of a number of 'free' services, the contribution of which is difficult to calculate. Publishers have two main adjusting financial mechanisms: the discount which they give to booksellers, and the royalty which they allow authors. In neither do they enjoy a free hand, since the level of both payments is influenced by the relative power of the other party involved.

THE VALUE SYSTEM AND OPPORTUNITY COST

We have already touched on the concept of the value system within the context of the technological development 'supporting activity'. The value system consists of the total series of value chains created – in this instance in order to produce and sell the book, by the publisher and all related and supporting industries. Thus, the bookseller has a link in the value system consisting of his/her own value chain of activities; the printer, paper producer and librarian have others. The linkages between these diffrerent elements of the value system are crucial to the overall value-adding process; and, as we shall see later, are currently altering the 'shape' of organizations themselves.

The value system does not operate in a vacuum; it is influenced by, and will itself influence, the broader external environment within which it has, at least, to survive, and strives to flourish. In the broadest sense, the business environment consists of the entire world; as progress in technology and communication accelerates, the world daily becomes (in practical terms) a smaller place.

We have considered the input of raw materials into a value chain. These materials may be tangible or intangible: human ingenuity continues to find ways of exploiting almost every substance, situation and geographical area, however unpromising it may seem. There is a price to pay for this ingenuity, both by the individual organization (at the micro level) and by national and international business communities (at the macro level). The simple fact is that some resources are finite; and those that are not will replenish themselves only if they are treated with respect. This means that organizations are in competition with each other for resources – be they tangible, such as raw materials, buildings, and land; or intangible, such as knowledge, expertise, or the cachet of an acknowledged brand name. Organizations that are successful in assembling the required resources for their activities also have to make a crucial decision: how best to exploit those resources. Every opportunity they take to deliver a product or service necessarily means, since resources are finite, that they have passed up an opportunity to deliver a different product or service. The forfeiture of the latter is known as **opportunity cost**.

Stakeholders revisited (i)

How can organizations best equip themselves to choose the activities that will bring them most success, and therefore enable them to continue to assemble resources to produce further products and services? A large part of the answer lies in keeping close to the customer, for whose benefit they are producing, and whose loyalty they are trying to secure. But it is also necessary for them to be aware of the other stakeholders in the organization and to try to accommodate their needs. This means being aware of all the stakeholders involved, establishing effective flows of communication and interaction with them, and gauging the relative amount of influence that they have. Customers are always important stakeholders; so are shareholders, staff and management. There are others whose 'stakes' may be more ambivalent: as Key Concept 1.2 explains, stakeholders may be 'neutral' but powerful – governments, for example – or hostile, such as competitors (who, on the other hand, may co-operate in order to compete – we shall examine examples of this).

Nearer the beginning of this chapter, we focused on the customer. We have now returned to the customer and identified him or her as a chief stakeholder in the value-adding process. To recapitulate, adding value is about creating what the customer requires, at a price that he or she is willing to pay, but which will also give the organization the return it must have to continue its activities, and take into account the needs of the other stakeholders involved.

Example Two: the Car Industry

Let us examine the components of another value chain – one which operates in quite a different way from publishing: that of the car industry. Refer to Case 1.3.

CASE 1.3

THE CAR INDUSTRY

The car industry operates worldwide, but with differing strengths and power balances in various countries and political arenas. The 1990s are expected to be a decade in which the selling focus is directed increasingly towards the demands of customers in newly developing markets, especially in Asia. Customer demands are changing in established markets: for example, in the United States, the passenger market is being shaped by a preference for 'luxury' trucks and robust four-wheel-drive vehicles. The Japanese car companies are seeking to increase their sales in the west by making capital investments in Europe, and achieving their high standards of quality and efficiency by training local workforces in their practices. (see Key Concepts 1.7 and 1.8.)

By 1994, Europe had become the major battleground of the industry. European car makers were being squeezed by what they identified as worldwide over-capacity. Ford lost more than $2bn in Europe in the two financial years 1991–3. Companies were being forced to rationalize or restructure. Workforces were being cut back, or required to work fewer hours. Hard bargains were being driven with components suppliers to cut prices. Although some worthwhile partnerships had been established between competitors in an attempt to decrease costs, the pressures to gain sales had resulted in some ugly battles; for example, in 1993, General Motors accused Volkswagen of industrial espionage.

German companies had experienced particular difficulties with quality and cost. Mercedes-Benz admitted that its luxury executive cars were 'over-engineered' – that is, that they were adding value that the customer did not necessarily need or want to pay for – and that it might end up being 'priced out' of world markets. Volkswagen in 1994 was in the unenviable position of being the highest cost volume car maker in Europe. To combat this, the company was reducing capital investments, putting increasing pressure on its components suppliers, and moving its vehicle assembly plants to other countries, including Mexico, Korea, Spain and the USA.

Erika Emmerich, the president of the German auto federation, said that German companies' problems stemmed from the following factors:

- high labour costs
- high energy costs
- high transport costs
- costs incurred by increasingly sensitive environmental legislation
- the German practice of working fewer hours per day than the rest of Europe
- Germany's higher-than-average taxes.

In Italy, Fiat launched the Punto towards the end of 1993 in an attempt to repeat the record success that it established with the Uno (launched in 1983, when it won the European Car of the Year Award, and still a steady seller ten years later). Punto's success would be essential if the company were to recover the position of market leader in its field, from which it slipped in the late 1980s.

Fiat had invested a tremendous amount of time and money in the effective design and efficient production of the Punto. They were relying on a combination of the following factors to capture the market:

- visual impact
- styling
- the construction of a new factory at Melfi, to ensure both manufacturing excellence and cost competitiveness

- manufacturing flexibility combined with a Just-in-time approach to their suppliers.

The high expenditure on research and development, combined with the major capital expenditure programme (amounting to 4,700 bn Lira) meant, however, that the company was experiencing cash flow difficulties, which were exacerbated by summer sales campaigns intended to relieve outlets of their stock prior to the launch of the Punto. In Italy itself, the market conditions were inauspicious, due to a combination of the economic, political and fiscal factors that issued from the worldwide recession, by which the country had been particularly badly hit, and the fact that foreign manufacturers had gradually eroded Fiat's share of the market.

The European car industry in general had also been forced to take notice of political demands placed upon it, which were originally driven by consumer organizations. The latter claimed that motor manufacturers used their franchized distribution systems (franchized dealers hold exclusive selling rights in the areas in which they operate, and are trained and monitored by the car companies) to stifle competition. They also pointed to a huge discrepancy in pricing between the same products sold in different European states. The manufacturers retaliated by arguing that, both from the safety and from the service perspectives, cars require specialized sales outlets; and that country-by-country comparisons of price lists can be misleading, because they need to take into account a range of complicating factors, such as varying discounts, local taxes, and the types and permutations of 'extras' available to the customer. Nevertheless, in July 1993 the European Commission required manufacturers for the first time to publish pan-European price lists, and it was likely that their block exemption from the Treaty of Rome statute, which prevented manufacturers from operating exclusive dealer systems, would not be renewed after it expired in 1995.

The car of the future would bring its own challenges to the industry. BMW and Mercedes were both experimenting with electric 'city cars' which had the very low emissions of pollutants that were likely to be demanded by coming environmental legislation. In order for these cars to run economically, they would have to be much lighter than today's conventional vehicle, and aluminium would probably be used extensively in their bodywork. This might mean, at least in the short term, that the car manufacturers would not be able to push their raw materials and components suppliers as fiercely for discounts as they had been accustomed to do in the early 1990s, since the resources, including skills, that the latter possessed would be at a premium; yet they would still have to produce the low-emission car with the design features and at a price which would make it attractive to the customer.

Source: adapted from a series of articles which appeared in the *Financial Times*, Sep 1993–Apr 1994)

Figs. 1.4a and 1.4b illustrate the major sequence of activities that takes place in the production, distribution and sale of cars. Car production begins with the design of the product – companies may spend many millions of dollars on this; the money is well-spent if it achieves

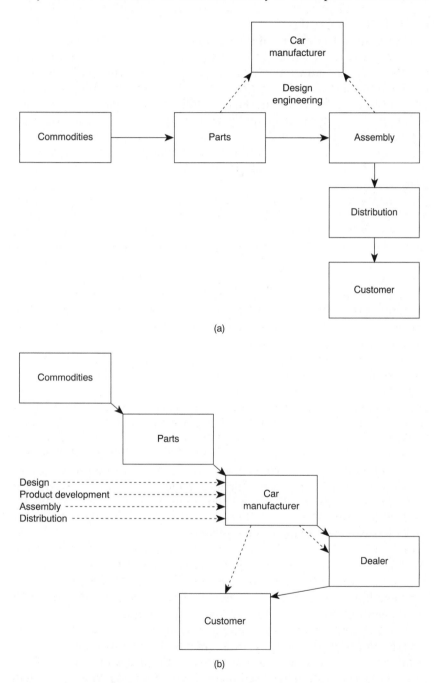

Figure 1.4 a and b The notion of added value: the car.

its objective – that of matching the demands of the customer. In their anxiety to excel, some car manufacturers have actually 'overshot' the demands of the customer by building in features that the customer does not wish to pay for. The technical terms for this is 'over-engineering'. It does not add value; in fact, it could be described as building 'negative value'.

The actual manufacture of the car has increasingly become an international process. Because of the intense competition between car manufacturers in an industry which has overcapacity (i.e., is capable of producing more than the market demands), they are obliged to seek the most cost-effective method of fulfilling each part of the value-adding process. This may mean the setting up of complex relationships, not only with vendors of raw materials and manufacturers of components, but also with other (rival) car manufacturers, so that some of the costs of research and development, design and assembly can be shared.

Political pressures increase the complexity. For example, in 1992 former US President George Bush visited Japan with American car industry executives, and Japanese car-makers agreed to a voluntary agreement to increase their local procurement of US-made car parts. The negotiations concerned the supply of parts to Japanese factories which had been set up in America, and for which components had originally been exported from Japan. It was partly undertaken in order to increase the acceptability of Japanese cars to the American market, partly an attempt to appease complaints that foreign access to the Japanese market was very restricted.

Some years later, the pressures had changed. In the mid-1990s, the greatest pressure on Japanese car-makers was the need to reduce costs and remain competitive. Therefore, they were planning not only to procure parts locally for the factories which they had set up in other countries, but also to import foreign parts for their Japanese operations. In 1994, Toyota was buying 90 per cent of its leather from US suppliers, and 10 per cent of its sheet glass. Mitsubishi Motors was considering buying steel from Korea to reduce costs, and also negotiating to procure the same parts for its Japanese-made cars as it did for those produced at the Diamond Star Motors factory in the US. By 1997, Nissan was planning to increase local procurement of US parts by 75 per cent (estimated value $980m).

Local sourcing of parts is consistent with the Japanese philosophy of efficient production (refer to Key Concepts 1.7 and 1.8), but importing components to Japan is an expedient born of necessity which may have questionable long-term effects (see Chapter Three for a discussion of the dangers of 'hollowing out' national industries).

Just as manufacturers are seeking to acquire components from the lowest cost producers, so they are searching for the most advantageous locations for the assembly of the vehicles. From the beginning of the 1990s, General Motors has used its profitable German subsidiary Opel to set up plants close to the emerging new markets of Asia and Eastern

Europe. Opel has an assembly plant in Turkey, and the Astra, its small family car, is produced in Hungary and Poland. In 1993, assembly of the Astra began in Taiwan; small volume production of the Opel Vectra (a larger family car) began in Indonesia in 1994 and assembly of the Astra started in India in 1995. Manufacturers like General Motors are not just looking for the cheapest and most efficient way of making their vehicles: they are also building networks for getting close to their customers.

Earlier, alliances between rival car manufacturers were mentioned. Such an alliance was set up between Honda, the Japanese car maker, and Rover when it was the UK subsidiary of British Aerospace. Subsequently, British Aerospace sold Rover to BMW, a German car manufacturer that Honda regarded with grave mistrust, and the complex series of supplier (for parts) and licensing (for designs) agreements between the two companies were thought to be in jeopardy. The example shows the pitfalls of such alliances, even though they may be dictated by economic necessity. Just how strong the latter is, however, is illustrated by the fact that the alliance has not in the event foundered. It has simply been hedged about with confidentiality agreements which protect Honda's intellectual property rights and expertise (i.e., the knowledge with which they add value for the customer). However, Honda is taking steps to ensure that the facilities which it gains from Rover in return – notably sheet metal pressing – can be sourced from its own plants in the future.

The final stage in the car industry value chain is that of sales and after-sales service. All the major car manufacturers operate on a 'franchise' basis, whereby they set up a network of dealers allowed to sell their product so that competition amongst dealers in a given geographical area is reduced. The resulting distortion of competition that would otherwise have taken place in a 'free' market has increasingly been regarded with disfavour by governments as they have sought to deregulate industries (see Case 1.3 and Chapter 2 for further details). The car manufacturers argue that franchising is necessary because of the high levels of product knowledge that are required from dealers, and also because of their need to work closely both with the car manufacturer and each other in order to deliver what customers want today, and monitor what they are likely to want tomorrow. It is, however, likely that franchising will come under increasing threat because of the exclusivity which it entails.

FOR-PROFIT AND NOT-FOR-PROFIT ORGANIZATIONS

Throughout this chapter so far, we have talked of 'organizations', though the two examples that we have examined in detail have referred to industries which are operated by 'businesses' – i.e., enterprizes which seek to make a profit from their activities. As we pointed out at the beginning, a Martian might not appreciate that there was a meaningful difference between the activities of a business and some other group engaged in a series of activities – the boy scouts, for exmple. The word 'organization' is at once more precise and all-embracing. Armies, churches, unions, peripatetic acting troupes, schools and universities are all organizations, as well as those entities to which we refer as 'businesses' – whether they are corner shops, or multi-national conglomerates. As Peter Drucker points out, collectively organizations form the constituents of the world that modern man has created for himself: they are the ' "social ecology" of a post-capitalist society'. The fundamental purpose of each one, and each individual within each one, is to contribute added value.

Therefore, although it is commonplace today to distinguish between 'organizations for profit' (a general reference to conventional businesses, though there are some 'hybrids') and 'not-for-profit' organizations (hospitals, social clubs, etc.), the distinction is a spurious one. Currency to continue their activities is the result of the successfully achieved output of all organizations. 'Organizations for profit' usually acquire this in a more direct way – straight from the customer.

MANUFACTURING AND SERVICE OPERATIONS

- A distinction is commonly also made between '**manufacturing**' and '**service**' organizations (and has as a result frequently generated fierce debate about which is the 'real' driver of national and world economic prosperity). Here, the distinction may seem easier to justify. It has been argued that manufacturing is about transforming **resources** into **goods** which can be transported, such as metal/components >>> cars; while service is about transforming **customers** by means of some intangible activity which cannot be transported, and is therefore typically produced simultaneously with consumption, such as hair unstyled >>> hair styled. Reflection may suggest, however, that in few organizations can such a distinction operate in a clear-cut fashion. Banks, for example, may process materials (cash) and turn them to assets (bonds, etc.). They may process information (a 'grey area' – intangible, but still a transportable resource) such as standing order instructions >>> cash paid to a third party at a certain date. But in carrying out these 'manufacturing' activities it could certainly also be argued that they are transforming the customer – in the first instance, by transforming him or her from someone with cash to someone with cash put securely to good use (resulting in a wealthier person with increased peace of mind); in the second instance, by transforming him or her from someone with a debt and the niggling administrative inconvenience of having to pay it on a regular basis, to someone with a debt taken professionally in hand and one chore fewer to worry about.

Even the industries on which much of this chapter has been based – book production and car production – though they may seem to sit squarely within the 'manufacturing' definition – transform the customer at the **end** of their respective value chains (the after-sales process which gives it its iterative nature and provides the lifeblood for its continual adaptation). The content of the book enters the customer's mind, and transforms him or her from someone with a need/desire for knowledge/entertainment to someone with that requirement satisfied. The possession of the car transforms a man or woman with a need or wish for personal transport, or a status symbol, or an aesthetically pleasing or environmentally 'correct' vehicle, depending on his or her particular definition of added value, to someone in that respect fulfilled.

Some 'service' organizations that make an income (it may not be 'profit' in the accepted sense) may be prepared to accept the lowest income that allows them to keep functioning. Their shareholders or patrons, if they have them, are likely also to recognize this, and not expect large or even 'normal' returns for their investment – they, too, are committed to what the organization perceives as its *raison d'être*. Value is added for them by being involved, and by being able to express their commitment (and perhaps receive praise for it). Many arts organizations come into this category. It may seem puzzling in the light of what has already been said about the necessity of adding value at a price which the customer can afford and is willing to pay. The anomaly arises when such organizations – 'experimental' theatre companies for example – cater only for minority audiences who cannot afford to bear all the costs of their activities, but where there is nevertheless a shared perception among the stakeholders (customers and shareholders included) that these activities are worthwhile and should be continued. In such cases, the importance of adding value in order to satisfy **all** stakeholders becomes apparent. (Their uncompromising adherence to their joint values may also be what necessitates the network of financial arrangements by which the organization exists: for example, few avant garde theatre companies would consent to generate income by staging a pantomime, since this would be regarded as breaking faith with their aesthetic ideal.)

The theatre offers a classic example of a service industry – its services are intangible, in the sense that it exists to operate upon the audio-visual senses, mind and feelings of the audience; plays are by definition produced and consumed simultaneously; and the quality or added value achieved depends on the outcome of the service – i.e., the customer's/stakeholder's perception of the delivery system.

The 'after-sales service' element of the value chain in service industries may be subtle and complex. This is important, because it is this part of the value chain which is responsible for generating future consumption. In the theatre, for example, it might be expected that if a theatre-goer likes a playwright, a play, a production, a theatre company or an individual actor, he or she will feel disposed to buy tickets for future performances featuring one or a combination of these factors. It may not be as simple as this, however. In almost all service industries, the personality factor creeps in. The theatre and the film industry offer obvious examples, because of the tendency of audiences to be curious about the lives of people in showbusiness: part of the value that is added for them takes the form of a kind of hero-worship, a larger than life appeal. This 'star quality' can be responsible for generating enormous sales, but can equally be catastrophic if the star 'fails' in some way not directly related to the service that they are providing. At a humbler level, similar problems are encountered by hairdressers, gym instructors and childminders. Those working in service industries need to be aware that it is part of themselves that they are giving to the value chain. Case 1.4 gives an example; Case 1.5 demonstrates how other forms of enterprise can be developed from this phenomenon, and become part of the value system.

CASE 1.4

ADDING VALUE WITH ONE'S LIFE AS WELL AS ONE'S ART

The Dublin Pinter Festival of 1994 received a letter from a feminist group denouncing three of the most famous post-war western playwrights: Harold Pinter, John Osborne and Ted Hughes, because they had 'fatally damaged' three women – Vivien Merchant, Jill Bennett and Sylvia Plath, all of whom died, two by suicide and one of alcoholism, after broken marriages with these writers.

Although the feminist group is extreme in believing that art is an extension of personality, their attitude does reflect a wider belief that the details of the artist's life should be available for public consumption. In an individualistic society, it may be logical for the writer to become a celebrity, almost a consumer icon, as well as the mouthpiece for our current social condition; and it is true that most literature is grounded in personal experience. It may even be argued that it is enriched by familiarity with that experience.

However, such relatively straighforward arguments become blurred by other cultural trends – political correctness, the tendency to conformism, to simplify and to be over-literal. Together, these encourage a conflation of an artist's life and work, and the passing of a moral judgment on both that is not related to the quality of the work itself.

When this type of perspective is taken, the work of the writer who is perceived as victim can be devalued just as much as that of the writer denounced for moral failure. Sylvia Plath, an internationally-renowned poet in her own right, gassed herself in 1963 leaving two young children. The storm of debate which this has engendered ever since about the position of the artist-mother/artist wife and wife-of-an-artist (Ted Hughes) in modern society has prevented serious evaluation of her work beyond those terms.

There is a paradox at work. Art may be timeless and universal; it is received wisdom that it means different things to different people in different ages. An artist's life, on the other hand, is conditioned by his or her time, and by the morality of the moment at which it is examined. Bearing in mind that the artist lives at the same time as those who buy his/her work, and therefore by whose approval he or she seeks to maintain his or her livelihood, how much of his or her 'true' self ought he/she to be expected to share with them? Or, to put it another way, in today's age of rapid media coverage on every possible subject, is a more sophisticated response required concerning the details of his life from the artist's 'customer' than the way in which it is frequently presented to him? Could one value-adding medium (e.g., the press) be cannabalizing or at least damaging another ('quality' literature)? (It is interesting that writers of 'popular' literature do not suffer from similar problems – their lives are allowed to be as scurrilous and lurid as they like!)

It is a truism that artists rarely lead lives which we would call 'normal'. They have always stood on the edge of society, and needed an ambivalent position as outsiders to distil, from their art, experiences which we can all share. They may or may not mind 'sharing' their lives with their 'customers'. But if, by doing so, the work which is their primary product is likely to lose its value, they may be trapped by a no-win situation: either they will be able to produce fine work but not sell it; or they will be constrained to lead 'respectable' lives, but lose the inspiration for the work.

Source: Adapted from Wullschlager, Jackie (1994) 'Danger of linking life and art', *Financial Times*, 6 June.

CASE 1.5

EXTENDING THE VALUE SYSTEM: THE VALUE ADDED BY THE 'PAPARAZZI'

'Paparazzi' is the quasi-disparaging, quasi-showbusiness name which has been given to professional photographers who specialize in taking photographs of famous people and selling them to newspapers and magazines. Paparazzi will go to great lengths to obtain 'scoop' photographs; they sometimes jump on to the bonnets of cars transporting their quarries, and a photographer once wrenched open the door of a cab containing John Cleese, the British satirical comedian, and began firing a flashgun in his face.

In the more sober 1990s, publications no longer pay the huge prices which routinely changed hands for photographs in the 1980s: in 1994, an unusual picture of a member of the British royal family might command £400; one of a film star leaving a night club, £75. Competition is fierce – there might be 40 photographers who have taken a similar shot, and each hopes that there will be an individual quality about his or hers that will make it sell.

It seems a hard way to make a living: why are so many people prepared to loiter for long hours on freezing pavements, when the outcome may either be no picture at all, or a picture that won't sell? The answer lies in their aspiration to chance upon the 'big shot' which would really add value by capturing public imagination and titillating curiosity – for example, a photograph of the Queen being escorted by someone other than the Duke of Edinburgh.

> 'That would be the ultimate picture in the world ... [it] would be worth at least £100,000 in this country. And abroad – well, it would be worth a million, maybe more.'

Bread-and-butter sales abroad from their archived materials are chiefly what keep the British paparazzi going. One of the better established has 300,000 pictures of royalty and celebrities. Photographs of the pop mega-star Madonna, for example, continue to sell steadily for several years in different parts of the world, and one may generate an income of £5,000 during the course of its life. A photograph of Joan Collins, the glamorous American film star, looking distinctly unglamorous as she shopped in London wearing a headscarf, made £8,000 from sales in all the countries in which her television soap operas had been shown.

Clearly, despite the uncertainty of their existence, the paparazzi have created a thriving entrepreneurial industry. They certainly meet the criterion of adding the value that the customer wants, and can sometimes command astoundingly high prices for this. The only question which remains is one of ethics. Should all forms of adding value, provided that they operate within the law, be encouraged?

Source: Macalister, Malcolm (1994), 'Paparazzi at work', *Livewire*, Jun–Jul.

MEASURING PERFORMANCE

We have put forward the proposal that ultimately all organizations are about adding value, and that they all need approval from their customers in order to generate present income for future activities. It is therefore vital that they measure their success in as exact a way as they possibly can. Clearly, different organizations will need different specific criteria to help them to determine how successful they are. The

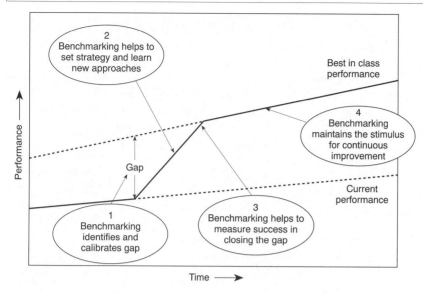

Figure 1.5 The concept of benchmarking.

practice of **benchmarking** can offer them the necessary tools (Figure 1.5).

Benchmarking was originally conceived as a way of measuring what the organization did against industry best practice; the most forward-thinking organizations are now finding this approach too narrow, and are seeking also (or instead) to benchmark themselves against best practice in other (possibly related) industries. Building societies, for example, as they increase the range of their activities, are comparing the way in which they add value to certain products with the way in which those products are delivered by banks and insurance companies.

KEY CONCEPT 1.4: BENCHMARKING

Benchmarking is the process of comparing business practices and performance levels between organizations in order to identify opportunities for making improvements.

By benchmarking performance levels, it is possible for the organization to identify and calibrate its performance gap (see **Fig. 1.5**). Benchmarking focuses upon understanding processes, determining how superior performance is achieved by others, and developing a strategy for closing the gap.

Benchmarking can be used throughout the supply chain of an industry, examining business relationships both within the organization, and with customers and suppliers; and it is increasingly being used to compare performance between industries. It can be applied in any situation where a function, process or activity is performing below expectations, or simply because the organization is committed to the idea of continuous improvement. (Though, as with any performance improvement technique, the greatest benefit is likely to be achieved by focusing on those areas of the business that are critical in driving competitive success.)

Benchmarking places emphasis on understanding the processes that deliver performance, and best practices in relation to those processes. The most profitable learning points are often discovered from organizations outside the industry.

The technique of benchmarking was developed by Xerox after they discovered in 1983 that their competitors, Canon, were retailing photocopiers at less than Xerox's own manufacturing cost. They sent a benchmarking team to Japan to compare their performance with those of their Japanese counterparts in a wide range of areas, and returned home to implement the measures they had learned.

Xerox realized that this approach need not be confined just to manufacturing, nor to direct competitors, and began to look at best-in-class companies in order to understand how they tackled a diversity of processes.

Leading-edge benchmarking is not therefore about comparison (since this is clearly not helpful when different industries are involved), but about processes and what can be learnt from them from those who conceive of and implement them with an extraordinary degree of excellence.

Source: Coopers & Lybrand (1993) *CBI Survey of Benchmarking in the UK*.

Stakeholders revisited (ii)

Ultimately, all measuring techniques are trying to establish how to add value for the customer at the least possible cost, and to charge for it a price which he or she will pay. It should be remembered that this cannot be achieved unless the demands of all the stakeholders are assessed and accommodated as far as possible (trade-offs will almost certainly be necessary, made on the basis of the relative power balance held by each stakeholder group; customers, shareholders and staff are all likely to exhibit a large influence on the stakeholder configurations for most organizations). Case 1.2 illustrates and explains a stakeholder map for British Coal. Fig. 1.6 offers a stakeholder map for the Toyota car company.

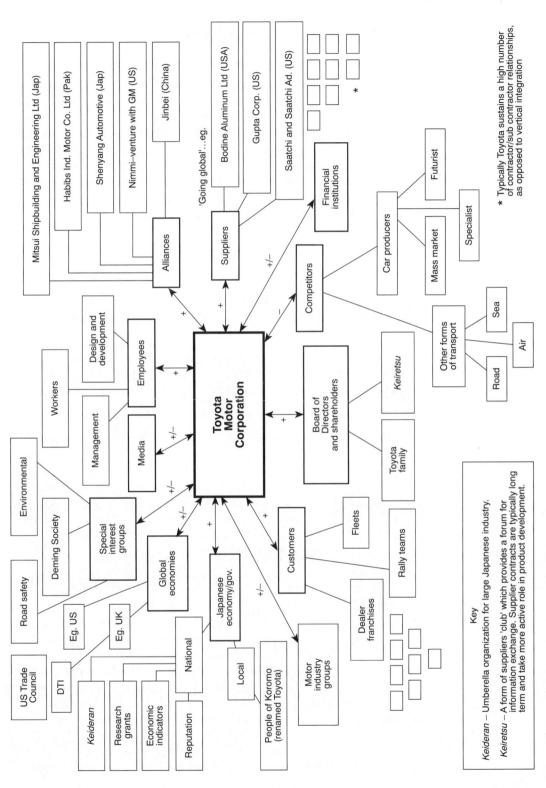

Figure 1.6 Stakeholder map for Toyota Car Company.

INDUSTRIES AND COMPETITION

We have established that organizations do not work within a vacuum; each belongs to an industry, and operates within a value system that will probably include organizations from other industries. Each organization also has **competitors**, who may exist both within and outside its industry. (Competitors **within** the same industry will be producing a similar product – e.g., types of soap powder; competitors from **outside** the industry may be competing for the same chunk of consumer 'disposable income' – e.g., theatre tickets versus compact discs; or they may be competing by finding a new way of fulfilling a particular consumer need – e.g., telecommunications versus air travel.)

KEY CONCEPT 1.5: MICHAEL PORTER'S MODEL OF COMPETITIVE ADVANTAGE

Michael Porter says that, when coping with competitive forces, there are three potentially successful generic approaches that a company can take in order to outperform other firms in the industry:

1 Overall cost leadership.
2 Differentiation.
3 Focus.

He says that it is rare, though not impossible, for a firm to pursue more than one of these approaches successfully at any one time.

1 **Overall cost leadership**
This requires a great deal of managerial attention to cost control, without sacrificing commitment to quality and service. Achieving a low-cost position means that the company can then gain above-average returns even when it operates in an intensely competitive industry. It gives it greater bargaining power with buyers, since they can only realistically drive prices down to the level of the next most efficient competitor; and it enables it to defend itself better against powerful suppliers, since, by starting from a low-cost base, it will have built in greater flexibility to deal with increases in the cost of raw materials.

It should be emphasized that 'low cost' does not mean 'cheap' or 'shoddy'. It is also difficult to achieve; and many (particularly western) companies experience great difficulty in understanding the real nature of their costs.

2 **Differentiation**

This means producing something which is perceived industry-wide as being unique. Such uniqueness may take many forms, and include design or brand image (e.g., Gucci shoes); technology (e.g., the Psion personal organizer range); customer service (e.g., Hertz hired cars); safety features (e.g., Volvo in Europe), etc. Each of these companies is able to charge a premium for the perceived differentiating factor, and, ideally, will develop and extend it over time. Therefore, differentiating is a viable strategy for earning above-average returns in an industry. Its principal advantage is that it leads to higher margins; its principal disadvantage, that it is an unlikely strategy for gaining high market share.

3 **Focus**

A focused strategy means concentrating on a particular buyer group, segment of the product line, or geographic market. Its entire objective is to serve a particular customer target very well, and much better than competitors who are trying to serve a broader range of customers.

The firm achieving focus may also potentially earn above-average returns for its industry. Focus means that the company has achieved a low-cost position, high differentiation, or both.

The relationship of the three generic strategies to each other is illustrated in **Fig. 1.7**.

In the face of challenge from competitors, the organization has to find its own particular route to attracting its customers: it has to establish a clear definition for itself of the nature of its **competitive advantage**. Key Concept 1.5 describes in detail Michael Porter's (1985) model of competitive advantage. Briefly, Porter says that there are two broad ways in which an organization can compete – on cost or differentiation. If it competes on **cost**, then it must succeed in being the industry's cost leader – it is impossible for more than one company to occupy this position, and illogical to compete on cost unless you have it. It is important to recognize that 'low cost' does not mean 'cheap'. It refers to a no-frills approach to producing the product; **some** of the resulting margin **may** then be passed on to the customer. By contrast, a company which competes on **differentiation** incurs costs by building in extra features; it has to ensure that the customer is willing to pay for these at an economic rate.

The organization therefore has to understand how it competes in order to be successful. The organization must by fully aware of its core

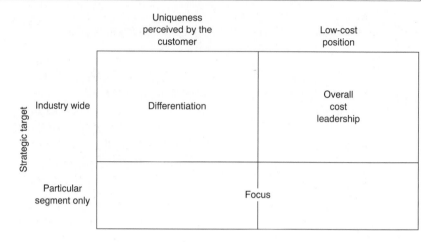

Figure 1.7 Michael Porter's three generic strategies.

competencies and then must match them with what customers require – the **'Key Success Factors' [KSFs]**, as they are often described. It can then analyze where its competitive advantage lies – i.e., what unique combination of attributes it possesses that distinguish it from its competitors.

Identifying key success factors may be a difficult task. Kenichi Ohmae (1983) offers the following advice:

- Dissect the market as imaginatively as possible to identify its key segments.
- Discover what distinguishes winner companies from losers and analyse the difference.
- Scrutinize the vertical chain of the business systems involved, from raw materials to servicing and after sales (i.e., the 'value chain').
- Recognize that improvement may provide the only means of differentiation (refer to Key Concepts 1.7 and 1.9).

Building on the work of Porter, Ohmae, and Prahalad and Hamel, John Kay (1993) says that competitive advantage can only derive from 'distinctive capability'; and a capability can only be distinctive if it is derived from a characteristic that other firms lack, that is also sustainable (persists over time) and appropriable (exclusively or principally benefiting the organization which holds it).

Kay identifies three types of distinctive capability:

1 **Innovation**. This is difficult to sustain because it invites imitation.
2 **Architecture**. Represents a system of relationships within the firm, or between the firm and its customers, or both.
3 **Reputation**. Kay says this is easier to maintain than to create, and meets the conditions essential for sustainability.

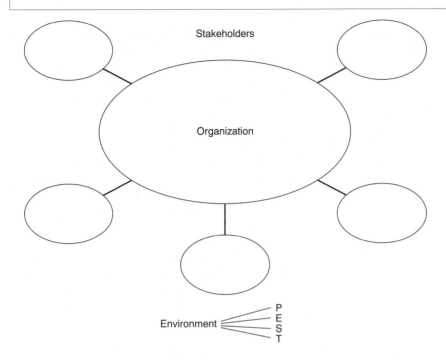

Figure 1.8 The impact of stakeholders and the environment upon the environment.

To these, Kay adds **strategic assets** as a potential source of competitive advantage. These are assets unique to the organization (such as a hotel which 'owns' a famous waterfall in its grounds).

Kay's main thesis is that although adding value is the basis of any successful enterprise, sustainable value-adding activities can only be achieved by developing a set of relationships which other organizations are unable to make. Hence he regards architecture as the most important source of competitive advantage.

PEST ANALYSIS

Box 1.1: An example of each of the PEST influences

1 Political: The importance of government credibility

How its government manages a nation's funds is clearly of great importance to the prosperity of that nation as a whole. Both profit-making and not-for-profit organizations hope that the decisions that their government makes will aid their value-adding processes. Those decisions are inevitably going to be swayed by other considerations: for example, the political 'colour' of the party in power, its strength relative to its opponents, and the influential effect of pressure groups (which may, however, include important businessmen).

All governments therefore have some system of economic management (and most are berated for the limited effects of the measures which they support). What happens when the government allows its grip on the economy to get out of control is illustrated by the case of Nigeria in 1993.

The country's debts had then escalated to 113 per cent of Gross National Product, and the military government had been discredited as both economically naive and financially corrupt. The result was that inflation accelerated as the Naira (national currency) plummeted in value, and western creditors became extremely wary of lending more money (Nigeria had already built up considerable debts in the West).

The only possible source of relief would come from throwing itself on the mercy of the international community, and begging funds from the International Monetary Fund (IMF). It was promised some support, in return for stringent reforms and tough economic measures, to be monitored both by its creditors and the World Bank.

However, a nation that has reached such a low state of credibility will take many years to recover. Its businesses will find it extremely difficult to trade internationally, which of course is likely to compound its problems for the future.

This example illustrates the close link which frequently exists between politics and economics in the context of **PEST** analysis.

2 Economic: the significance of stable exchange rates

Example (1) refers to the significance of a nation's having a currency that inspires the confidence of its trading partners. Trade is also affected by the stability or otherwise of exchange rates – since the time gap between a firm in one nation producing and delivering goods to another nation, and receiving payment from that nation may mean a sizeable difference in the amount of revenue received, if the exchange rate frequently fluctuates. Attempts to achieve the desirable control are sometimes made at an international level. The most significant of these in recent years was the setting up of the European Monetary system (EMS) by the then European Economic Community (now the European Union) in 1979.

Countries which joined the EMS agreed to abide by a system which operated:

- a scheme of permitted margins for exchange rates between their currencies, and permitted margins around a central artificial unit of currency called the **Ecu** (now called the Euro)
- a policy of 'managed floating' between the currencies of the countries operating within and outside the system.

The short-term objective of the EMS was to push inflation rates down to what was then regarded as the exemplary German level. (This was before the economic aftershocks of the reunification of Western and Eastern Germany made their impact post-1989.) Its long-term objective was to promote economic convergence in Europe (an ambition which was immeasurably complicated by the collapse of the former Soviet bloc in 1992).

For a while, the EMS seemed to work. It achieved some lowering of inflation across Europe as the result of the broad adoption of similar economic policies by its member states, and the (slow) acceptance of the Ecu as a unit of currency in international commerce.

But during the early 1990s, the frequent realignment of currency values undermined the stability of the exchange rates for whose maintenance it existed. Individual currencies at the top or bottom end of permitted margins around their central rate came under strong speculative attack, and were pressured to revalue or devalue.

A 'run' on the pound in the autumn of 1992, which the British government at first sought to stave off by drawing heavily on reserves, eventually led the United Kingdom to secede from the EMS. In 1993 the Danish krone and the French franc were similarly squeezed, and avoided devaluation only with difficulty. (In 1996, a gathering of economic 'wise men' in Brussels suggested that no European currency would be sufficiently stable for homogenization by the year 2000.)

In 1996, the pound was 'floating' against other currencies, including those within the EMS. This was of great significance both to industry and consumers: its relatively weak state made conditions more favourable for companies wishing to export (because foreign buyers could gain more per unit of their own currency) and made imports less affordable (because customers in Britain had less buying power per pound; it also followed that raw materials imported from abroad were proportionately more expensive).

3 Social: two examples of the commercial effect of changes in work and leisure habits

(i) **Japan**

Japan has made huge strides in economic development in the last 50 years. Although the Japanese have always been avid buyers of the state-of-the-art, the rapidly obsolescent electronic products on which the country has built most of its wealth, the traditional Japanese family has also been thrifty, keen on saving and keen to work; until recently, the husband was the only member of the family who would be working unless there were grown-up children, and he would be committed to a work schedule which left little time for leisure pursuits.

By the beginning of the 1990s, this was beginning to change. Educated women were beginning to join the workforce, and some were choosing not to leave it when they married, or in certain cases, when they had children. The current generation of Japanese workers increasingly resents spending all of its time at work; whilst many people are still careful about spending, they want life to be more rich and varied. Some have even discovered the pleasures of extended credit. Since Japan is a country in which shortage of space means that most homes are small, the goods its inhabitants wish to buy are often luxury goods of a personal nature – French perfumes, Italian shoes, designer fashions, etc. The desire for these (largely European) articles with high added value has been encouraged by the Japanese government, which is concerned about a trade surplus that its trading partners are viewing with increasing discontent.

The rich new market opening up in Japan is a boon for the producers of the luxury goods, at a time when famous names are losing the appeal they held for European customers in the 1980s – some of these former European customers have been impoverished by recession; others, though they might be able to afford the products, regard it as 'politically correct' not to spend ostentatiously. Therefore, there is a growing perception in Europe that value is not added by the name tag attached to the product – in other words, brand names are less powerful in commanding a premium. The luxury goods companies are thus faced with the choice of either 'going downmarket' in Europe, in order to match customers' requirements by adding value in a new way, or of finding a new market for continuing to charge for prestige. The latter is clearly likely to be the more rewarding, both financially and in terms of fitting in with their existing culture – particularly if other rapidly developing countries also cultivate an appetite for luxury goods as prosperity generates the desire for social change.

(ii) **Iran**

A different kind of social value-added service may be offered by a philosophy, religion or creed. This was the case in Iran in the 1990s, where Islamic fundamentalism had achieved enormous popular appeal.

Until the late 1970s, Iran was ruled by the Shah, a hereditary monarch. The country was semi-westernized, but there was a huge social and economic divide between rich and poor. Eventually the mullahs, or Islamic religious elders, managed to marshal the prolific but disorganized populace to rebel, and the Shah was forced into exile. The people received comparative social security, and also the spiritual security of belonging to the religion of Islam, which was taken back by the religious leaders to its extremist 'fundamental' roots.

Added value was thus offered in the form of the creation of a new national lifestyle, with which everyone could identify, and which offered a degree of protection to all. The organization that supplied it was the church – and the state (now essentially the same body). What the nation's leaders (now more moderate since the death of Ayatollah Khomeini in 1988) had to find for the future was a way of funding this 'service' in the long term, by establishing effective external trading partnerships.

The strictures of the religion itself make this extremely difficult. Eventually, a compromise may have to be reached of accepting some of the western ideas and practices which the fundamentalist movement originally sought to stamp out from the country, in order to enable fundamentalism itself to flourish. As well as the people of Iran, Iranian businesses and potential trading partners (and the international community as a whole) have an interest in the successful resolution of this problem. The conundrum is an interesting one: the supplying organization is adding the value that the customer requires, but the price (paid only indirectly by the customer) is at present too great.

4. **Technological: the contribution made by scientific research to adding value**

Other examples focusing on the impact of information technology may be found in the Case studies of Chapter Six.

'Plastic that grows on trees'

A partnership has been formed between Massachusetts Institute of Technology and Metabolix, the US biotechnology group, to develop a type of plastic that can be grown organically – what they term a 'harvestable polymer'. Various attempts have been made since the late 1970s to develop a kind of plastic that grows in plant form, but only advances in genetic engineering in the 1990s have made it possible.

There are two main reasons for wanting such a product: first, various oil crises have not only pushed up the prices of petroleum-based plastics, but also, on occasions, made them scarce or put their future under threat; secondly, petroleum-based plastic is not only one of the most difficult materials to recycle, it also has an inconveniently long life – it is calculated that it will take hundreds of years to decompose.

In 1994, a team headed by Professor Anthony Sinskey succeeded in capturing the genes in certain bacteria that are responsible for producing biosynthetic material. Advances in molecular biology mean that they can move this genetic information either to other bacteria which reproduce more rapidly, or to plants. It was hoped, ultimately, to transfer the plastic-producing genes to seeds, so that host plants such as potatoes and mushrooms could make polyester fibres. The sunlight that plants tap is cheaper than petroleum, and therefore each plant would not have to manufacture a lot of the organic polymer to make it worthwhile.

Metabolix still had quite a long way to go, however: the scientists had only been able to produce the desired reaction in a test tube. There was also formidable competition in the field of producing biodegradable polymers from bacteria. In Britain, Zeneca had perfected biodegradable shampoo bottles, using the brand name 'Biopol'; Vargill, an American company, was also making biodegradable plastics, and had set up a new plant to make plastics from cornstarch. There were, however, problems with these alternative biodegradable plastics: they were expensive to make, costing up to three times as much as petroleum-based plastic to produce; and their quality might be in doubt – tests had shown that they might disintegrate under certain conditions (though the companies concerned were improving their products all the time). Other customer imperatives had to be fulfilled – for example, the new plastics must be easily used in current moulding machines, since businesses would be unwilling to buy new machines to accommodate the product.

But the companies concerned believed that further research and development, possibly aided by communities and organizations worried about landfills and the high cost of recycling conventional plastic, would result in the resolution of all of these problems. The real key to success would be to produce a cheap, easy-to-use material of exceptional quality. When that happened, the whole plastic industry would be revolutionized.

Source: Griffith, Victoria (1994) 'Plastic that grows on trees', *Financial Times*, 15 Feb.

We have already said that the organizations that we have been discussing do not work within a vacuum; they have to take into account their stakeholders and their competitors. They also have to work within, accommodate, and, if they are skilful, try to shape, their wider external environment. We have seen how both stakeholder analysis and models of competition help them to assess the impact and the relative power balances of the factors external to the organization which affect them.

There is a further tool, simple in concept but often complex in application, which aids in the identification of the many external variables to which the organization should remain sensitive. It is commonly called **PEST** analysis (Box 1.1). 'PEST' is an acronym for **P**olitical, **E**conomic, **S**ocial and **T**echnological factors. (PEST analysis is sometimes referred to as STEP analysis. The etymological meanings of both acronyms are relevant: PEST indicates that the organization has to deal with sets of circumstances that can 'plague' its work; STEP signifies the systematic and progressive analysis that may be undertaken to adjust to or combat such factors.)

In the following chapters, we deal in detail with each one of the PEST factors; an overview of them follows.

Political Factors (Chapters Two and Three)

All organizations are affected by the politics of the nation or nations within which they are operating (and the more countries in which an organization operates, the more complex the political considerations become). Political factors that have a direct or indirect influence on both the value chain of the individual organization and its entire value system include taxation policies (direct and indirect); employment policies; the standard of management achieved by governments of individual nation states, and of larger political communities such as trading blocs; how foreign trade is conducted both nationally and internationally; and the stability of the government(s) involved.

Economic Factors (Chapter Four)

The economic factors which affect organizations are often closely tied in with political factors, because they are influenced by various types of government intervention (or the absence of it). Relevant issues include: banks' base rates; a country's balance of payments figures; share prices; the exchange rate of the national currency, and of the countries that the organization is doing business with; and the Retail Price Index or its equivalent.

Social Factors (Chapter Five)

It is often difficult for an organization to make a helpful appraisal of the social issues that are likely to affect it, as these tend to be both diverse and insidious. The most creative and successful leaders are those who not only become expert at spotting social trends in their early stages, but also develop an intuition for the ones that will have a significant bearing on the society that the organization is positioning itself to serve in the future. The trick is to separate the true sea-change from the passing fad (though the latter can also be capitalized upon, provided that its transitory nature is recognized). Examples of social issues of which the organization needs to be aware if it is to remain viable and healthy are: changes in taste and demand for goods; demographic changes; changes in work and leisure habits; changes in patterns of illness and health; and general shifts in attitude.

Technological Factors (Chapter Six)

Today, when people talk about technological change, they often mean the impact which the adoption and development of information technology is having on the value chain and the value system (but it should be remembered that there are other important kinds of technological development, as the first example in **Box 1.1**, point 4 illustrates).

The use of computers, and more especially networked computer systems, has revolutionized the way that thinking organizations operate. It reinforces the importance of 'knowledge workers'; it means it is less important where people work from, and will ultimately revolutionize how they buy things; and it enables resources to be used in the most efficient way. It is now difficult to argue, however, that Information Technology is a source of sustainable competitive advantage – more often than not, industry leaders in technological developments have not recouped their investment before competitors catch up by using 'copycat' tactics, and sometimes overtake them by passing on the lower costs that they have achieved (with a much lower investment) to customers by lowering prices.

Technology and its future development are therefore essential considerations when an organization is developing its strategy for adding value. There are also philosophical factors which may contribute to its successful deployment (see Key Concepts 1.6–1.8).

THE INTERNAL ORGANIZATION AND ADDING VALUE

The last section of this chapter deals with how the organization may be arranged internally in order to deal with all the factors which we have discussed. In considering this, we focus on a group of stakeholders to which we have so far only made passing reference: the management and staff of the organization.

Value is added **for** the customer, but this can only be achieved **through** the people of the organization. Traditionally, organizations set about tackling how they would fulfil the necessary tasks by dividing themselves up into functions. A typical manufacturing company, for example, might have a structure consisting of five main functions: Research and Development, Personnel, Operations, Sales and Marketing, and Finance, each of which might be headed by a director who made the most important decisions in his or her respective area, and reported to the Chief Executive.

A large number of organizations still operate in this way. Starting in the 1980s, and gathering momentum in the 1990s, however, forward-thinking organizations (including many of the largest and most powerful) have subscribed to the belief that there are better ways than this for their people to achieve added value.

The reasons for this are as follows:

- Traditionally structured organizations compartmentalize their activities; this may cause duplication of effort, rivalry and lack of communication between departments.
- Traditionally structured organizations are hierarchical. It means that the authority and responsibility for taking important decisions rests with those at the top. This may not only have the effect of demotivating staff, but also means that the full potential of the organization is not being tapped – people with innovative ideas lower down in the hierarchy may have no way open to them of being heard.
- The hierarchical layers of traditional organizations usually mean that the organization carries a lot of 'fat' – middle management levels that are not adding value, and are making the organization less cost effective, and less responsive to the needs of customers. The widespread use of information technology has made the jobs fulfilled by many middle managers redundant; new uses need to be found for their talents.

Instead of dividing up the work within a structure better suited to the pre-technological-revolution era, many organizations – whether they are for-profit or not-for-profit, service or manufacturing – have therefore tried to arrange what they do in terms of **processes**, and usually sought to give an overall coherence to the series of processes they have developed by marrying it to an overall concept or philosophy. By this means, strenuous attempts are made to cut out all activities that do not have a direct impact on adding value.

Not all organizations who have embraced the idea have made the final step of moving entirely away from functions; but they have all recognized that processes cut across functions. Thus an order-fulfilling process might involve activities that were once separately handled by the operations, finance, and marketing departments.

Adopting the process method of running organizations does not mean discrediting much that has been learnt from the functional way of managing. Operations Management, for example, is about finding efficient ways to transform resources and/or customers, as we have already discussed; Marketing is essentially about effectiveness: getting close to the customer, finding out how present products match his or her needs, and trying to gauge what his or her future needs will be.

The chief difference in emphasis in the focus on processes as a mechanism for adding value is that it deliberately sets out to eliminate 'waste' – activities that do not contribute to the customer's needs/desires, and therefore for which he or she will not or should not be expected to pay.

The focus on waste reduction is the crucial idea underpinning the philosophy of **Total Quality Management (TQM)**. An organization which adopts TQM is committed to the idea of continuous improvement, which is achieved, not by quality assurance, or inspecting quality in, but by making each employee not only responsible for, but trusted to take pleasure in, their own workmanship. There are various tools

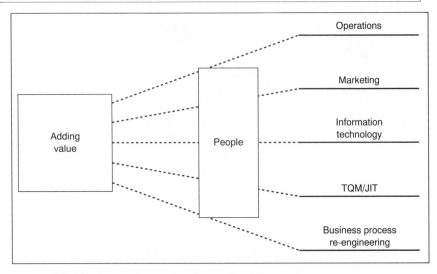

Figure 1.9 The internal organization and adding value.

and techniques associated with the philosophy, which is also heavily reliant on cross-functional teamwork. Key Concept 1.6 describes TQM in more detail. Closely associated with TQM is **Just-in-time (JIT)** supply management, which involves sharing a TQM philosophy with other organizations within the value chain. Key Concept 1.7 explains JIT.

KEY CONCEPT 1.6: TOTAL QUALITY MANAGEMENT (TQM)

What is total quality management? It has been defined by John Oakland, one of its leading exponents, as 'an approach to improving the competitiveness, effectiveness and flexibility of a whole organization.' If this claim can be fulfilled, then clearly TQM can be used as a powerful tool for adding value. TQM is a **philosophy** and embraces the following concepts:

- TQM's major objective is to get rid of all wasted effort.
- That there is a way of planning, organizing and understanding each activity within an organization.
- To be truly successful, TQM depends on the involvement of each individual at every level in the organization.
- TQM can be applied to all types of organization.

TQM focuses on **problem prevention**. Commitment to it within the organization needs to start from the top, because it is primarily an attitude of mind. It is not a cost-cutting or productivity improvement device; its effective implementation depends on the people who use it. Therefore, it is chiefly concerned with changing attitudes and skills, so that the culture of the organization becomes one of preventing failure – i.e., doing the right things, right first time, every time.

It therefore focuses on **attitudes**, **abilities** and **participation**.

There is an identifiable cycle involved in bringing these attributes into play. Oakland calls it the 'EPDCA' cycle. The acronym can be briefly explained as follows:

E	**Evaluate**	– the situation, and define objectives
P	**Plan**	– to achieve objectives fully
D	**Do**	– implement plans
C	**Check**	– that objectives are being achieved
A	**Amend**	– take corrective action if they are not

The Total Quality goal is therefore never achieved, since the process is an iterative and never-ending one.

Oakland offers ten points that he believes are essential for senior management to take into account if they are to introduce TQM successfully:

1 The organization needs long term COMMITMENT to constant improvement.
2 It must adopt the philosophy of zero errors/defects to change the CULTURE to right first time.
3 It must train people to understand CUSTOMER-SUPPLIER relationships.
4 It should not buy products or services on price alone, but look at the TOTAL COST.
5 It must recognize that the improvement of the SYSTEMS needs to be managed.
6 It has to adopt modern methods of SUPERVISION and TRAINING, in which the imperative is to eliminate fear.
7 It should eliminate barriers between departments by managing the PROCESS – and improving COMMUNICATIONS and TEAMWORK.
8 The following should also be eliminated:
   - arbitrary goals without methods
   - all standards based only on numbers
   - barriers to pride of workmanship
   - fiction – get FACTS by using correct TOOLS.
     In order to achieve this, it is advisable to BENCHMARK against best practice (within the industry, and also outside it).
9 It is necessary to EDUCATE and RETRAIN constantly.
10 A SYSTEMATIC approach has to be adopted to manage the implementation of TQM.

KEY CONCEPT 1.7: JUST-IN-TIME (JIT) BUYER-SUPPLIER RELATIONSHIPS

Just-in-time management is closely associated with Total Quality Management, and depends on the same philosophy of adding value by aspiring to ever-greater levels of quality and the elimination of waste. It was first developed in Japan in the 1970s, and the three main factors which led to its conception were the adoption of new quality techniques, lack of space, and the development of the Toyota Production System by Taiichi Ohno. Ohno, who has been called the 'father of just-in-time', put into practice the precepts of two American management gurus called Deming and Juran. At Toyota, he caused buffer stocks to be removed completely, allowed workers to stop the line, and developed 'kanban' tickets which enabled linkages to be formed in the production process, so that there was no over-production or shortage of parts.

In JIT, the drive towards elimination of waste is directed at two areas:

- **Machinery**
  by reducing operation times
  reducing set-up times
  eliminating over-production.
- **Manpower**
  by eliminating unnecessary tasks or parts of tasks
  speeding up some tasks
  making some tasks easier.

The objectives are achieved by setting up continuous improvement teams that tackle individual aspects within these areas. Poor quality is always caused by variation in standard. The question to be addressed is, what causes it? Once this has been established, Just-in-time seeks to combat the variation by a variety of methods such as Statistical Process Control (SPC), or 'fishbone diagrams'. As we have already found within the context of TQM, the underlying philosophy demands that the responsibility for quality lies with the individual operator.

Quality therefore moved from being something that is **inspected** into a product or service, to something that is **built** into it. The premise is that workers **want** to produce quality goods.

Once the company has adopted this philosophy and the accompanying techniques, it can begin to look at Just-in-time purchasing. JIT is an important cost (and therefore waste) saver because:

- Most businesses need to buy in components and materials to make the products that they sell, and the proportion of the total cost represented by bought-in items is generally increasing (cross-refer 'core competencies' and the 'make or buy' decision).

- Some organizations buy in virtually all that they sell – e.g., retailers, distributors.
- JIT means working closely with suppliers, and therefore spreading the wast-saving concept to other organizations, with the resulting salutory effect on other parts of the value chain and the value system. It can be used as an incentive to improve supplier performance, and usually results in a reduction in the supplier base – which again reduces waste by simplifying operations procedures; it is easier to deal with ten companies than 110.

Establishing such relationships with suppliers implies a considerable shift from the traditional attitude towards them. Purchasing managers have historically seen their role to be to exact the keenest possible prices from suppliers, and threatened loss of business for non-co-operation. These so-called 'arms-length' relationships are wasteful of time and lead to haggling, arguing and quality problems and late deliveries. Even more importantly, the two parties hold no shared objective. The traditional way of securing low prices – discount for quantity – generates wasted space and ties up resources through having warehouses full of materials not yet needed.

JIT, in contrast, means long-term relationships with suppliers, and treating them as partners, not adversaries. The participating companies then each benefit from enhanced performance. Obviously, the particular benefits to be gained differ depending on the nature of the organizations, but they generally include:

- lower stock levels
- smaller, more frequent deliveries
- shorter lead times
- simpler systems
- better quality
- lower costs.

JIT means ensuring that there is a **flow** of inputs through the value-adding system, which, ideally, are matched to the production rate. Therefore, there is less stock in the system; faster response times are possible; innovations can be introduced more quickly; and market trends can be followed more closely.

Obviously, developing the necessary internal and external linkages takes time, and there may be some trade-offs to consider. For example, the size of the supplier may be significant – how important is the company's business to it? Small companies tend

> to have more flexible systems; but they are not necessarily the leaders in innovation and product development, therefore they may be riskier in terms of viability.
>
> Once the supplier has been selected, supplier assessment can be undertaken to drive continuous improvement programmes; such assessment has always been done, but in the past it had punitive overtones. In JIT, the assumption has already been made that the supplier is the best for the job; an alternative supplier is not being sought, just more effective ways of the joint elimination of waste. Joint continuous improvement teams can also be effective.

Employees who are enabled to take responsibilities and make decisions which were previously the preserve of their superiors are said to be 'empowered'. Connected with empowerment is the philosophy of '**intrapreneuring**' – which means, literally, the tapping of entrepreneur-like qualities of initiative, innovation and drive from employees at all levels within an organization – in return for which they should expect to receive respect, a degree of security, proper remuneration, and an established level of licence to take risks which might not come off.

Business process re-engineering [BPR] is a philosophy, or a meta-discipline, which has been developed in the 1990s. It goes by a variety of other names, including business redesign, business re-engineering, and network redesign (the last embraces larger areas than one organization, maybe even the whole of the value chain). More than any other management philosophy, it has proselytized the idea of management by process. It differs fundamentally from TQM in not taking an incremental approach – instead of trying to build on what the organization has already achieved, BPR says that it should start afresh, and examine everything it does from a new perspective – that of adding value for the customer and making the most economical, efficient and effective use of the resources at its disposal. This includes people, and information technology, the latter often being the enabler of such an approach. Key Concept 1.8 explores BPR more fully.

> **KEY CONCEPT 1.8: BUSINESS PROCESS RE-ENGINEERING**
>
> Between the years 1984–9, the Massachusetts Institute of Technology co-ordinated a major research programme entitled 'Management in the 1990s'. Understandably, it had a technological bias, but it was concerned with every aspect of the strategic and operational management of the organization in the immediate future.

In 1990 Davenport and Short observed that successful organizations were using information technology systems in ways that were more advanced than the traditional automation of clerical and operational tasks; and, in 1991, Venkatramen elaborated on these observations by identifying business process re-engineering [BPR] as the third of five levels of IT-induced organizational transformation. He used the term BPR quite precisely to describe how IT can transform the way in which an organization works internally, rather than simply automate the way it worked pre-IT.

The idea of BPR was popularized by Hammer in 1990, when he coined the catch phrase 'Don't automate – obliterate!' What he meant was that organizations should rethink their businesses by capitalizing on opportunities provided by the new information technologies.

Business process re-engineering is therefore:

- a top-down approach to radical organizational change – it needs commitment from the organization's **leader** if it is to work.
- an approach to organizational improvement that seeks opportunities for fundamental transformations by focusing on the **processes** by which it delivers products and services to its **stakeholders**.

It is **not** synonymous with TQM, which seeks to achieve continuous incremental improvement.

Note: Organizations tend to embrace the need for radical change only when there are significant external threats and pressures; but the environment is increasingly turbulent in any case.

The successful implementation of BPR depends on a number of internal circumstances being in place; therefore, a detailed effort needs to be made to understand the organization's **current** processes. Once the existing processes are understood, a creative/ intuitive leap has to be undertaken to establish where the organization should want to be in the future. This involves asking a number of crucial and far-reaching questions:

- How can it encourage creativity and radical thinking in managers who are immersed in current day-to-day operations?
- How do managers assess the opportunities provided by information technology when IT literacy is still low?
- What sources or guidelines are available? In a sense, there is too much detailed information about these: there is copious up-to-date information obtainable about such concepts as the virtual organization, the hollow organization, the intellectual

holding company and the modular corporation, but none of the literature on these offers clues about how to decide the choice of one form over another.

Implementation of BPR also raises some fundamental questions:

- Is it possible to implement radical changes in a step-by-step fashion, or must a 'big bang' approach be adopted?
- Is it possible to pilot a change in a subset of the organization, when change will involve the whole organization?
- Is IT able to deliver the applications/technical infrastructure to support new processes quickly enough, or is a new set of IT development skills, approaches and tools required?

Sophisticated **measurement** processes (perhaps based on the techniques that have arisen from benchmarking) need to be put in place by those practising BPR so that they know when they have got there – because the processes which they are redefining and refining will cut across several functions. **BPR therefore means transforming the organization to turn on a pattern of processes, not functions**. The measurements established need, if possible, to capture an understanding of each process and its capabilities.

The move towards process-based organizations consequently involves an attempt to understand the impact of such nebulous but potent concepts as power, authority and culture.

Recent writers on BPR have alleged that, because of its roots in IT, proponents have accorded too little weight to the social issues it involves. Tinaiker *et al.* have pointed out that the processes that lie at the heart of its philosophy are socially constructed – i.e., defined in terms of their meaning to the people who carry them out. It is a well-known fact, for example, that most people who work get more from the workplace than the tasks they have to perform and the salary or wage that these generate. Work, and the configurations of people, place and practice that it involves, is an intensely social activity.

Therefore, if an organization is bent on re-engineering its processes, it must be aware of the fact that it is proposing to change the patterns of social interactions, and it must be able to envisage what this will mean to the chain of processes that it is hoping to establish. It can only hope to succeed if it is able to capitalize on a body of shared meanings and values (i.e., a strong **culture**) already in place.

There is consequently an overwhelming argument in favour of the belief that the social world of BPR must include the **worker** as well as the **re-engineer** and the **customer**.

We return to these ways of running organizations later in the book. At present, it remains to be emphasized that organizations cannot run without people; that people have to co-operate to make organizations work; that they cannot co-operate unless they understand; and that understanding derives from a mixture of training, shared values (culture) and shared experiences. In other words, in order to flourish, every organization must become a '**learning organization**'.

The following chapters of the book look at the **political** environment within which organizations operate at both the national and international levels, and at world-level shifts in ways of operating, such as trading blocs. They also look at the **economic** environment that underpins the individual business (micro-economics), and national and international economies (macro-economics), and discuss how politics and economics can aid or hinder the value-adding process.

We then go on to examine the **socio-cultural**, **technological** and **competitive** environments that the orgnaization needs to be aware of in its attempts to add value, and following these chapters, make a further, more detailed study of **stakeholders** and their impact on adding value. The final chapter will consider **strategies** for adding value.

Exercise. Now that you have read this chapter, including the information in the Key Concepts and Case 1.3, it would be useful if you were to construct a value chain for the car industry based on Porter's model.

SUMMARY

In this chapter, we have achieved the following.

- Examined the concept of adding value, and what it means for for-profit and not-for-profit, servicing and manufacturing organizations. Some definitions of adding value have been offered in order to clarify understanding of what it involves.
- Examined a range of themes arising from the value-added process, including the chain of activities involved; the idea of objectives and stakeholders; the concepts of core competencies, culture, systems and synergy – an understanding of which is vital to an effective exploration of the underpinning factors of adding value.
- Looked in detail at Porter's idea of the value chain, and constructed a specific example of it in relation to the publishing industry. Students have also been invited to construct their own value chain from details provided about the car industry.
- Examined the idea of opportunity cost and its relevance to adding value.
- Discussed (briefly) the idea of performance measurement.
- Explained the key ideas of competitive advantage, and industries and competition, drawing on the work of Michael Porter, John Kay and others.

- Touched briefly on the concept of PEST analysis, and how it is used as a connecting theme for the rest of the book.
- Looked at adding value within the context of the internal organization, and
- briefly, suggested potential strategies for adding value.

REFERENCES AND FURTHER READING

Ansoff, I. (1988) Synergies and Capabilities Profile', published in *New Corporate Strategy*, J. Wiley, Chichester.

Drucker, P. (1993) *Post-Capitalist Society*, Butterworth-Heinemann, Oxford, 1993.

Itami, H. and Roehl, T.H. (1987) *Mobilizing Invisible Assets*, Harvard University Press, Harvard.

Kanter, R.M. (1984) *The Change Masters: Corporate Entrepreneurs at Work*, Allen & Unwin.

Kay, J. (1993) *The Foundations of Corporate Success*, Oxford University Press, Oxford.

Oakland, J. (1993) *Total Quality Management* (2nd edition), Butterworth-Heinemann, Oxford.

Ohmae, K. (1983) *The Mind of the Strategist*, Penguin, London.

Peters, P.J. and Waterman, R.H. (1982) *In search of Excellence: Lessons from America's Best Run Companies*, Harper and Row.

Porter, M.E. (1980) *Competitive Strategy*, Macmillan, London.

Porter, M.E. (1985) *Competitive Advantage*, Macmillan, London.

Porter, M.E. (1985) *Competitive Advantage: Creating and Sustaining Superior Performance*, Free Press, pp. 42–3.

Prahalad, C.K. and Hamel, G. (1990) 'The Core Competence of the Corporation', *Harvard Business Review*, May–June.

Pumpin, C. (1987) *The Essence of Corporate Strategy*, Gower.

The political environment: governments and the value-adding process

2

LEARNING OBJECTIVES

- To understand how governments can, should and do affect the value-adding process.
- To understand the four major types of policy option that governments can pursue and assess their significance for adding value.
- To define pressure groups; explain how they behave, and assess their impact upon government.
- To give the arguments for and against the power of trade unions within the context of adding value.
- To understand how governments affect adding value through direct and indirect taxation, employment, education, training and economic policies, with examples.
- To put the arguments for and against privatization and nationalization.

INTRODUCTION

In this chapter, we examine what can governments **can**, **should** and **do** do to contribute to the process of adding value and to help national and international value systems. We begin by looking at four major types of policy that governments **can** pursue within the context of adding value, and then continue by examining the historical relationship of government to business. We go on to consider the importance of the rise of pressure groups in contemporary society, and then address in more specific detail the impact of governments' relations with trade unions.

A discussion of what governments **do** do begins with a description of both direct and indirect taxation policy, and its effect on business. How far governments do (and should) intervene in combating unemployment follows, with a detailed look at some specific measures taken in recent years. This leads into an account of government's role in the educative process, and the relationship of education to training. The chapter moves on to reflect on governments' economic policy within the context of the ownership of strategic industries, and the arguments for and against the nationalization or privatization of industries are put forward.

GOVERNMENTS AND ADDING VALUE

Michael Porter, who developed and popularized the idea of the 'value chain', is almost definitive in his view of what the aim of government should be when it tries to shape the national value-adding effort.

> 'The only meaningful concept of competitiveness at the national level is productivity.'
>
> (Michael Porter, 1990, p.6)

Associated with this is the idea that the goal of all nations is to achieve an ever-higher standard of living. Governments cannot of themselves add value, but they can facilitate or hinder the adding of value, and therefore the accumulation of wealth, by others. They should, according to Porter, recognize that this is their key role when formulating their policies. Kenichi Ohmae (1990) says that the role of government has been superseded by the philosophy and aims of the 'global' organization. Peter Drucker endorses this:

> '. . . the players on the stage – politicians, diplomats, civil servants, political diplomats and political writers – speak and write in yesterday's terms and, by and large, act – indeed, have to act – on yesterday's assumptions and on the basis of yesterday's realities.'
>
> (Drucker, 1993, p.10)

Whatever the truth of these views, it has to be accepted that governments wield powers of decision-making which affect organizations directly or indirectly in almost all the activities which they pursue in their initiative to add value. A government is a major stakeholder, which makes both a direct and an indirect impact on other stakeholders. An example of the first is the taking of legislative measures, say, concerning employees' health and safety at work rights, which affect specific employers. An example of the second is that of the 'knock on' effects of such laws – they might boost or depress industry confidence, and therefore the amount of investment the industry is prepared to make. This will have an impact on its supplier industries, and so on.

Government actions cause ripples throughout the whole value-system, and it is therefore important to understand how and why governments behave.

TYPES OF POLICY OPTIONS THAT GOVERNMENTS CAN PURSUE

Historically speaking, governments have adopted specific identifiable stances in relation to their dealings with industry. These are obviously linked to the central ideological beliefs which underpin their administrations. Turner (1989) identifies four major types of policy option that governments can pursue:

1 The 'pure' free market approach.
2 The 'social market' approach.
3 Selective intervention.
4 An economy planned by the government.

It is worth considering the implications of each of these in some detail.

1 **The 'pure' free market approach**
The principle behind this derives directly from the thinking of the nineteenth-century 'political economists'. Its development can be traced from Adam Smith to John Stuart Mill to Ricardo, and it has found its modern mouthpiece in the work of Milton Friedman. Its central tenet is that if everyone works for selfish interests, the aggregate result will be the greatest possible economic benefit to society as a whole. Government invervention can play no part in such an economy, because it will simply have a degenerative effect on the overall market, and add to any weaknesses which exist.
Implicit in the thinking of political economists are three key assumptions:
• That people are fundamentally rational and well-informed about the options open to them.
• That people do and should pursue self-interest, and that this is not morally reprehensible.
• That organizational activity should operate freely, without interference from the law (though all but extremists accept that there should be some minimal restraints on individual behaviour).

The effect of the 'pure' free market approach on adding value

First of all, it encourages countries and individual companies (or individuals) to specialize in a narrower range of goods and services, because it relies on the efficacy of the 'law of comparative advantage' (See Key Concept 2.1 for an explanation).

KEY CONCEPT 2.1: THE LAW OF COMPARATIVE ADVANTAGE

There are two countries, A and B. Both produce two goods – corn and computers. Both countries have an equal amount of capital and labour, but A has rich farmland and a suitable climate for growing corn, while B has a less favourable climate and less fertile soil, but a more highly skilled workforce. There is no unemployment in either country. When both countries are using their resources equally to produce both goods, output is as follows:

Country	Corn (units)	Computers (units)
A	800	300
B	300	800
Total production before specialization	**1100**	**1100**

[The relative value of each unit of output is the same]

If, however, each country specializes in the production of the goods at which it is most efficient (i.e., A specializes in corn and B in computers), then output becomes:

A	1500	Nil
B	Nil	1500

The net gains of specialization are therefore 400 units of corn, and 400 of computers. (In specializing, A gave up the production of 300 units of computers, and B gave up the production of 300 units of corn, leaving a net gain of 400 of each. Obviously, the example is unrealistically over-simplified; but it illustrates the gain both for each country and the world economy if they devote themselves to producing the goods in which they have comparative advantage.)

While this would appear to satisfy some of the needs of the consumer, by adding value at the lowest possible cost, it may also restrict consumer choice, since the total range of goods and services available might be more limited than they would otherwise have been. In terms of the effect on national economies, and therefore productivity and standards of living, it accepts the desirability of the 'survival of the fittest' axiom: that some nations will grow and prosper because their organizations are adding value in a way that both national and foreign consumers find attractive; others will become poorer.

Secondly, because of the international interdependency of organizations necessary in order for the law of comparative advantage to work, it encourages the development of inter-related value systems that support the concept of adding value. In this respect, the philosophy appears to be entirely laudable; but critics would say that it is wrong to ignore the implications of taking such an approach when procuring, for example, a nation's energy, or its defence equipment. Whether views such as these, coloured by nationalist values, are old-fashioned or a matter of fundamental common sense is subject to opinion. What they do highlight is that the ideology, taken to its logical extreme, views everything as a commodity – and this would include complex 'packages' such as health care and education.

The role of the state in such a context is minimalist and specific – the state addresses such issues as defence, policing, enforcing contracts and maintaining a stable currency. Since it wishes to motivate businessmen to create wealth, but does not concern itself with the redistribution of it, a key aim of the state operating the free market approach is to keep taxation to a minimum. The advantage to governments is that they are thus enabled to absolve themselves from a range of economic problems.

From the adding value point of view, this is where the greatest weakness of the philosophy lies. Despite its use of the word 'free', which has popular appeal, it can be argued that the fostering of great disparities between wealth and poverty ultimately has the effect of not only restricting choice, but also of allocating resources badly (thus deviating from the principle that the required added value should be achieved at the lowest possible cost). The wealthy are in a position to commandeer resources, whilst the poor, whatever talents they possess which might be harnessed towards the creation of value, are disadvantaged from birth and therefore unlikely to make their potential contribution.

2 The 'social market' approach

The 'social market' approach was upheld as a shining example of how governments could properly help organizations to add value throughout the 1980s, although exact definition of what the expression means has proved elusive. What users of the term have tended to do is to extol the political management of West Germany that proved so successful prior to German reunification in 1989.

The 'social market' approach endorses the 'political economy' ideals of free markets, free trade, and keeping government intervention to a minimum. However, this minimum intervention wears a more human face, and does involve the construction by government of considerable social safeguards to counteract poverty and social inequality. In other respects, it comes closest to Porter's view of what the appropriate role of government should be – that government should concentrate on developing an economic climate in which business and industry are able to flourish. (See Box 2.1 for Porter's account of the effects governments have.) This involves lowering

---

Box 2.1: A summary of the views of Michael Porter on how government affects the 'strategy, structure and rivalry' of a nation's industries

1 **Factor conditions.** These are affected through subsidies, capital market policy, education policy, etc.
2 **Product standards and regulations**. These are established by governments to mandate/influence buyer needs. A company or industry can turn them to competitive advantage – e.g., Volvo in Sweden made a virtue of necessity when the Swedish government imposed strict safety standards on vehicle manufacture by adopting safety as their key marketing ploy.
3 **The Government** is often a major **buyer** of the industry, for instance, if it operates in defence goods or telecommunications equipment. This may help or hinder the industry – the former, by pushing it to excel; the latter, by 'cushioning' it against foreign competition.
4 **Government** can **shape** the circumstances of **related** and **supporting** industries, for instance by controlling advertizing media or regulating support services.
5 **Government policy** influences **firm strategy**, **structure** and **rivalry** through devices such as capital market regulations, tax policy, and so on.

Source: adapted from Porter, M. (1990) *The Competitive Advantage of Nations*, Macmillan.

---

taxes, keeping 'red tape' to a minimum, imposing less regulation, encouraging society to adopt an 'enterprise culture', and, by implication, obliging it to support only a very small 'dependency culture' (i.e., people living on state benefits).

The effect of the 'social market' approach on adding value

It is clear that this philosophy has the great virtue of providing a fertile environment for the adding of value without demanding the extremes of self-interest dictated by political economists. Whether it is really possible to achieve is a different matter. Even prior to unification, West Germany by no means lived up to the ideal – for example, it did and still does heavily subsidize its coal industry; and, in the early 1990s, many of the European Community countries were to claim that Germany kept the value of the Deutschmark artificially high in order to help to buttress itself against some of the economic consequences of amalgamation with the East. (This is discussed in more detail in Chapter Four.) German unification meant that Germany acquired, almost overnight, a colossal 'dependency' problem, which at the time of writing is far from being resolved. The best that

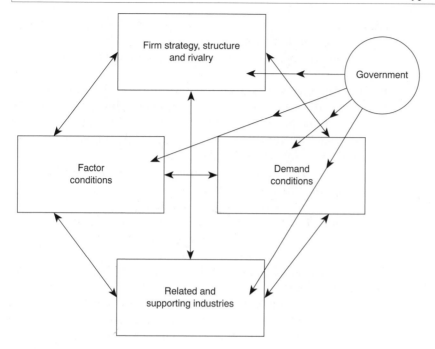

Figure 2.1 Diagrammatic explanation of Michael Porter's view of how government affects the 'strategy, structure and rivalry' of a nation's industries.

can be said of the 'social market' approach is perhaps that, whilst commendable as an idea, it can only be partially achieved, and then by economies which have already attained a high degree of affluence. They will probably not be able to remain true even to the aspiration of it if they experience a change in circumstances.

3 **Selective government intervention**

The philosophy behind the idea of selective government intervention in an economy is that a government's macroeconomic management (for a detailed discussion, see Chapter 4) is insufficient to ensure the achievement of particular economic goals. Examples of these might be the objective of full employment, or the avoidance of a balance of payments deficit.

Devine, Lee and Jones (1989) identify two broad types of intervention:

(i) **Competition Policy**. This seeks to affect industrial performance indirectly by maintaining or creating a framework within which the pursuit by individual firms of their private interests results in a desirable economic outcome. (See Case 2.1 on the Net Book Agreement for an example.)

(ii) **Industrial Policy**. This involves state intervention at the level of specific industries, firms or sectors, or aimed at a particular geographical area, which is designed to bring about directly a desired outcome that would not otherwise occur. It therefore has the effect, to a greater or lesser degree, of supplementing or supplanting market forces.

The policy tools of intervention might include the following:

- Direct financial assistance for development. This might mean cash grants or tax incentives for firms or industries to invest in new technology, or the setting up of elaborate facilitating networks such as the 'Enterprise Zones' devised by the British government in the mid-1980s.
- Financial assistance to stop producing. The European Union is currently pursuing a massive 'set aside' programme, which involves paying farmers not to use their land for agricultural production. The reasoning behind this is that it is cheaper (and ecologically more sensible) to do so than to cope with the problems ('wine lakes', 'butter mountains', etc.) associated with overcapacity. In political terms, such a policy is known as 'positive inducement'.
- Some governments, conversely, may impose sanctions (known as 'negative inducement') against products which they feel are not beneficial to the national economy. They may be trying, for example, to persuade manufacturers to make farming machinery instead of weapons. From the government's point of view, such policies often have the additional appeal of public popularity. They promote 'socially useful production.'
- Public ownership of companies or ultilities ('nationalization'). This is discussed in detail later in the chaper.
- The setting up of new publicly-owned companies to fulfil a national need – e.g., the creation of Girobank in the UK in 1968.
- Greater control by the government in the way that industry is regulated and run – for instance, by preventing the merger of two large companies which would have the consequential result of creating a monopoly situation.
- Sometimes, a government may deem it necessary to 'write off' the bad debts of a company in order to give it a new start, particulary if the company is about to be 'privatized'. The British government adopted such a procedure when it sold Rover to British Aerospace in 1988.

CASE 2.1

THE NET BOOK AGREEMENT

This case illustrates how a practice allowed by government represents direct intervention by imposing competition policy.

The Net Book Agreement was a **restrictive practice** which operated in the United Kingdom for almost 100 years. It imposed a **resale price maintenance** on new books, which meant that the price was decided by the publisher in advance of their supplying the book to the bookseller. It was originally set up in 1900, because publishers were afraid that the cut-throat competition among booksellers had become so fierce that price wars were fast driving many of them out of competition, with the result that there were too few book retailing outlets.

The Net Book Agreement was set down in its final form in 1957, and defended in court in 1965, when it was allowed to survive on the grounds that 'books are different', and that 'selling a book is not like selling an egg or an orange'. The arguments in its favour were that it offered consumers a wider degree of choice, because without it many books would not be published at all, and that it kept the price of books down, because using some books as 'loss leaders' would have knock-on effects in other bookselling areas. Resale price maintenance has only been allowed in Britain for 'special' cases such as this.

In the late 1980s, Terry Maher, then Chairman of the Pentos bookselling group, campaigned for the abolition of the Net Book Agreement on the grounds that it encouraged bookshops to be inefficient by protecting their margins, and in fact led to fewer book sales, because people were discouraged from setting up new bookshops. Shortly afterwards, the Reed Publishing Group decided that it would no longer impose resale price maintenance on its titles. Several other large publishing houses eventually followed suit.

Both the political and economic climates had changed since 1965. The Conservative government of the 1990s was ideologically opposed to restrictive practices; and some of the reasons for upholding the Net Book Agreement – such as the detrimental effect to the industry of price wars – had lost their significance now that there were two substantial bookselling chains operating in the UK, Dillons and Waterstones, neither of whom would be likely to be driven out of business by a price war. Pressure on the publishers from supermarkets to be allowed to stock a selected range of books and sell them at prices of their choice, and a change of management and consequently attitude towards the Net Book Agreement at W.H. Smith's, the leading high street chain, undermined its chances of survival still further.

In November 1993, the UK government announced that it had referred the Net Book Agreement to an investigation by the Office of Fair Trading. It seemed likely that the government no longer felt that circumstances were right for it to interfere in competition within the book trade; and in the event, it did not need to. In September 1995, Random House and HarperCollins, pressured by W.H. Smith's, the supermarkets, and the need to meet their own performance targets with boosted pre-Christmas sales, announced that their books would no longer be sold 'net'. The Net Book Agreement was almost immediately declared 'unenforceable' by the Publishers Association.

The case is interesting, in that it illustrates that government-permitted self-regulation within an industry in the last analysis operates in the interests of suppliers, and not the customer. This is not to say that the Net Book Agreement did not contribute to added value while it was in force; whether in fact this was so is not clear at the time of writing (May 1996), as more time is needed to assess the impact of this major change to the British book industry.

It will be evident that almost all interventionist policies are capable of provoking controversy, and that some of them also raise profound questions of ethics.

Historically speaking, interventionism derives from the approach of John Maynard Keynes and J.K. Galbraith. It has been called 'national political economy'. In its more advanced forms, it looks at capitalism with a suspicious eye, but does not seek to abolish it. However, as can be seen from some of the examples above, even governments that fundamentally support the free market approach feel compelled to take some interventionist measures.

The effect of government interventionism on adding value

If interventionism succeeds in fulfilling its objectives, then it could be argued that it helps to add value by making both individual companies and the economy as a whole stronger – in the adding value spectrum, it is therefore an enabler. Conversely, if it doesn't work – by failing to stimulate innovation, productivity and demand in the way that the government envisages, or by perpetrating inequalities in the market that the government has failed to take into account or not foreseen – it can have a negative effect on the adding of value, particularly at the lowest possible cost to the consumer. Critics of interventionism would say it is impossible to gauge the results of 'meddling' by the government once it has been done, because of the complex nature of market, industry and economy, but that it is undesirable *per se*, because anything that interferes with 'free' market forces is not likely to be beneficial to the consumer. The theory is impossible to test, since at any national and certainly at the international level, a totally free market mechanism cannot be said to exist.

4 **An economy planned by the government**

Worldwide, government planned economies are in decline, following the break-up of the Soviet bloc in the late 1980s. China is the only large nation which now has a planned economy.

Planned economies reflect the Marxist school of political economy; they view society and the economy in terms of class antagonism, in that they believe that any form of capitalism is bound to lead to conflict between workers and owners. The other schools of thought accept that at least there is potential for co-operation between workers and owners. For Marxists, this is a contradiction in terms.

Consequently, the public ownership of industry, business and commerce plays a key role in the Marxist school. The argument it puts forward is that if society is inherently exploitative, then one means of removing the opportunity to exploit is to remove the means of exploitation – i.e., the ownership of industry and business – and thus also prevent the creation of a ruling class. The ideal is always deviated from in practice, because a ruling class does emerge in planned (or 'command') economies, but it usually consists, not of leaders in industry and commerce, but of politicians. This has clear implications for the products planned economies produce, and the level of added value they are able to achieve.

The effect of a command economy on adding value

Historically speaking, command economies have cushioned themselves against market forces by having huge captive markets in both their own countries and associated command economies, and therefore have made little response to demand. This means that they do not necessarily produce even the broad type of goods that the consumer requires, much less differentiate them to appeal to market sectors. Once produced, the goods may be badly distributed, so that the people who might be interested in buying them do not have access to them. One feature of such products is that they might be very cheap, because command economies do not operate on the productivity principle embraced by market economies – i.e., that each worker is more or less responsible for generating the added value which creates the profit to pay his or her wage. Clearly, there is little attempt to add value in the command context – the concept has no relation to the objectives of output.

Former command economies are therefore suffering from the severe disadvantages of producing uncompetitive (in the innovatory/technological sense) goods, and achieving very low levels of productivity when they attempt to convert themselves to market economies. They may find temporary markets for goods which are of inferior quality but cheap, but they are under great economic pressure to make themselves competitive rapidly. There are bound to be significant social casualties, and possibly some social unrest, as this process takes place. Russia's attempts to create a market economy are described in Case 2.2.

The critical issues surrounding the four main government approaches to policy options are summarized in Key Concept 2.2.

CASE 2.2

RUSSIA'S DIFFICULTIES IN ATTEMPTING TO CREATE A MARKET ECONOMY

In August 1993, two years after abandoning its command economy, inflation in Russia had reached nearly 30%. Manufacturing production was falling, oil production was declining, the budget was operating under a huge deficit, and the tax 'take' was falling. Many of the Russian people clearly felt that they had been better off, and that, at a national level, 'things worked better' under a command economy.

On the face of it, they were right, because Russia, in common with all the former 'Iron Curtain' countries, was suffering from the difficulties of setting up a market economy almost overnight. The old system was no longer appropriate, but the new system required immense resources – including expertise – which could only be developed over a period of time.

President Yeltsin's government, with considerable backing from western governments, had devised a plan for creating these resources, but naturally people whose cost of living was rising daily were afraid, and impatient of waiting for matters to improve. The increasing lack of popular support for the fledgeling democratic government, compounded by the powerful influence of many surviving members of the communist 'old guard', led to an abortive coup to depose President Yeltsin in September 1993. The political uncertainty, and fears about the power gained by the Russian army in its support of the President, caused the International Monetary Fund to delay administering an elaborate international support programme designed to make the transition to a market economy as easy as possible.

This combination of events meant that in late 1993, the balance of power seemed to be swinging against the creation of a true market economy in the country.

Source: details taken from the *Financial Times*, October 1993

KEY CONCEPT 2.2: THE FOUR MAJOR TYPES OF POLICY OPTION GOVERNMENTS CAN PURSUE, AND THEIR IMPLICATIONS FOR ADDING VALUE

1 **'Pure' free market approach**
  Assumes:
  - People are rational and well-informed
  - They do and should pursue self-interest

- Organizational activity should operate with minimum interference from government

Effects on adding value:

- Encourages companies to specialize in narrower range of goods and services – relies on 'law of comparative advantage'
- Encourages the development of inter-related value systems between nations
- Taken to its extreme, views all goods and services as commodities
- By causing great disparities of wealth, may become self-defeating – i.e., not only restrict choice, but cause the poor allocation of resources

2. **The 'social market' approach**

   Endorses:

   - Ideal of free markets and free trade
   - Keeping government intervention to a minimum

   But:

   - Involves government in construction of social safeguards

   Effects on adding value:

   - Commendable as an ideal, but requires affluence and social stability
   - Therefore, difficult to put into practice in the long term
   - Companies/industries may find such governments turn to either free market or more interventionist behaviour if circumstances change

3. **Selective government intervention**

   Two broad types:

   - **Competition policy** – seeks to affect performance by creating a favourable environmental framework
   - **Industrial policy** – involves state intervention in specific industries

   Intervention may include:

   - Direct financial assistance
   - Financial assistance to stop producing
   - Sanctions ('Negative Inducement')
   - Nationalization
   - The creation of new publicly owned companies
   - Greater control of the industry in the way it is regulated
   - Giving a company with bad debts a clean start

   Effects on adding value:

   Depends on whether the interventionism works. If it **does**,

   - Government acts as an enabler
   - National economy and individual industries and companies grow stronger

   thus creating benefit for the consumer. If it **doesn't**:

- Innovation is not stimulated
- Productivity and demand don't follow the expected pattern
- Inequalities in the market are fostered

and it has a negative effect on adding value for the consumer.

N.B. At any national/international level, a totally free market mechanism cannot be said to exist.

4 **A command economy (planned by the government)**

Follows theory of Marxist school:

- Views society and economy in terms of class antagonism
- Believes that all forms of capitalism lead to conflict between workers and owners
- Therefore subscribes to public ownership of industry, business and commerce, as a means of obviating the main means of exploitation by a ruling class

But

In practice, an elite does emerge, of politicians rather than industrialists

Effects on adding value:

- Cushions industries against market forces; therefore there is little response to demand
- Goods consumer requires may not be produced
- Even if they are, they may be poorly distributed
- Workers often achieve very low rates of productivity, thus making goods uncompetitive in international terms
- Goods are often of inferior quality; they may attract by their cheapness, but achieve no real 'added value'

N.B. Governments seeking to abandon command economies, as in Eastern Europe, may find that they have to deal with widespread economic casualties, and probably social unrest.

THE RELATION OF GOVERNMENT TO BUSINESS

Leaders of industry often have uneasy relationships with governments, whatever their political hue. Even in market economies, businesspeople frequently express the view that it is a significant objective of the state to collect power for itself, and therefore to exercise unnecessary control and thus inhibit business activity. Some western countries – America is a strong example – have **pluralist** societies, in which the power of the state is limited by the power exercised by (often very highly organized) public opinion and special interest groups. This also is not always pleasing to businesspeople: since there is a considerable counterbalancing of power going on all the time, it often takes a long time for political decisions to be made, again with an inhibiting effect on what their organizations do. Moreover, special interest groups, particularly if they can harness the support of the media, have been known to bring even large companies to their knees by exposing them systematically to adverse publicity.

Governments which support a generous social safety-net programme – i.e., 'welfare states' – frequently exasperate or, it is said by others of a more 'right-wing' persuasion, demotivate businesspeople by levying high taxes at both the corporate and the individual level. Both employers and their employees are further incensed by the 'black' economies which sometimes flourish in welfare states (where those claiming unemployment benefit are also working 'unofficially' and gaining untaxed income as well) and add further to the tax burden.

There is a tendency for businesspeople to regard politicians as self-serving and, sometimes, incompetent. This view is reinforced by the emergence of political scandals, especially those relating to the financially corrupt behaviour of politicians. The likely corollary to such disenchanted perception from businesspeople is that they will themselves take the initiative to manipulate governments and, as far as they are able, bend the state towards operating in their favour. Large and multinational organizations, of course, wield the highest 'clout' when it comes to thinking in these terms; the more concentrated, and internationally concentrated, industries become, the greater their manipulative powers, should they choose to exercise them. As long ago as 1969, Edward Epstein, of the University of California, wrote:

> 'The fear exists that large corporations, acting either in concert or through intermediaries such as trade associations or national business organizations, will be in a position to overwhelm other social interests competing in the political process and, thereby, to achieve dominance over the formal and informal institutions of American government'.
>
> (Epstein, 1969)

Business and government, therefore, often act in uneasy symbiosis with each other; their activities may be mutually beneficial, but the basis for trust is often missing from their transactions. Businesspeople themselves may form pressure groups that exert power over governments; governments will shy away from alienating their business supporters. Ultimately governments hold the trump card of the authority to legislate while they are in office, but the fear of losing the office itself, all other motives aside, will oblige them to take into account a powerful business lobby.

Despite their sometimes strained relationship with governments, however, most organizations feel the need for relatively stable government. In order to be able to plan and invest in the future with confidence, they have to believe that they can reasonably trust the measures that the government has put into operation or is planning for the future; that the government is capable of managing the economy competently and will continue to do so; and that the government is strong enough to make day-to-day decisions that are not simply dictated by political expediency. Case 2.3 illustrates why it is necessary for governments to have stability.

CASE 2.3

THE IMPACT OF UNSTABLE GOVERNMENT: TWO EXAMPLES IN 1993

Example 1

Italy has had a succession of short-lived, weak and corrupt governments since the Second World War. The nation has been afflicted throughout by the influence of organized crime, which is said to have penetrated to the highest levels of government. There is a real threat that this will now lead to the break-up of the country, with the more prosperous heavy-industrial North cutting itself off from the poorer and more crime-ridden South. Business organizations in the North feel incensed that corruption is eroding the value that they are able to add, because of its consequent effect on the cost of taxation, building an appropriate infrastructure, etc. The implications for the country's southern-based industries, which include tourism and cottage-industry textiles, are serious, because if they lose the subsidies which they have hitherto enjoyed from the North, they may no longer be able to compete with similar industries in other nations. In November 1993, the country's political turmoil was reinforced by chaotic general election results, with victories in certain geographical areas for every political persuasion, from communists to neo-fascists, and no clear-cut political leaders.

Example 2

The uncertain future of Hong Kong after its official hand-over to Communist China in 1997 means that companies are reluctant to continue to invest there. Some are actively seeking other bases in South-East Asia. The possibility that many of the colony's best eduated and most able workers will choose to leave before 1997 presents a significant threat to the prosperity of individual organizations, for which a likely solution is also that they will decamp. The long-term effect of this will be to preserve added value for customers, provided that the particular geographical base is of no significant importance to them, and that they remain loyal; but in the short term, such upheavals will result in the waste of many physical assets and the loss of use of the highly sophisticated infrastructure, with the inevitable effects on costs and service. The situation is almost the converse of the problem in Italy.

THE EFFECT OF PRESSURE GROUPS ON GOVERNMENTS

Pressure groups have proliferated in the past 20 years. Both governments and businesspeople are now obliged to be attuned to the voice of public interest groups, and to allow them to help to shape public policy concerning the way government, industry and commerce operates.

Pattakos (1989) offers the following definition of a pressure group:

> '... a self-appointed cadre of people who derive their mandate (they believe), strength and motivation from the people.'

Pressure groups may attack the policies of government itself, or they may target the activities of certain firms and institutions in such a way that the government is obliged to take action. Research into the ways that such activists operate has discovered that they tend to share the following characteristics:

- they take a long-term view, and are prepared to stick to their goals for years
- frequently two or more groups will form coalitions to achieve a mass that they would not gain on their own
- in recent times, they have become more sophisticated; they now make use of information technology, and their members plan and train
- they are perceived by the public at large as being altruistic; they are therefore able to generate a great deal of sympathy for their cause, which makes them powerful.

In addition to lobbying the government and specific organizations directly, activists will seek to generate support from the media, religious groups, unions, universities, legal and regulatory bodies, and international bodies such as the United Nations and the European Court. They always seek grass roots support from the public.

They tend to choose their targets well, and to develop campaigns that bring tremendous pressure on those targeted. Their tactics include economic boycotts, shareholder resolutions, legal action, marches, demonstrations and sit-ins. Extremists resort to emotional blackmail (prayer vigils, etc.) and even to violence and law-breaking.

The implications of their activities for adding value are complex. On the one hand it could be said that, especially in a political climate wedded to the idea of market forces and minimal regulation, they act as a safeguard. They either warn consumers of hidden dangers in products of which they would otherwise be unaware, or protect them 'in spite of themselves' from products that they may want, but that are 'bad' for them or society at large; in other words, that they add value in the larger 'quality of life' sense. On the other hand, it should be acknowledged that on occasion pressure groups have generated ill-substantiated hysteria aginst certain products, with the resultant loss of added value to the consumer and of its investment to the relevant industry. Furthermore, evidence that pressure groups exhibit a reluctance to disband once a campaign is over, instead taking up some other cause, suggests that they sometimes operate on a dynamic which is not impelled by altruism.

TRADES UNIONS AS PRESSURE GROUPS, AND GOVERNMENTS

As well as 'ad hoc' pressure groups, there are other groups of people who have significant powers to pressurize governments and affect the decisions they make. The most organized of these are trades unions. Trades unions often have strong political bonds with socialist governments, and may also make a significant contribution to party funds, which can cause governments to be influenced in an ethically questionable manner. Right-wing governments that allow individual companies to make substantial donations to party funds equally run the risk of compromizing themselves.

Trades unions have often been blamed, especially in Britain, for national economic problems. Samuel Brittan, an eminent British journalist, has argued that trades unions are not only dangerous to the economy, but to the workers themselves, because they have used the threat of strike action to force post-war governments into a range of unwise economic policies, viz:

- **Price controls**. These interfere with market forces, and are often also asociated with wage controls. (If wages are not also controlled, so that they outstrip prices, this is bound to lead to increased unemployment, as employers can no longer afford to maintain the same workforce.) The result is a depressing effect on standards of living, and a questionably desirable manipulation of the labour market.
- **Subsidies** given to companies and consumers to keep prices down. They lead to an inefficient use of the total resources available to the national economy (i.e., they do not produce the best possible added value).
- **High taxation**. This is one of the direct knock-on effects of subsidization.
- **Excessive government borrowing**. Socialist governments, particularly, will not want to compromise parts of their programme for the nation (e.g., health, education, housing) that they may have difficulty in funding, partly because they have been cushioning the workforce with subsidies and may not be able to raise enough money from taxation to bridge the gap. The government will therefore have to borrow from other sources, with the consequent impoverishing effect on the nation as a whole.
- **Excessive increases in the supply of money in the economy**. Monetarists believe that inflation is caused by an increased money supply (this is explained in Chapter Four).

- **'Protecting' certain groups in the workforce**. This prevents the movement of workers from declining sectors of the economy to expanding sectors, because there is insufficient incentive for them to do so; therefore overall economic growth is slowed.

Other observers point out that the more militant a union is, the more likely employers are to replace its workers with a machine, thus accelerating the pace of unemployment. It should be said that this is a short-term view. Drucker asserts that all future workers will be 'knowledge workers' – people with skills and expertize that cannot be replicated by machines. from the value added point of view, almost all tasks that can be done as well by a machine as by a human should be – because they will almost invariably be done at a lower cost.

Defenders of trade unions do not refute the economic arguments, but they defend unions for the following reasons.

- **The nature of trade union power is defensive**, and should be viewed in relationship to the power of capitalist companies. The latter often carries more 'clout'.
- Trades unions **react** to events; they do not set the agenda for investment, marketing and design decisions, therefore they have no influence on the value-adding process.
- **There has to be protection for workers**, because capitalist firms can shift production to where they choose, and increase or decrease production levels as they see fit, as well as choose to update designs and equipment or not; again, the workers have little say in the value-adding process. Since these decisions are made by mangement, management should take the blame for poor industrial performance. (This is a traditional, not to say old-fashioned, adversarial stance; more is said in Chapter 5 about the contribution that people at all levels of an organization can make.)
- In any case, much more time is lost through illness and accident than strikes.

It is hard to disagree with the claim that in the late 1960s and 1970s, the unions exerted a stranglehold on industry and government in Britain. It is for governments to legislate to define union powers, and in the past ten years they have chosen to diminish these almost everywhere in western Europe. Yet some form of worker association to monitor the way the workforce is treated is not only socially desirable, but can also have a beneficial effect on adding value – since over-exploited, under-trained and underpaid workforces are unlikely to perform, certainly in the long term. The answer, which is 'single' unions for each company or industry, so that negotiations are kept simple and practices such as 'multi-skilling', which are beneficial to the value-adding process, do not attract resource-wasting hostility and haggling, may already have been found in countries such as Germany and Japan.

WHAT DO GOVERNMENTS DO WHICH AFFECTS THE VALUE-ADDING PROCESS?

So far, we have examined different government ideologies and discussed their impact on adding value, and considered the potential tensions and conflict in the government/business community relationship. This section takes a detailed look at how governments operate in practice to try to stimulate industry to deliver the ever-increasing added value that leads to national prosperity, whilst taking into account the constraints.

1 **Taxation policy**

   (i) **Direct taxation**. This consists of the following:

      (a) **Corporation Tax** levied upon the profit of the business itself. This makes a significant impact on the type of financial planning carried out by the organization. It has already been said that some governments will offer tax incentives to businesses to plough back money into investment in equipment, training, etc. Conversely, a government which endorses a punitive corporate taxation system may discourage businesses from either setting up or staying within its national boundaries.

      (b) **Income tax**. If income tax is levied at a higher rate than by the countries with which a nation most closely identifies (British earners, for example, would probably expect to compare their situation directly with that of other people working within the European Union), then a company's potential customers within that nation will have less net income to spend upon its products. This will have a greater impact on the company if its goods are aimed at 'disposable income' – i.e., are not necessities. It may mean that some of the 'value added' features that customers would otherwise have been prepared to pay for are not in the circumstances considered to be affordable. (In an economist's terms, it will have a significant effect upon products for which demand is elastic.) Direct taxation levied upon specific products by a government (e.g., spirits, tobacco), has a similar effect, the difference being that it is possible for the industry concerned to anticipate and measure more precisely, since it is already aware of what its share of disposable income would probably be. It should be pointed out that governments often target inelastic products for such levies because this makes calculation of the likely tax revenue more accurate.

   (ii) **Indirect taxation**. There are several forms of indirect taxation which affect businesses. The most significant in Britain is probably VAT, or value-added tax. This is currently levied at a rate of 17.5 per cent on the manufacturers' selling price on all but a narrow range of goods, which may be either exempt (like food) or zero-rated (like books). Zero-rated products may be reviewed periodically and the decision to give them a zero rating modified. Many developed nations, including most of the European Union countries, have some form of value-adeded tax.

Other forms of indirect taxation include road taxes and tolls – important considerations in nations which have road-based or car-based economies, particularly for companies that do not operate close to their customers.

From the value-added perspective, it could be argued that the country itself produces advantages related to the product (technical expertise, effective distribution, etc.) which makes the payment of such taxes worthwhile. The argument falls down when whatever national advantages the country has are eroded by competitors operating in countries which do not attract similar taxes.

2 **Employment policy**

Unemployment in developed countries rose by nearly three million in 1992–3. High and rising unemployment has become a pressing political issue, because governments often stand or fall on their employment records. Therefore few governments, however enthusiastic their views on market forces, believe it is acceptable to allow unemployment to find its own level. The problem is complicated by other considerations. In Europe, for example, it is recognized that rising unemployment presents a threat to the future economic and monetary integration of member states of the EU; on the other hand, **low inflation** – the goal of almost every European country – is usually associated with high unemployment figures.

The Organization for Economic Co-operation and development (OECD) undertook a survey into the causes of persistent joblessness in 1992–3, in which it concluded that the rise in unemployment that has occurred steadily in developed nations since 1960 is due to:

- a shift in developed economies away from manufacturing
- competition from developing countries
- technological change

Each of these results in what economists call 'structural unemployment', the most difficult type of unemployment to address, because it is associated with fundamental economic and social changes. Structural unemployment tends to affect whole regions, sometimes whole nations. The concentration of unemployment in such areas is difficult to combat, partly because people are unwilling to abandon old skills and acquire new ones (known as occupational immobility), and they are unwilling to move to vacancies in other areas because of their cultural and personal ties to the region (known as geographical immobility).

Governments have the tricky task of addressing these issues without undermining the long-term prosperity of their economies. Arguably, government initiatives to encourage industry to create high added value – provided that they work – could help to solve the problem. The difficulty also lies in the complexity of the situation which they are trying to remedy. The following examples of ways in which UK governments have tried to tackle unemployment illustrates what is meant.

i) **Regional Policy**

In the UK, a variety of regional policies was developed in the 1930s and expanded in the 1960s. A new system was established by the 1972 Industry Act. It was aimed at producing greater economic growth by enabling a fuller use of resources – both labour and capital. Between 1972 and 1988, the main instrument used was the regional Development Grant, which consisted of a capital grant of 15% payable to firms in designated 'Special Development Areas' for them to invest in plant, buildings and machinery.

Critics of the scheme argued that capital grants merely served to intensify capital production, which did not result in job creation, and that they failed to discriminate between good and bad investment, or between the more and less needy. In other words, money was being given to firms who would have made the investment anyway.

Consequently, the Regional Initiative was introduced in 1988. Under this scheme, Regional Enterprise Grants were awarded by the Department of Trade and Industry on a case by case basis. (Box 2.2 explains how the DTI operates, and what is included in its brief.) The grants were of two types: either Investment Grants, designed to aid projects in most manufacturing and some service sectors (the DTI paid 15 per cent of the expenditure on fixed assets for the project, up to a maximum grant of £15,000), or Innovation Grants, which led to the development and introduction of new products and processes (the DTI paid 50 per cent of eligible costs, up to a maximum grant of £25,000). The DTI also provided factories for sale or rent on reasonable terms, or even rent free for a period. Regional Selective Assistance, consisting of a variety of further grants for capital and training costs where it could be shown that the investment would result in the creation of jobs, was made available.

ii) **Enterprise zones**

The creation of these in the mid-1980s represented an attempt to deal with the problems of the inner cities. They went beyond regional policy, since some of the Enterprise Zones lay outside designated Development Areas. The rationale behind their creation was to release young, small businesses from the bureaucracy, which could impose a crushing burden on them and stifle initiative. The main incentives offered were:

Box 2.2: An explanation of how the Department of Trade and Industry (DTI) operates in Great Britain, and the scope of its activities

The Department of Trade and Industry is a collection of Ministries within the UK government, headed by its own President, who is an inner cabinet minister. He or she is reported to by the Ministers for Industry, Trade and Energy, and the Parliamentary Under Secretaries for Trade and Technology, Corporate Affairs and Consumer Affairs and Small Firms respectively.

The aim of the DTI is to help UK businesses compete successfully at home, within the rest of Europe, and throughout the world. In order to fulfil this aim, it provides advice, practical help and expertize, and seeks to exert its political influence favourable in the cause of British business.

Its stated objectives are therefore as follows:

- to seek to identify the needs of UK business through a close dialogue with individual sectors and an understanding of what influences competiveness at home and abroad.
- to ensure that those needs are taken into account by government and within the European Union.
- to work for trade liberalization worldwide, and help UK business to take full advantage of UK and overseas market opportunities.
- to widen choice and stimulate enterprize by promoting competition and privatization.
- to promote the economic development of UK energy resources and ensure that the nation's needs are met cost-effectively.
- to maintain confidence in markets and protect customers by fair, proportionate and effective regulation, while working to reduce regulatory and administrative burdens on business.
- to stimulate innovation and encourage best practice throughout business in quality, design and management.
- to foster the creation and development of small and medium-sized businesses.
- to respond flexibly to the needs of different regions and areas with special difficulties.
- to take proper account of environmental issues in the development of all its policies to stimulate an effective business response to environmental developments, and ensure that the Government's overall environmental policy takes proper account of the impact on business.
- to manage and develop the people in the DTI so that they provide a professional, high quality, accessible and responsive service to business and the community in line with the principles of the Citizen's Charter.

Source: DTI (1993) *A Guide for Business*, DTI.

- Exemption from Development Land Tax
- 100 per cent allowances for commercial and industrial buildings
- Exemption from rates on industrial and commercial property
- Simplified and relaxed regulations for planning procedures
- Simpler and speedier administration of remaining controls, and government requests for statistical information to be kept to a minimum.

Both the development of Regional Policy after 1988 and the Enterprise Zone Initiative represented a movement towards a more market-orientated approach to solving the problem of unemployment.

Despite the strong 'self-help' element introduced into them, however, and the potential they offered for producing quality goods at competitive prices, it could not be said that they were other than interventionist, nor denied that the goods were indirectly subsidized. Therefore these initiatives were disapproved of by free market purists, who argued that regional problems would eventually resolve themselves if they were left to market forces, because regional unemployment was an indication of labour market disequilibrium – i.e., an excess supply of labour at the prevailing wage rates. Consequently, the argument continued, what was required was a reduction in wages, which could then be passed on to the consumer in the form of lower prices. If unemployment was high in a region, then wage rates would be lower, and some labour would be attracted to other regions by the higher wage rates obtainable there; similarly, new firms would be attracted to the depressed region because they would understand that by locating there they could reduce their costs. Therefore, in time, an equilibrium situation would be restored to the area.

This viewpoint is simplistic in that it does not take into account, for example, the timescale involved, nor any of the main reasons for the growing trends in unemployment analyzed by the OECD (see above). However, it does imply social costs which might be politically, as well as ethically, unacceptable to any government. When the idea of Enterprise Zones was first developed, the 'minimizing' of regulations was to be extended to relax employment legislation relating to working hours, minimum wages, and health and safety at work in these areas. In fact, the express aim was to create a series of 'mini-Hong Kongs' almost solely responsive to market forces, but the government drew back from this, afraid that such a radical departure from the state's role as a safeguarder of human rights would be politically unwise. The overall effectiveness of a regional policy in improving the employment situation is however open to some doubt. Studies in the UK suggest that unemployment would have been worse without a policy, but that the effect has been only marginal, with the creation of between 200,000 and 350,000 jobs in two decades at the cost of approximately £50,000 per job. (This is a crude measure, and does not take into account the social costs and benefits involved, or the financial costs if these people had been 'long-term unemployed'.) Regional policy does more than pay lip service to the unemployment problem, but its main value to the government lies perhaps in being seen to be tackling the issue.

The examples show that even a government ideologically committed to the market economy feels impelled to take significant steps to intervene when addressing major issues such as unemployment, and that, in western economies at least, it is not possible for the government to draw back from its role as citizens' protector. If follows that 'free market forces' are permitted only to obtain to a greater or lesser degree, not entirely, in the value-adding process. The OECD findings indicate that governments keen on developing an employment programme that is going to be effective in the future also need to link it to a proper analysis of skills requirements, education and training.

3 **Education and Training**

Unemployment is a complex phenomenon related to government attitudes to education and training, and skills issues generally, especially the development of expertise in new technologies.

Providing the appropriate educational climate within a country, and the right skills base, is seen by Michael Porter as one of the 'legitimate' influencing roles of government in the quest to add value. How governments should do this can be a matter of controversy. In the first place, there is the question of the age-old debate of the fundamental purpose of education – is it primarily to provide people with factual information that will enable them to develop successful careers and thus contribute to their country's economic prosperity, or should it seek first to 'lead out' the innate qualities of creativity and reflection, which will then, hopefully, result in the creation of a society which is both prosperous and civilized? In Britain in recent years, industrial leaders have criticized educational establishments for preferring the second, more academic stance, to the former, more practical approach, and claimed that it is one of the reasons for the country's loss of competitiveness. In other nations, the links between industry and educational establishments have long been more closely forged – German engineering companies, for example, have since the middle of the nineteenth century both sponsored universities and helped to establish the curriculum that their future workforce will study.

Believing that other nations have succeeded better with an educative programme that is more vocationally orientated, the British government has since 1980 taken some radical measures to facilitate directly work-related education and training in Britain. One such initiative consisted of the setting up of CTCs, or City Technology Colleges, which were directly sponsored by businesses and governed by boards of businesspeople who acted as advisors on the curriculum. These subsequently suffered from a falling-away of business support as businesspeople were forced to concentrate their minds and their chequebooks on dealing with the post-1989 recession. Throughout the 1980s, also, it became progressively more difficult for students wishing to pursue non-vocational courses, particularly if they were arts-orientated, to obtain state support. The government countered charges of philistinism by pointing out that the amount of support that the state could offer to higher education was finite, and that to increase the nation's wealth by providing people with the necessary skills had to come before the 'luxury' of supporting the arts – which would be better served in the long run by this course of action. In 1992, the country's polytechnics, with their more vocationally-orientated teaching programmes, were accorded university status, in an endeavour to remove the image of superiority enjoyed by the universities. These moves in further and higher education were supported earlier on in the educative process, by supplying schools with better technological facilities, and by emphasizing the need for all children to gain proficiency in the basic learning blocks of writing, reading, and mathematics. Again, some of the legislative measures taken to facilitate this, notably the imposition of a National Curriculum, were dogged with controversy.

Training people already in the workplace, and measuring the standards that they had achieved, was also attempted. National Vocational Qualifications, which gave credit ratings for particular skills obtained in the workplace so that future employers could be offered some yardstick to assess an individual's achievements and potential, were one manifestation of this. Direct training programmes that businesses could tap into, some of which were tailored to their individual needs, were also set up. One of these was the Investors in People [IIP] programme, developed primarily for small businesses. When participating businesses had reached a government standard, they were awarded an IIP qualification. Case 2.4 describes this in more detail.

It has already been said that some of these government reforms attracted controversy, and some achieved at best only a partial success. The same was true of similar initiatives that took place in other countries. What they perhaps illustrate is the need for government, industry and educators to work together closely all the time to forge national prosperity – and this does not necessarily imply taking the totally pragmatic, vocational approach. Some of the steps taken by the British government were imaginative and enterprising, and certainly better than a 'do nothing' attitude; but it takes time for such radical shake-ups and complex new networks to function effectively. In the meantime, their success in terms of contributing to the adding value process can only be patchy.

THE INVESTORS IN PEOPLE PROGRAMME

Investors in People [IIP] was developed by the Department of Employment with help from human resource development experts. It was administered in England and Wales by 82 government Training and Enterprise Councils (TECs), which were in 1992 given £10m to improve the training of people in work, and in Scotland by the 14 Local Enterprise Companies, also government sponsored.

IIP was slow to take off, partly because many small businesses viewed it with suspicion, believing the administration of it to be unacceptably bureaucratic and time-consuming. However, most of the 253 companies who had been awarded the status in June 1993 were enthusiastic about its effectiveness, and experts said that it provided one of the most useful checklists, based on best practice, of how companies should be developing staff.

The standard is not awarded to companies for spending large sums on training; rather it measures their approach to the problems they encounter, and which they are helped to resolve in brainstorming sessions involving all the staff. Some TECs have refined their input to include diagnostic help with problems, and to establish whether or not the business already has in place basic essentials, such as a business plan. Then the agenda might include such diverse issues as the latest profit forecasts, the technical problems arising from a new order, or whether the premises comply with health and safety rules.

Assessors acting for the TECs eventually decide whether or not the company qualifies for the award by examining how it measures up to the following questions:

1 Have goals been set for the business?
2 Have these been explained to the workers?
3 Have workers the right skills to meet the needs resulting from the goals?
4 Has the investment in skills been evaluated against the performance of the business?

Source: Adapted from Wood, Lisa (1993) 'A wider view for the workforce', *Financial Times*, 15 June.

4 **Economic Policy**
   Governments' economic policies as they affect the money supply and interest rates of their respective countries are dealt with in Chapter Four. There are other government policies that are designed to have a direct effect on how and what a country's industries and organizations deliver, and these are described below.

i) **Nationalization/privatization**

A nationalized industry is one which is publicly owned by the country to which it belongs. It may have been bought by the nation's government, using funds provided by the taxpayer, or it may have been developed by the government from the outset. Many western governments nationalized industries (railways, coal, etc.) in the 1930s, after the Great Depression, because they believed that this would provide a means of safeguarding against some of the worst privations caused by economic slumps. Some companies came into the public sector as part of the post-Second World War reconstruction effort. National monopolies, such as power grids, where investment costs were huge, usually were developed by the public sector because no private enterprise could amass the capital required. There can be a variety of other motives for nationalization:

- **Ideology**. Left-wing governments are likely to favour nationalization, because it represents a manifestation of the Marxist ideal of common ownership.
- **Strategic**. A government may wish to have complete information about, and control over, an industry – for example, oil – which plays a key part in its economy, and be reluctant to allow such an industry to take its chance with market forces.
- **Pragmatism** (from a largely socialist viewpoint). The government may think that national control will make the industry more efficient (and therefore better at delivering added value).
- **Control**. This relates especially to monopolies. The government may believe that it is in the national interest if the product, commodity or utility produced by the industry is not in the hands of private ownership.
- **Crisis Management**. A government may intervene to save a company or an industry from decline or liquidation by buying it, because it believes that it is in the national interest for it to survive and flourish.
- **'National Champion'** approach. The government may feel that the nation it represents is importing too much of a particular product, or that there is a need for a national presence in a certain industry. It will then nationalize in order to develop what it feels is required.

In the 1990s, nationalization is no longer popular. Even in its heyday, there were frequent expressions of uneasiness at the difficulty of assessing the aims and performance of publicly-owned industry. The 1980s saw a wave of privatization of national industries throughout the world, with Britain taking the leading role. Governments saw privatization – selling shares in formerly nationalized industries to the public – as a way of simultaneously raising revenue, sloughing off financial responsibilities that had become unworkable, thus reducing public borrowing, and getting rid of companies which had been, quite frankly, 'bad buys'. Other reasons for privatization include the following.

- **Ideology**. The belief that market forces should govern all organizations, and that what they charge for their product, how they manage costs, and ultimately whether they survive, should be dictated purely by demand. On the face of it, such an approach should deliver the best possible added value.
- **Pragmatism** (from a largely 'liberal' viewpoint). A government wedded to the concept of privatization believes that private enterprize makes business more efficient.
- **Fairness**. The idea that governments should not intervene to prop up their nation's industries.
- **Widely-held ownership of shares**. It has been a recent goal of many economies to encourage share ownership by 'ordinary' people. The rationale is that not only does this create a significant redistribution of the nation's wealth, but it gives people a vested interest in contributing towards the effort to make companies excel, thus increasing national competitiveness.

CASE 2.5

PRIVATIZATION: THE GERMAN EXPERIENCE

The following extract illustrates how other political considerations must also be taken into account when a government commits itself to a major policy such as that of privatization.

West Germany's privatization effort in the 1980s was modest, and raised approximately one tenth of the amount raised in the UK for the same period. Most of the DM 9.4 bn was generated by privatizing four industrial companies, and of these, only Salzgitter, a steelmaker and shipbuilder, was sold outright. The others were sold by floating shares on the stock market. The four companies constituted most of the state's direct industrial holdings in west Germany.

After these sell-offs, the public sector in west Germany consisted of banking, transport, housing and research and development, worth an estimated DM 7.9 bn, and the state service monpolies: Deutsch Bundesbahn, which in 1990 lost DM 5 bn, and Deutsche Bundespost.

The state's holding in Lufthansa, the world's fourth biggest airline by turnover, was reduced from 80 per cent to 52 per cent in the years 1982–90. Selling off the rest would present a problem over staff pension arrangements, because although the airline operated as a private company and received no state subsidies, its employees had the same pension rights as civil servants.

The privatization of Deutsche Telekom and Deutsche Bundesbahn would similarly raise problems over pensions and other employee rights, and require a constitutional amendment. Both enterprizes in any case needed considerable investment in order to cope with the unequal standards inherited from the East German post and rail systems in the wake of German reunification (the reuniting of east and west Germany after the dismantling of the Berlin wall in 1989).

The financial burden of German reunification might have appeared to be a catalyst to generate further sales to the private sector, but politically Germany was deeply divided over the merits of privatization. In the east, an organization called the Treuhandanstalt was set up to facilitate the sale of formerly state-owned east German companies (practically speaking, all of the large companies, since East Germany was a command economy). Initially, the federal (western) government had briefed the Treuhandanstalt to be ruthless about closing down companies that could not pay their way; but when east German industry turned out to be far less competitive than had been hoped, interventionist steps were taken to ensure that at least some of the 8,000 enterprizes being offered survived. Rising unemployment and anger in the east made the government in Bonn decide in 1991 that although privatization remained the goal, it must not be bought at the cost of social stability.

Source: Adapted from Watkins, Georgina (1991) 'New Stock Goes on the Block', *International Management*, Dec., pp.41–2.

Privatization has been a controversial practice. In the first place, it has been argued that it is morally wrong to sell back to the public that which they owned originally (since the nationalized industries were bought and developed with public funds). Then the sell-offs have included public utilities (water, gas, electricity), which have traditionally been regarded as being safer in the public domain if they are to provide a fair service for all. In the UK, each privatized utility is monitored by a regulator (OFWAT, OFGAS, etc.) in an attempt to ensure protection for the consumer. The regulator, which is a direct representative of the government, is a stakeholder of considerable power. It has the authority to stop any of the regulated industry's activities if it does not think they are being carried out and charged for properly. In practice, the fierceness of the regulator depends on the attitude adopted by its chief officer. There is still conflict, which the regulator acknowledges to a greater or lesser degree, between the demands of the shareholders and the statutory duty of the companies to charge consumers an affordable price, and in industries that require a great deal of investment, these two needs can only be satisfied at the expense of quality. Many governments that have engaged in privatization have been more interested in the financial benefits that it offers than in the ideological justification for it. Internationally, in any case, tougher measures – for example, through EU directives, or GATT agreements (see Chapter 3) – are making it increasingly difficult for governments to offer aid that distorts competition; if governments cannot favour their own industries, then it could be argued that there is little benefit to be gained from a public sector existence. The objective of widely-held share ownership also raises a complex web of ethical questions. Some governments undoubtedly underpriced shares, and offered immediate gains for investors, to boost their privatization programmes; companies interested in buying ailing public industries have also been offered financial 'sweeteners' in return for taking on their debts and problems. And although the number of 'ordinary' shareholders has increased in privatizing countries, the trend may be a temporary one, and has made little impact on the steady concentration of ownership into the hands of institutional investors (pension funds, insurance companies, etc.).

The ultimate test of privatization must rest on assessment of how a company performs after it is privatized. This, of course, means appraising how it adds value at the lowest possible cost. The real question is how 'value' should be defined in the context of the complex environment of many privatized industries – for example, should it take into account a collective responsibility to posterity?

The very sensitivity of the privatization issue highlights the difficulty experienced in all dealings between government and industry of establishing and assessing both quantitative and qualitative performance measures.

Exercise. Devise a table of key industries privatized in Europe during the past five years, and compare them with their counterparts in America. The return for shareholders that they are achieving at the time of publication, and other performance measures, should also be given where possible.

SUMMARY

In this chapter, we have examined the contributions of government to the value-adding process. We have considered what governments **can**, **should** and **do** do, following the premise of Michael Porter that productivity is the only meaningful yardstick of national competitiveness.

Specifically, we have studied:

- Four major types of policy that governments can pursue, viz.,
  1 The 'pure' free market approach
  2 The 'social market' approach
  3 Selective intervention
  4 Government-planned economy
  in the value-adding context.
- We have considered the traditional relationship of government to business, and the effect of pressure groups on governments; and we

have looked at the impact of governments' relations with trade unions.

- You are now able to describe Taxation Policy, both direct and indirect, in terms of its effect on business.
- Employment policy and its importance to governments, and therefore how it affects the decisions which governments make to stimulate industry, have been studied, with a detailed look at UK regional policy and the enterprize zones.
- Education and training, their relation to industry, and government's role in reconciling the needs of the latter with the broader aims of education, has been discussed.
- Economic policy has been looked at in the context of the ownership of strategic industries, and the arguments for and against nationalization and privatization put forward. This has led to a consideration of the importance of both qualitative and quantitative performance measures throughout industry, and the role government can play in this.

REFERENCES AND FURTHER READING

Devine *et al.* (1989) *An Introduction to Industrial Economics* (4th edn.), Unwin Hyman, London.

Drucker, P. (1993) *Post-Capitalist Society*, Butterworth-Heinemann, Oxford.

Fuller, N. (1990) *Fundamental Economics*, (2nd edn.) Tudor Publishing, Merseyside.

Ohmae, K. (1990) *The Borderless World*, HarperCollins, London.

Pattakos, A.N. (1989) 'Growth in activist groups: How can business cope?', *Long Range Planning*, 1989. Reproduced in Mercer, D. (Ed.), *Managing the External Environment*, Sage, London, 1992.

Porter, M.E. (1990) *The Competitive Advantage of Nations*, Macmillan, London.

Sturdivant, F.D. (1981) *Business and Society* (revised edn.), Irwin, Illinois.

Turner, R.L. (1989) *The Politics of Industry*, C. Helm, Bromley, UK.

Reference has been made throughout to contemporary business newspapers and journals. As with any aspect of business, but most especially when dealing with politics, students are advised to make close reference to these contemporary sources of information.

National and international changes: trading groups, political alliances and the value-adding process

3

LEARNING OBJECTIVES

- To understand the views of Michael Porter, Kenichi Ohmae and other well-known writers on how international trade is best undertaken to aid the creation of added value.
- To understand the economist's principles of international trade.
- To understand the attitudes of governments to international trade, and offer definitions for the several measures that governments may take to influence it.
- To understand the way in which the following international organizations, which have been set up to promote world trade, work:
  - The General Agreement on Tariffs and Trade [GATT]
  - The European Economic Union [EU]
  - The European Free Trade Association [EFTA].
- To grasp some of the difficulties which have existed in the trading relationship between the EU and Japan.
- To understand the unique role which America occupies in world politics currently, and the significance of the Asia Pacific Economic Co-operative [APEC] and the North American Free Trade Agreement [NAFTA].
- To describe how the power-balance between the 'superpowers' arose after the Second World War, and make some assessment as to whether the concept of 'superpower' is still relevant.
- To understand the role of the 'Group of Seven' [G7] nations.

- To comment on the post-war rise of multinational corporations; to offer a definition of what types of organization these are, and understand the implications of their present and future influence on world trade, and the significance of this to the added value concept.

INTRODUCTION

In this chapter, we continue our examination of what governments **do** do to contribute to the process of adding value, moving now from the national to the international stage. We will take a further look at the economic principles of international trade, and then examine what key writers on management and strategy say that governments **should** do within this context. We will then define and assess the various measurements that governments **can** undertake to influence the trading process.

Descriptions follow of a number of prominent international organizations which have been set up to shape international trade, and after this the specific difficulties that have afflicted the trading relationship between the EU and Japan are discussed. America's role in world trade is considered, particularly within the context of new trading arrangements currently being set up by the USA which look east rather than west for their alliances. The rise of the 'superpowers' is explained, and an assessment made of whether the term is still relevant, and, if so, which countries are qualified to occupy the role. The power and position of the 'Group of Seven' [G7] nations is considered and the importance and relevance of these organizations to adding value in the future is offered as a subject for debate.

Finally, we move on to discuss the post-war rise of the multinational corporation; we examine different types of multinational, and the definitions which significant authors have applied to the term. We review the controversy as to whether they make a beneficial or harmful contribution to the growing strength, to the idea of adding value, and to the future shape of the world economy.

INTERNATIONAL TRADE

1 **The principles of international trade**

The economist's law of comparative advantage has already been described in Key Concept 2.1. In a simple and, in practice, unachievable international trading situation, trading between two countries will continue as long as the domestic opportunity cost ratios in them are different. In the example given, trade would cease when it cost more in terms of resources for B to import corn than to produce it. If B could produce corn more cheaply than A in terms of computers by transferring resources to corn production, then trading would stop.

However, it is necessary to realize that A does not have to have an absolute advantage over B in producing corn for B to carry on trading with it; what it needs to be able to do is produce corn more cheaply than B relative to world market prices. If B has devised a means of producing corn slightly more cheaply than A, but the opportunity cost of this is that resouces are diverted from building computers, which B can produce much more cheaply than A, then from B's government's probable point of view, B should carry on specializing in computers and buying corn from A, because then the overall profits made by Country B would be greater. However, governments are likely to try to find ways of achieving the best outcome for their nations. A's government might try to maximize the benefits accruing to its own country, and alter the efficiency outcome, by imposing tariffs on computers imported from Country B. In this case, A's government would be taking what is known as a **mercantilist** stance – its goal is the creation of the most favourable distribution of wealth. A liberal economist, on the other hand, would place most emphasis on the shared interests which arise from economic exchange. **Liberalism** considers that the most important goal of a government's economic policy is the maximum creation of total (i.e., global) wealth by achieving optimal efficiency. These are called **Pareto-optimal** benefits – see Key Concept 3.1. Optimal efficiency is achieved by producing what the customer requires, in the right quantity, at the lowest possible cost (i.e., with minimal waste). The concept lies at the heart of the added value philosophy. It explains why most western governments claim to be wedded to the idea of free trade. How they operate in practice forms much of the substance of this chapter.

2 **Attitudes to trade in practice**

Despite the virtues of Pareto-optimal ideals, which are endorsed by most western governments, there are many other political considerations which are in practice taken into account when international trading decisions are made. The 'ideal' of free international trading is routinely upheld, and GATT as an institution (see below) is continually working towards it, but it is still the norm for governments to attempt to restrict the amount of trade they allow in order to protect their domestic economies from some of the less desirable effects of foreign competition. The resulting policies are known as 'protectionist' policies. Restrictions on trade may include any of the following measures:

(a) **Tariffs**. These are taxes on imports, otherwise known as 'duties'.

KEY CONCEPT 3.1: PARETO-OPTIMAL BENEFITS

The reasoning behind Pareto-optimal analysis is as follows:

1 In any free economic exchange, both parties gain, because they place different values on the products being exchanged. Each party values less than the other party the product that it is offering for trade. For instance cash, which may, for example, be spent on education for his son, is more important to a Saudi oil producer than the oil of which he has a plentiful supply; the oil is more important to a British manufacturer, who needs it to generate power for machinery. This has been the basic principle of bartering since trading began.

2 However, both parties may not gain equally. The oil producer may gain greatly from the exchange – particularly if he belongs to a cartel such as OPEC – whereas the businessman may only gain slightly, e.g., he may be paying more for oil than he would for other fuels, but he may not wish to incur the expense of adapting his equipment.

3 Liberal economists are interested in the point which is reached when the **joint overall** benefits from the exchange are maximized. This is called the **Pareto-optimal benefit**. Establishing where this point lies, and then achieving an outcome which realizes it, is a matter for bargaining, and usually involves the governments of the countries concerned. Political power is important, but (at least, so the theory goes) it is used positively and not punitively to achieve the most favourable result. The rationale behind this is that each nation will be sensible enough to see that it is better to have a share of the resulting wealth, and therefore to support a system which generates as much wealth as possible, rather than to try to adopt measures which will curb the wealth-producing efforts of other nations.

4 International borders are therefore of less importance to economists and all those interested in the maximization of global wealth than the wealth-generating processes themselves.

(b) **Import quotas**. They consist of quantitative restrictions placed on specific imports. Under the General Agreement on Tariffs and Trade (see below), they are illegal; nevertheless, in the European Union alone, member states were protecting more than 1,000 different products through national Quantitative Restrictions (QRs) in 1993, and strong local pressures in some cases had led to demands of elevating QRs to Communitywide levels. The fact of this illustrates how difficult it is, both politically and economically, to remove the practice of upholding import quotas. Where progress has been made in achieving it, transitional phases are often needed. These may take the form of Voluntary Restraint Agreements (VRAs) in which the exporting country promises to honour a quota arrangement, as it were, by gentleman's agreement, rather than because it is legislatively binding.

(c) **Reciprocity**. This is a complex concept, which is often not clearly spelt out even by countries engaging in it. Simply, it requires that the status of, and opportunities for, firms conducting business abroad be equivalent to those that they enjoy at home. More commonly, it implies 'mirror-image reciprocity', where a nation's government insists that opportunities for its firms abroad are equivalent to those provided by it for foreign firms before access is granted to its markets. In contrast, 'national treatment' is also often applied, meaning that the competitive rules operate in exactly the same way for domestic and foreign companies trading in a country, regardless of the conditions existing in the outside market – i.e., that equality of opportunity is absolute and unmanaged. The relative merits of reciprocity and national treatment have been the cause of heated debate. One compromise alternative is an overall balance of concessions, which is another kind of reciprocity measure, but one which examines the degree of market access provided for the nation's, or trading bloc's, firms in all sectors, not just in specified industries.

(d) **Subsidies**. These are already referred to in Chapter Two in the section on trades unions. Direct financial help from governments, in the form of cash payments, tax concessions, etc., either allow domestic producers to reduce their prices below those of foreign competitors, or simply make it possible for them to compete. They are, of course, one of the more extreme manifestations of 'interventionism', and alien to the market forces concept.

(e) **Exchange control regulations**. These place a limit on the amount of foreign currency available to pay for imports, in effect restricting the number of imports the country is able to accept.

(f) **Physical controls**. A complete ban or embargo may be placed either on a specified product, or the products of a specific company or nation. In the latter case, the government is often using sanctions to indicate its disapproval of or displeasure at some political practice being carried out by the vetoed country. For example, many nations operated sanctions against South Africa in protest against the apartheid regime, and governments of the world united to impose sanctions on Iraq after its invasion of Kuwait in 1990. In the latter case, sanctions were imposed in an attempt to force the Iraquis to retreat from Kuwait without the necessity of military action, but the measure was unsuccessful.

Sanctions imposed for political reasons are frequently ineffective because they take too long to work, or because they are not universally observed.

(g) **Rules of origin and local content**. This is another complex procedure which has primarily been developed by the European Union, but which is likely to be adopted by other regions and trading blocs as trading worldwide becomes increasingly polarized. It is directly related to the value chain concept, and more particularly to which nation's firms gain most from the value-adding process. The 'local content' percentage of the end product is identified and measured in order to try and gauge the amount of added value contributed by the local community. A standard percentage is then established (this is not uniform; it varies from sector to sector, but in the European Union if it does not reach the 'safeguard rule' of 45 per cent, the company producing the product is likely to attract a tariff, thus increasing the cost of the finished article) with the aim of preventing the companies operating within the country from becoming mere 'screwdriver' plants.

A more sophisticated variant of this is known as 'substantial transformation' content, where an attempt is made to determine the origin of the essential value-added component (i.e., that which builds the margin) rather than through its overall local content percentage. This would seem to make more sense in high technology industries, where, for example, complex but tiny components attract many times more added value than the larger artefacts which house them.

Are such policies beneficial to the consumer, or ever defensible in terms of creating quality at the lowest possible cost? On the face of it, the answer is no. Writers such as Michael Porter have argued vehemently and with some logic that protection from competition can only lead to inefficiency and paucity of innovation; and moreover, that when industries eventually (as will inevitably happen) have the prop of government support taken away from them, they will be even more weak and ill-equipped to face international competition. Not only do consumers have to bear the higher costs incurred by protectionism, but the choice of goods to which they have access is artificially restricted. Trade is also a great civilizer, and forges links between countries, promoting co-operation; attempts to interfere with the trading mechanism frequently result in retaliation, and can even lead to wars.

In practice, as we saw in Chapter Two, all governments are interventionist to a degree. The arguments usually put forward in favour of their intervening in trade are most commonly:

- that it is necessary to protect a new or developing industry
- the country needs to control its balance of payments deficit

- the domestic economy needs protecting against unemployment caused in part by an influx of imports (see above)
- strategically important industries need protecting
- the domestic economy needs protection from 'unfair' competition – which might include 'dumping' (the selling abroad of excess production to cover marginal costs only), or 'sweated labour' from economies where there are few or no safeguards for employees.

The questions raised by these issues serve only to illustrate that, taking the widest perspective, there can be no cut-and-dried answers. The knock-on effects of allowing a country's economy to decline without coming to its aid, or allowing another country to gain an unstoppable ascendancy, may in the long or even the medium term militate against the best interests of the consumer. The consumer is, after all, usually a member of a local community, and may not have the necessary information, let alone the vision, to understand the impact of his or her short-term buying decisions on posterity. To take this stance would be all very well if governments could be relied on to make decisions that were not only well-informed, but also ethically correct and accounting for the implications of all the variables involved. The task is, in truth, superhuman. Perhaps the status quo of piecemeal interventionism is the best that can be hoped for in the forseeable future, with an international consensus moving gradually closer towards allowing market forces to decide as individual nations become stronger. However foremost experts take a stronger line.

CURRENT THINKING ON INTERNATIONAL COMPETITION: THE VIEWS OF PORTER AND OHMAE

Michael Porter's work *The Competitive Advantage of Nations* is an exploratory thesis which sets out to discover why some nations excel in some industries. In Chapter Two, Porter's view that productivity alone offers a meaningful gauge of competitiveness was quoted. Porter goes on to offer four other central tenets which underpin his arguments, as follows.

1 That international trade and foreign investment provide both the opportunity to boost the level of national productivity, and a threat to increasing or maintaining it.
2 That government intervention serves only to slow down the upgrading of the nation's economy and limits long-term living standards.
3 That the influence of the nation itself may be applied to specific industries, and segments within those industries. Most successful national industries consist of groups of firms.
4 In many industries, especially high-tech ones, factor comparative advantage (as already discussed) offers an incomplete explanation for the success of that industry in a particular country.

To what, therefore, does Porter attribute the success of the national industries that he has identified? To explain it, he has developed a model, which he calls the 'diamond' of national advantage. He says that successful industries depend upon the home nation to give them a complex interlinking base of favourable circumstances, which are described by the four 'points' of his diamond:

- demand conditions
- factor conditions
- the contribution made by related and supporting industries
- firm strategy, structure and rivalry i.e., ('jockeying for position') within the nation.

According to Porter, it is this complicated, and difficult to reproduce, set of circumstances existing in the home nation that not only enables an industry of world-class standing to be developed, but also makes it difficult for other nations to achieve the same success. Key Concept 3.2 explains the facets of the 'diamond' in some detail. The contribution that each of these facets makes to the value chain are indicated.

KEY CONCEPT 3.2: THE COMPONENTS OF MICHAEL PORTER'S 'DIAMOND'

1 **Demand conditions**

Porter identifies three broad attributes of home demand which are relevant to international success:

(i) **Composition** (the nature of buyer needs). The more sophisticated and therefore demanding the home buyers of an industry's products are, the more they will help it to establish international competitive advantage by continually pushing it to add value in new directions, and therefore to innovate and upgrade before its compeitors.

(ii) **Size** and **pattern** of growth. For example, is the industry a 'sunrise' industry (Drucker's term), which has been developed by exploiting new technologies? If so, then the way it is marketed at home will have a significant influence on the way it is presented abroad, and therefore on its future success.

(iii) **Mechanisms** for transmitting the nation's preferences to foreign markets. If the nation's values and culture are being exported (e.g., by the media, or by businesspeople, say, demanding the same standards of hotel abroad to those they are used to at home), then a competitive advantage established by the demanding home consumer is reinforced.

2 **Factor conditions**

Porter builds on the classical economist's concept of the factors of production – land, labour and capital – but updates the idea by devising what he calls a 'Hierarchy of Factors':

(i) **Basic factors**

These are similar to those taught by classical economists, and include the following:

- natural resources
- climate
- location
- unskilled/semi-skilled labour
- debt capital.

He points out that nations may be poor in one or more of these factors, and turn such impoverishment to competitive advantage, because it has forced them to think sooner than their rivals about.

(ii) **Advanced factors**

These are based on the idea that what Drucker calls the 'knowledge worker' is the main creator of added value today, and will become even more important in the future. Examples include:

- modern digital data communications infrastructure
- hghly educated personnel
- university research institutes in sophisticated disciplines.

These examples indicate that factor advantages most likely to contribute to a high value-added component will not only be specialized, but will need continual investment in order to be sustainable. High-tech skills become outdated quickly. Therefore a delicate balance has to be achieved between training and paying people to produce the goods that add value for today's customer, and those that will fulfil that function in the future.

(iii) **Related and supporting industries**

By 'related industries', Porter means industries which operate co-ordinated or sharing activities. For example, ink manufacturing supports the printing industry, and printing supports the publishing industry. It could be said that both ink-making and printing are publisher-related industries. Porter says that if the **linkages** between related and supporting industries are strong and mutually reinforcing, the following benefits are likely to occur:

- The creation of **new** competitive industries. For example, 3M developed the Stick-On Notepad from its knowledge of and experimentation with adhesives.
- Opportunities for **information flow** and **technical interchange**. These are particularly valuable in establishing added value for the customer, since, as will be clear from the publishing example above, each industry is the customer of its immediate 'upstream' supplier in the value chain. Of supreme importance is the feedback communicated by the ultimate consumer – in the case of publishing, by the book-buyer to the retailer. Efficient channels need to be established to relay this information. Case 3.1 describes Booktrack, a new product consisting of a subscribers' database set up to exchange information between the book retailing and publishing industries.
- New approaches to **opportunities** and **competition** such as joint ventures that help spread cost and risk.
- International success can pull through demand for **complementary products and services**, thus strengthening the national base.

(iv) **Firm strategy, structure and rivalry in the domestic market**

Porter argues that rivalry among domestic producers acts as a powerful competitive stimulus. For example, in industries where the Japanese have established worldwide leadership, there may be many home rivals. Porter's research team identified 112 machine tool manufacturers, 34 making semi-conductors, 25 making audio equipment and 15 making cameras.

Although Porter maintains that all four attributes of the 'diamond' are necessary for sustained competitiveness, domestic rivalry, especially when it is associated with geographic concentration, is particularly powerful, because it has the ability to 'transform the diamond into a **system**.' [Porter]

The virtue of this phenomenon is that clusters of competitive industries are therefore set up, linked both vertically (the next step in the value chain) and horizontally (through rivalry), so that an efficient national network for adding value is created. Therefore success is not just a random happening, but the product of close co-operation and continual industrial drive.

Source: Adapted from Porter, M. (1990) *The Competitive Advantage of Nations*, Macmillan Press.

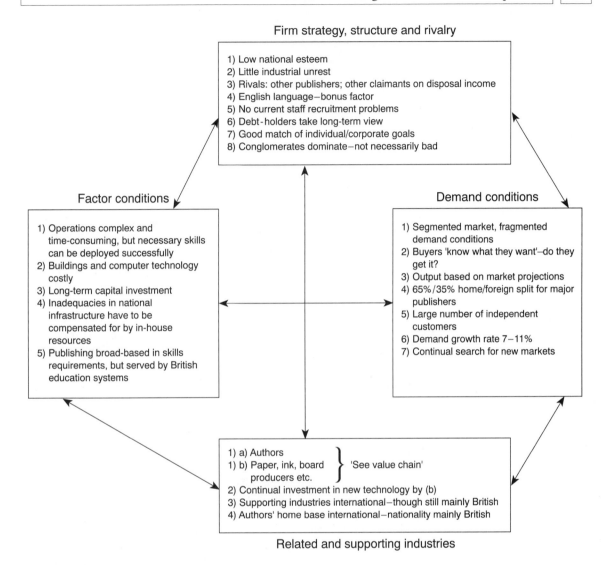

Figure 3.1 Porter's 'Diamond': publishers.

Porter goes on to say that there are two other factors which have a bearing on the 'diamond' – chance and the role of government. These do not properly belong to the diamond, because they cannot contribute directly to the adding of value, but they do influence the way in which that is achieved.

He offers the following examples of chance:

- acts of pure invention
- major technological discontinuities (e.g., in biotechnology, micro-electronics, see case 3.1 for an example of these).
- discontinuities in input costs (e.g., oil shocks)

- significant shifts in world financial markets/exchange rates
- surges of world or regional demand
- political decisions by foreign governments
- wars.

CASE 3.1

BOOKTRACK

'Booktrack' is an enterprise which was set up jointly in late 1993 by J. Whitaker Ltd., a company which generates and disseminates bibliographical information for the book trade, and an American company which gathers and sells statistics on the recorded music industry.

For more than 100 years, Whitaker has occupied a unique position in the British book industry as the official cataloguer of all books and the publisher of *The Bookseller*, the trade journal. Since the mid-1970s, it has also allocated ISBNs (International Standard Book Numbers) to publishers, so that each book published may have a unique reference number and accompanying bar code. It pioneered the use of first the microfiche and then the CD ROM (Compact Disk Read Only Memory) for storing this data in an accessible form. Most libraries and publishers, and many booksellers, now use the CD ROM on a regular basis. It may be networked if users are prepared to pay Whitaker an additional charge.

Throughout the 1980s, while Whitaker was making these technological advances, bookshops also were undergoing a technological revolution. First of all, a teleordering system was launched by Software Sciences Ltd., so that booksellers' orders to publishers could be sent via a dedicated telephone line on a daily basis. This cut down massively on the costs of paperwork and postage, and helped both to prioritize orders and speed up deliveries. Secondly, the major bookselling chains installed EPOS (Electronic Point of Sale) systems, so that they could continually keep track of which books were selling and in what quantities. This helped them to add value for the customer by means of good service, since they were more likely to have in stock the books which people really wanted to buy.

Publishers, also, developed sophisticated computer systems which told them which items were moving out of their warehouses, and to which retailers.

Clearly, a great deal of information was being gathered by all the parties involved, but it was not being effectively disseminated. If this were to happen, the process would surely be of benefit to everyone, especially the consumer, and Whitaker was quick to spot the potential here for a new offshoot of the book information industry.

It took the first step by acquiring Teleordering Ltd. in 1990. It then formed an alliance with the music data company, in order to tap into areas of expertize it did not have in gathering market statistics of this nature. Finally, it set up pilots with publishers and booksellers to find out how much support the product would achieve, what sort of price people were willing to pay for the added value that they were being offered, and what the possible pitfalls of the venture might be.

By September 1993, having resolved some of these questions in advance as far as was possible, the venture was ready to 'go live', and a director for the project had been appointed. If it is successful, 'Booktrack' will provide an exciting example of how some high-tech industries can give birth to others, if their potential is imaginatively explored.

There are still some issues that will have to be addressed, however. For instance in the related fields of ethics (how much information about customers should be generated by EPOS systems, and to whom it should be released) and competition (both in the areas of bookselling and publishing), rival companies will be asked to contribute sensitive data on the assumption that it will be beneficial to everyone; but it might be argued that some organizations will benefit more than others from the arrangement. No doubt the resolution of these problems will set precedents for other industries engaged in the use of high technology for information sharing.

Source: various editions of *The Bookseller*, and promotional material.

Many of Porter's examples are outside the scope of control of an industry or business; the most any leader can hope to do is to manage the effects of them as imaginatively and efficiently as possible as they arise. The relationship with government is, however (as we have seen) more complicated. Porter gives instances of how governments may affect each of the 'points' of the diamond, as follows.

1 **Factor conditions** are affected through subsidies, capital market policy, education policy, etc. Of these, Porter endorses government's role in the last. According to him, it is the proper task of government to provide an enabling **infrastructure** for business activity, not to meddle in the market mechanism.
2 Product standards and regulations are established by governments to mandate or influence **buyer needs**. These may create competitive advantage by moving the industry forward, giving the home firms the lead in adding value. For example, the Swedish government's insistence on strict safety regulations for vehicles led Volvo to make a virtue of necessity, and base its strategy upon the distinctive safety features of its products.

The government itself is often a major buyer of high added-value items such as defence goods and telecommunications equipment. Its role in this respect can help or harm the industry, depending on whether the government exhibits 'favouritism' towards it, or encourages it to remain internationally competitive by judging its goods impartially with those of other nations. For example, some years ago the British government faced a dilemma when making a choice between buying British or American tanks. The American tanks clearly suited their needs better, but to place an order for them would have resulted in the loss of many jobs in the British defence industry. In the end, the political argument was the more powerful, and British tanks were bought.

3 Government can shape the circumstances of **related** and **supporting industries** by, for example, controlling advertising media; regulating support services. Exhibit 3.1 gives a shortened version of the remit of the Advertising Standards Authority.

4 Government policy influences **firm strategy**, **structure** and **rivalry** through devices such as taxation policy (we have already considered this, and it is discussed in more detail in Chapter Four). Again, Porter states that by being as little interventionist as possible, a government is helping to promote the competitiveness of its nation's industries.

Conversely, he says, government policies can themselves be affected by determinants of the 'diamond' already in place, such as the location of educational resources, and an industry's early introduction of safety standards.

Finally, Porter makes the point that there are important differences of national approach towards such key issues as training, background, management style, attitudes towards customers and international activities. These are essentially cultural differences, and are discussed at length in Chapter Five, but it is important to be aware of them at this stage.

Kenichi Ohmae, in direct contrast to Porter, identifies what he calls the 'Three Strategic Cs', and says that they are applicable to all industries, regardless of the nation in which they are operating. (see figure 3.2)

The three Cs are:

1 **Customers**. They are divided into segments, and need to be targeted (and listened to).

2 **Corporation**. The company itself. Ohmae divides this into traditional functions, but his model nevertheless operates on a value-chain-type basis

3. **Competitors**. He says the company should concentrate on understanding the key aspects of competition – i.e., where competitors' core competencies lie and how they add value uniquely.

Exhibit 3.1

The mandate and activities of the Advertising Standards Authority

The Advertising Standards Authority of the UK acts independently of both the government and the advertising industry. It acts as an adviser to and as a watchdog of the latter. Its mandate is to promote and enforce the 'highest standards in all non-broadcast advertisements in the UK'. It does this in the public interest, and it seeks the co-operation of the whole of the advertising industry by ensuring that everyone who commissions, prepares and publishes advertisements observes the British Codes of Advertising and Sales Promotion.

The Codes are established by a sub-committee (CAP: the Committee of Advertising Practice), which consists of representatives from advertisers, promoters, agencies, the media and service providers. The first Code appeared in 1961. Subsequent revisions were made every four or five years as more sections and rules were added. The first Code of Sales Promotion Practice was introduced in 1974, the Alcohol Code was appended in 1975, and the Cigarette Code in 1976. All these Codes were rewritten and redesigned in 1995. The Codes require that advertisements and promotions should be:

> . . . legal, decent, honest and truthful; prepared with a sense of responsibility to consumers and to society; and in line with the principles of fair competition.

In 1994, the USA tackled issues as diverse as the use of speed claims in car advertising, the persistently misleading claims made by some slimming advertisers, and advertising aimed specifically at children. It sought to clarify the issue of what actually constitutes an advertisement (since some advertisements are now couched in the guide of 'editorial copy' in newspapers). It investigated the protection of religious sensitivities in advertising, and kept a watching brief on the development of the 'information superhighway' as an advertising medium.

During 1994 the ASA received 9657 complaints relating to 7334 advertisements. To try to ensure that it retains an overview of compliance of its codes and trends in advertising generally, in October 1995 it conducted a National Advertising Review, which it described as 'a statistically valid trawl of advertising appearing on posters, in magazines and in the national and regional press'.

The ASA is a member of the European Advertising Standards Alliance (EASA), which has its offices in Brussels. The Alliance is an umbrella organization that co-ordinates advertising controls and promotes best practice among its membership, while not controlling them. It has been successful in launching a system of cross-border complaints, by which consumers in any member state can have complaints investigated against advertisements originating from other member states.

Source: *ASA Annual Report*, 1994

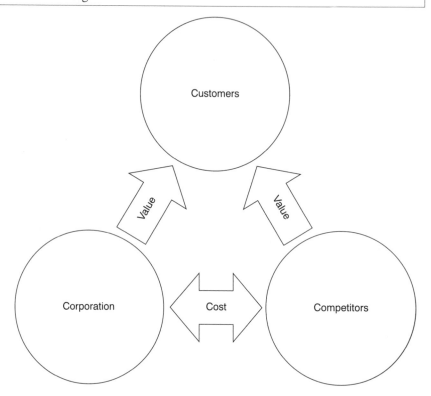

Figure 3.2 The three strategic Cs, after Kenichi Ohmae.

Ohmae claims that the power of the corporation cuts across national boundaries, and that all forward-thinking companies simply think of the whole world as their marketplace. Governments and their activities, and the concept of the nation itself, are redundant and irrelevant to this business environment. While this attitude may seem too futuristic at present, especially in view of what we have said about governments and their power, Ohmae's ideas are worth considering within the context of the rise and continuing power of the multinational corporation, which is discussed at the end of this chapter.

INTERNATIONAL POLITICAL MOVEMENTS TO PROMOTE TRADE IN THE WORLD

1. **The General Agreement on Tariffs and Trade [GATT]**
   The General Agreement on Tariffs and Trade was negotiated after the Second World War to promote world trade and investment. Its purpose was to regenerate forces driving the exchange of goods and services, which had not been fully effective since the Depression of the 1930s. Currently, 108 of the world's countries belong to GATT.

GATT has a creed among its member nations, who subscribe to the belief that it is important to:

- raise the world's standard of living
- secure a growing volume of real income and demand by developing the world's resources
- expand the worldwide production and exchange of goods.

GATT therefore sets out to create reciprocal and mutually beneficial arrangements that reduce tariffs and other barriers to trade and eliminate discriminatory trade practices. It provides an international framework for settling trade disputes, and in the 1990s is taking into its remit issues relating to services, investments and intellectual property.

The main mechanism by which GATT operates consists of a series of multilateral trade negotiations (collectively known as a 'round') which can last for several years. The first five of these to take place encouraged exchanges and a building of trust between the countries involved, but produced little material effects. The 'Kennedy Round' (1963–7) was credited with producing the first major GATT accomplishments. It resulted in the eventual reduction of tariffs and duties by 30 per cent, which substantially increased world trade. After the first oil crisis occurred in the 1970s, however, trade barriers began to reappear: countries began to circumvent GATT restrictions on protectionism by turning to voluntary restraint agreements (whereby nation's 'promised' or came to 'gentlemen's agreements' to, for example, limit the number of goods they would attempt to export to their trading partners), public subsidies, and national procurement policies. It will therefore be apparent that GATT negotiations are closely influenced by political decisons taken within the participating countries. The complexity of considerations that influence politicians when negotiating in a GATT round is illustrated by Case 3.2, which describes some of the problems considered in the Uruguay round of talks.

As the brief account in Case 3.2 of GATT and its activities indicates, there are a number of important trading blocs operating in the world at the moment. These operate with varying degrees of power and efficiency. Their general effect is to force even powerful governments to compromise on trade issues, though of course in trading agreements a *primus inter pares* is likely to emerge. What is certain is that national and international politics always form some part of the equation in the value-adding process.

Perhaps the most powerful, and certainly the most complex of all the current trading blocs is that of the European Union (EU). A brief account of its structure follows.

2 The European Union (EU)

Note: the European Union was known as the EEC (European Economic Community) until its name was changed to reflect wider membership and ideals at the end of 1993.

CASE 3.2

THE URUGUAY ROUND OF THE GATT TALKS

The Uruguay Round was launched in the coastal resort of Punta del Este in 1986, and should have been completed in 1990; but deadlock on the reform of farm trade blocked progress in all the areas in which it proposed to be involved after 1990. This culminated in French farmers taking to the streets in protest at the end of 1992. Negotiations which took place in Geneva at the time involved pressure from the USA, with the backing of other exporters of farm produce, for the elimination of the EC's farm subsidy scheme, from which France, with a very significant agricultural sector, benefited particularly. Eventually, it was agreed to cut the subsidies rather than to abolish them. (Such a reform would be unlikely to provide significant new export opportunities into Europe for non-European countries, but would still be valuable if world food prices rose, because there would be a decline in the volume of EC food surpluses being 'dumped' onto world markets.)

GATT negotiators were also seeking to press countries to open their markets to trade in services. The USA and the EU jointly called for 'maximum liberalization and minimum exemptions', but a number of areas remained fiercely controversial:

1 **Financial services**. Banking, securities and insurance were especially important to some countries (the USA, France, Germany and Britain). In 1992, American and EC negotiators were able to agree a common position, and next planned to force compromise from other key countries – Japan, Korea, and the five Asean nations of Singapore, Indonesia, Thailand, the Philippines and Malaysia, none of whom was showing the inclination to co-operate.
2 **Telecommunications**. The world's 12 main telecommunications markets – including the USA, the EC, Japan, Canada and Australia – were close to agreeing an 'extended negotiation' which would last two years. It was envisaged that this would lead to rules for opening up basic telecommunications to international competition.
3 **Audio-visual services**. Within the GATT context, this meant the international marketing of films, videos and television programmes. It was important to the US, whose second most important export to the EC in 1991 was films and TV programmes. However, France was insisting that 60 per cent of its prime time television programmes should be of EC origin, while other member states were asking for between 40 per cent and 50 per cent.
4 **Maritime services** attracted a great deal of controversy, but it was uncertain whether mooted 'cabotage' arrangements – allowing foreign ships to carry cargo between two ports inside any one country – would be made possible. GATT was pressing generally for

liberalization of international shipping, along with action against 'closed' shipping conferences, which at the time allowed shippers plying a route to block new entrants.

5 **Government procurement contracts** had long been closed to international competition, but reforms would be resisted by powerful domestic industrial lobbies, especially in the construction industry. The USA, although pushing for reform, was likely itself to generate controversy: in many states, the 'Buy America' act, which required state and local authorities to buy US-made products where available, was operational, and widely used to ensure that local companies secured government contracts.

The Geneva conference had a third task of negotiating tariff cuts across a wide range of industrial and non-industrial goods, and to persuade governments to replace non-tariff barriers to trade (such as quotas) with simple tariffs. Negotiations at this level were cumbersome because they had to be undertaken bilaterally between all 108 of the countries involved in the Uruguay Round, and because they involved the resolution of the following difficult issues:

- **Zero-for-zero tariff peaks**. The USA was pressing for the EC to eliminate entirely its tariffs on a number of goods, particularly in the chemical and pharmaceutical industries, but the EC was unwilling to do this unless the USA agreed to reduce some of its tariffs on glassware and ceramics.
- **Rice imports for Japan and South Korea**. This issue revolved around the question of farm trade and market access. Japan and South Korea had kept their local rice markets firmly closed, bowing to pressure from vocal farm lobbies. Following the agreement between the USA and the EC to liberalize farm trade, these countries would come under pressure first to open at least 3 per cent of their markets, and then gradually to cut tariffs – which at first might be set as high as 700 per cent.
- **Banana imports**. Bananas had become a controversial issue for Europe. Preferential import quota regimes targeted at former British and French colonies had attracted criticism inside GATT itself. Demands for comprehensive replacement of quotas with tariffs would force the dismantling of these quota arrangements, causing great difficulty for Caribbean island exporters especially. Banana trade might appear to be an arcane area for controversy, but its symbolic importance would be great if Japan or Korea chose to use it to prevent concessions on rice trade. The point illustrates the international political ramifications of all GATT proceedings.

Source: Dodwell, David (1992) 'Now the tough talks can begin', *Financial Times*, 23 Nov.

The EU was set up in an attempt by some of the countries of Europe to rationalize their business environment under the Treaty of Rome in 1957. In 1979, the Cassis de Dijon established two key principles for the Community:

(i) That products and groups of products which met essential safety criteria must be allowed free circulation in the EU. There was, thereafter, no attempt to legislate detailed technical standards.

(ii) For product differences based on non-essential requirements, there was mutual recognition of national regulations and industrial standards.

In 1985, the Cockfield White Paper established that deregulation would take place within a new regulatory environment. This built on the principle of mutual recognition, and proposed to remove physical, technical and physical barriers which conflicted with the goal of a single united market. The deadline for realizing these steps was set at the end of 1992. The White Paper was followed in 1987 by the Single European Act, which made major amendments to the Treaty of Rome. The most important of these were as follows.

• A unanimous vote on decisions was no longer required, and therefore progress was no longer slowed down to the pace of the most reluctant member state (of which there were now 12).

• New powers of veto and legislation would be conferred on the European Parliament.

• New policy areas would be addressed, including the environment, research and technology, regional development, and economic and monetary co-ordination.

• The Community would aim for stronger 'social and economic cohesion'. A Regional Development Fund (cf. the UK's efforts on its own behalf) was set up to provide funds to the less developed member states, to help counteract the increase in regional imbalances within the Community.

• Poorer regions would be allowed to delay the implementation of EU directives.

The EU consists primarily of four bodies:

(i)   The **Commission**, which initiates legislation and administers Community policy.

(ii) The **Council**, which approves legislation.

(iii) The **European Parliament**, which can modify or impede legislation.

(iv) The **European Court of Justice**, which interprets laws, and frequently establishes precedents of far-reaching impact.

The Commission drafts proposals, and sends them to the Council, which decides whether to accept or reject them via one of three methods: Unanimity, which is required for votes concerning tax harmonization, the free movement of people, and human rights; simple majority voting, which requires the support of seven of the member states, and qualified majority voting, which requires 54 of 76 votes. Although most legislation needs only a qualified majority for approval, the Council has adopted the practice of adopting virtually all proposals by unanimity. When an issue forces a qualified majority vote, the member states carry different powers. In 1993, the arrangement was as follows:

- Germany, France, Italy, UK   10 votes each
- Spain   8 votes
- Belgium, Greece, Netherlands, Portugal   5 votes each
- Denmark and Ireland   3 votes each
- Luxembourg   2 votes.

The European Parliament consists of 518 members (MEPs) who are elected by a direct vote in the member states. Representation varies, according to the state's size, from 81 to six. The Parliament meets in Strasbourg for one week in each month. It has three main functions:

(i)   **Legislative**. The Parliament is consulted about most legislation proposed by the Commission and can make amendments to it. It can delay legislation until the Commission responds to the suggestions for amendment. Decisions are presented to the Council, but are not binding on it.

(ii) **Financial**. The Parliament can request changes in some expenditure items and unilaterally make changes in others, as well as reject the Community budget.

(iii) The Parliament can put **oral and written** questions to the Council and Commission. It can bring both to the European Court of Justice for failing to act in accordance with the Treaty of Rome. It can dismiss the Commission from office through a two/three majority vote.

The European Court of Justice, which is based in Luxembourg, has the power to settle disputes and award penalties. It consists of 13 judges, one from each member state, and one appointed by the large member states in rotation, plus six advocates-general, appointed by agreement among the national governments. They all serve six-year renewable terms. There is also a Court of First Instance to relieve the heavy workload.

The nature of law in the European Economic Community is as follows:

- **Regulation**. This is achieved by means of a legal act which is passed with general application to all the member states, and is immediately binding on all of them, it therefore supersedes their national laws, and it may be issued by the Council or the Commission. In 1993, its scope had been limited to establishing and developing market organizations for agricultural products.

- **Directives**. Directives are binding, but only in respect of their results; the implementation which leads to these results is left to the discretion of the national governments. They may be issued by the Council or the Commission, and generally a period of time is allowed for implementation. Consequently, many countries are slow to put them into practice.

- **Decisions**. Decisions are acts directed specifically to particular parties: member states, companies and individuals. They are binding, and of the powers exercised by the EU, they have the greatest impact on competition. In the same area, the EU may also make recommendations which are not binding, and do not give rise to legal obligations. These tend to have a limited effect on the individuals and companies concerned, but they do serve a purpose: to prepare the ground politically and psychologically for subsequent legal acts, as the powers of the Community gather momentum.

- **Taxation**. Taxation has proved a tricky area for the EU. The original goal was to achieve a standard corporate rate throughout the Community. In 1995, this was replaced with an affirmation of mutual recognition of individual countries' taxation procedures. Some refinements were made in 1990 to prevent multinational companies from 'cheating' or avoiding the payment of tax. The 'Parent/Subsidiary Directive' eliminated the withholding of taxes on dividends paid to a parent organization in one member state by a subsidiary in another. The 'Merger Directive' allowed the deferral of capital gains tax on acquisitions, but only if the acquired company continued to pay taxes in its home state. An arbitratory panel was also set up to address tax disputes.

The EU thus has the effect of imposing a supra-national government authority on member state organizations. Whether or not this helps competitiveness, and therefore the most effective creation of added-value, is a far-reaching and controversial question. On the one hand, it could be said that the EU is seeking to create the largest (in transactional terms) free trade area in the world; on the other hand, there is some truth in the claims of those who represent it as the world's largest cabal – a group which does not deal with non-member nations on a 'level playing field' basis. There is considerable mistrust of its aims and achievements in the USA, for example.

Moreover, its record for creating a 'level playing field' even among its own nation states, has been at best patchy. The issue of government procurement illustrates this. Government procurement in the 12 states of the Community was estimated as being worth $490 bn per annum in 1990, but most contracts were awarded to firms based in the countries whence they originated. A directive was therefore issued to encourage member states to buy on the basis of cost and quality of product, not on the nationality of the supplier, but it was acknowledged that there would be major delays in the implementation of this, because so much was at stake, and because many national firms were not competitive. The directive was ambivalent about whether it was also encouraging competition from outside the EU.

Community decisions made in the 1970s, and recommendations passed in 1984, for the opening up of telecommunications contracts, proved ineffective because the following infringements took place:

- invitations to tender were not published
- 'exceptional bid' award procedures (where companies were allowed special treatment because of a situation peculiar to themselves, or because they could demonstrate that they had a special area of expertise) were abused
- the bid conditions were incompatible with the legislation that had been passed
- some tenderers were unlawfully excluded
- discrimination was exercised during the appraisal of the tender awards.

However, it could also be argued that in principle the EU promotes better trading conditions, and that many of its objectives necessarily have to be long term, partly because of the complexity of the problems involved (not discounting emotion based or 'irrational' issues), and partly because rapid change in some areas would cause too many casualties (*pace* free market forces advocates). Its at times excessive bureaucracy is an unfortunate by-product of attempts to deal with these matters. Throughout its history, too, it has tried to counter charges of being inward-looking and insular by forging trading agreements with other trading blocs and individual nations – see 3, 4, 5 and 6 below:

3 **Comecon (the Council for Mutual Economic Assistance)**

Comecon is now defunct, but an understanding of it is useful, both in demonstrating how non-market economies make use of trading blocs, and in demonstrating the differences, and indeed the similarities, that existed between Comecon and 'free market' unions such as the EU.

Comecon was the trading bloc established in 1949 for the so-called 'iron curtain' countries, consisting of the former Soviet Union and its political satellites. It was Stalin's response to the Marshall Plan, a wide-reaching aid package sponsored by the Americans to revitalize Western European trade in the aftermath of the Second World War. The countries originally involved were the Soviet Union, Poland, East Germany, Bulgaria, Czechoslovakia, Hungary and Romania. Later Vietnam, Cuba and Mongolia were included.

For many years after the foundation of the EEC, COMECON was hostile to the Community, principally because it regarded it as the trading arm of NATO (the North Atlantic Treaty Organization, set up to establish and maintain a nuclear deterrent against the Soviet bloc). During the 1970s, however, despite continuing Soviet hostility, Bulgaria, Czechoslovakia, Hungary, Poland and Romania found it useful to conclude agreements with the EEC for items such as textiles, steel, and meat. In 1985, Mikhail Gorbachev, newly appointed to the Soviet presidency, authorized general negotiations between the EEC and COMECON, and in 1988, after ten years of talks, the two trading blocs finally recognized each other. In 1989, when the Communist governments were swept away throughout the COMECON nations, western businesses, partly as a result of the efforts of the EC, were already interested in their markets. In March 1990, the EEC increased its stature and its credibility as a political entity by being appointed by the United Nations as a co-ordinator of western aid to eastern Europe, and the EEC itself (not its individual members states) embarked on reaching new trade and co-operation agreements with the former COMECON nations.

The EEC conceived the ambitious plan of creating a free trade area to embrace the whole of EC and former COMECON territories, but in 1993 this was still beset with the difficulties attendant upon the inconvertibility of Eastern bloc currencies, political instability within their nation states, and the degree of modernization and reform they individually needed to put in place in order to be able to compete in a free market economy. Case 3.3 describes the specific problems experienced by the Carl Zeiss Stiftung, a company that developed as two separate entities after the Second World War; these entities were amalgamated as the commercial showpiece of German reunification after 1989. (The case is expanded in the *Lecturers Resource Manual*)

4 The European Free Trade Association [EFTA]

EFTA was founded via the Stockholm Convention in May 1960. Its impetus was the wish of non-EEC nations not to be left out of the west European economic integration process integration process in the wake of the inception of the EEC. Its original members were Austria, Denmark, Norway, and Portugal, Sweden, Switzerland, and the UK. Finland joined later, and Iceland followed in 1970. Denmark and the UK left to join the EEC in January 1973, and Portugal left in 1976. The Stockholm Convention also applies to Liechtenstein, since it forms a customs union with Switzerland.

The central difference between the EU and EFTA is that the former is a customs union, whereas the latter is a free trade association. A customs union is defined by GATT as having a common external tariff; a free trade association leaves each member free to determine its own external tariff policy. EFTA depends on numerous informal and unbureaucratic ways of co-operating between small nations, whereas the EU is highly bureaucratized and centralized.

THE CARL-ZEISS-STIFTUNG

Founded in 1889, the Carl-Zeiss-Stiftung was a successful, innovative manufacturer of high-tech opthalmic and measuring equipment, which was divided by the political carving-up of Germany in the aftermath of the Second World War. It subsequently developed as two separate companies, one at Oberkochen in the west, and the other at Jena, in the east. After German reunification, the Zeiss company at Jena was reunited with the Zeiss company at Oberkochen, mainly through the offices of the Treuhandanstalt [Treuhand], an enterprise set up to achieve the privatization of the almost exclusively state-owned east German companies. The Treuhand chose Zeiss as an emotive flagship for its activities, an example of what might be achieved by the marrying of west and east after reunification.

The western Zeiss had continued in the tradition of its founder, Ernst Abbe, and was a high tech company which enjoyed a reputation for quality and technological innovation. Abbe taught that excellence derived from providing a secure, supportive working environment for the workforce, and allowing individuals to develop their talents to the full. The name of Zeiss is to be found in advanced scientific institutions worldwide on a range of high quality, state-of-the art scientific and optical instruments.

It was quickly realized that Zeiss at Jena was technologically backward by western standards, and that its employees, used to an autocratic regime, were in no sense 'empowered' or receptive to the idea of using initiative. In common with most east German companies, it had little concept of free market competition or profitability. The notion of adding value in terms of customer requirements was alien to the philosophy of a firm that had gained its prestige within the precepts of a command economy.

The reunited Zeiss company therefore became a pawn of political forces. Its respective managers were constrained both by the impact of their past environments, and by the determination of the political authorities that the amalgamation of the western and eastern firms should succeed. From becoming a flagship symbolizing the national triumph of the German nation, it came to represent a microcosm of the German predicament following reunification.

In the future, Zeiss has to find a way of reconciling the high-tech, high-added value approach which it has built up in the west with the damage that must result from the marketing of the admittedly cheaper, but inferior eastern products to sophisticated customers in all countries. In the process, a number of fundamental ethical and cultural clashes seem inevitable. The question is whether the solid and loyal customer base, with whom the western Zeiss has collaborated closely in its search for continual improvement and the consequent adding of value, will remain staunch during the traumatic shake-out which is bound to take place.

This case is a much shorter version of 'The Carl-Zeiss-Stiftung' which appears in Thompson, J.L. 1993 *Strategic Management: Awareness and Change Lecturers' Resource Manual*, Chapman & Hall.
The material used for the original case was supplied by Dr. Bernd Raebel, of Carl Zeiss Oberkochen, and by Carl Zeiss (Welwyn) UK, as well as from published sources.

EFTA is very preoccupied with the EU, aspects of which consume 80 per cent or more of its agenda. In 1993, nearly two-thirds of EFTA's noninternal exports had EU countries as their destination, but only about 10 per cent of EU exports were going to EFTA nations; although EFTA still represented the EU's largest single market, it was clear that EFTA would lose more than the EU from any deterioration in trading arrangements. The primary basis of EU/EFTA relations consists of a set of Free Trade Agreements (FTAs) signed in 1972–3 between each EFTA country and the then EEC. These eliminated virtually all import duties on industrial products by July 1977 and in 1993 were still being administered bilaterally through joint committees.

In 1989, the EEC and EFTA agreed to start negotiations to establish throughout their countries the same freedoms of movement for goods, services, labour and capital that were the goal of the 1992 EEC programme, but these negotiations made slow progress. The most difficult issue to address was that of the decision-making apparatus which a closer relationship would need. The EEC appeared unlikely to be prepared to share its powers to make the final resolutions. One solution – which might not prove acceptable to EFTA – was that EFTA should participate in future discussions, but carry no voting powers. The very stickiness of relations between these two groups suggests that power, and not the promotion of free trade or adding value, is the fundamental issue which exercises the minds of those involved.

5 **The EU and Japan**

A major impetus behind the EU's 1992 programme was to address the challenge to Europe represented by Japan, and to counter both the aggressive behaviour of Japanese companies in Europe and Japan's own numerous barriers to imports.

After the 1973/4 oil shocks, Japan was protectionist in its attitude to trade; at the same time, insatiable world demand for Japanese exports, combined with limited domestic imports, low inflation rates, and its large trade surplus, made Japan's trading record much better than those of its partners and competitors in the west. The implications of having a trade surplus, and the reasons why countries seek to achieve a trade balance, are described in Key Concept 3.3.

KEY CONCEPT 3.3: THE BALANCE OF TRADE

1 In the simplest possible terms, a nation has a balance of trade (otherwise described as 'a current account in equilibrium'), if the goods and services (including 'intangible' items such as professional expertise) that it **imports are equal in value to those which it exports**. Because of such things as variations in times of payment and national accounting conventions, it does not make sense to look at one year's figures in isolation when trying to establish whether a nation's current account is in deficit, in surplus, or indeed, balanced. Instead, the figures need to be examined over a period of several years, so that the prevailing **trend** can be perceived.

2 The balance of trade in a country can only be said to be **stable** if
   - Credits and debits are equal in value.
   - The exchange rate of the currency remains stable.
   - The government does not feel obliged to introduce measures which create unemployment or raise prices, sacrifice economic growth, or impose trade barriers.

3 A **trade deficit** occurs when:
   - Export performance is affected by a high exchange rate, thus making the price of home goods too high to compete in foreign markets **or** inefficient production methods make the costs of output too high, with a similar result.
   - There are excessive imports of consumer goods.
   - A large amount of raw materials and capital goods are being imported by home country organizations with the intention of boosting their own output. Clearly, this can have a beneficial outcome, and should only be a temporary phenomenon, because the raw materials should enable the creation of added value which will lead to improved productivity and true national prosperity.

4 The **consequences** of a trade deficit are:
   - The country is importing more goods than it exports; therefore, the general standard of living is being improved, but true national prosperity is not being achieved (if it is accepted that this is directly related to productivity, and therefore the adding of value). It will be evident that such a situation is dangerous if allowed to continue for any length of time; it is directly analagous to a household living on credit which it cannot afford to pay back.
   - The country therefore needs to import capital from abroad. This, however, is only likely to be forthcoming if interest

rates are high, so that foreign investors gain a good return on their investment, and if they are confident that the country's economic prospects are healthy in the medium to long term. If the country is unable to attract such foreign investment (which puts it in the position of moving further away from true prosperity, because it will be paying interest from the proceeds of all its **future** adding value activities for what its people are **now** enjoying), there will be pressure on its government to devaluate the currency. The reason for this is that there will be a surplus of the currency in the foreign exchange markets. Of course, such a step would immediately make the nation poorer and move it even further away from achieving prosperity, or reaping the rewards of its efforts.

5 A **trade surplus** occurs when, year after year, a country's exports exceed its imports in value. The surplus can either be used to make overseas investments, or added to the nation's own reserves (reserves are kept by governments to 'bail out' their countries in times of economic adversity).

6 That this should be a problem may not be immediately apparent: you might argue that the country has succeeded in finding ways to add value that others have been unable to emulate, and that it should be congratulated. However, a persistent surplus will eventually cause the following problems:
   - If the country, like Japan, is a major trading nation, then the fact that it is continually in surplus means that its trading partners, such as the USA or the EEC, are continually in deficit. These countries are therefore obliged either to continue importing the goods of the nation in surplus until all their official reserves are run down, at which point there will no longer be any scope for either side to trade; or, what is more likely, they will seek to find ways of interfering with the free trade mechanism, and therefore, in value added terms, affect the choice of the ultimate consumer, by imposing trading restrictions such as tariffs or import quotas (see main text).
   - It is therefore in the interests both of world trade, and of the individual consumer, of whatever nationality, for each country to have a reasonably healthy balance of payments.

7 The only alternative to this is **autarky**, the term used to describe a nation which seeks to be entirely self-sufficient. In recent years, Albania has tried to follow this path, having isolated itself both from the west and the Soviet bloc, to which it was originally allied, for political reasons. The result has been a nation caught in a time warp, many of whose people are living below the minimum acceptable subsistence level. It is an extreme example of the law of comparative advantage at work

> – for no nation can excel or even preserve a competence in each of the many economic acticities which now contribute to human civilization.
> 8 Both the importance and the complexity of the balance of trade, and its relevance to the adding value process, therefore become apparent.

A useful exercise would be to find and study a set of Britain's (or any other country's) trade figures. In 1,000 words or fewer, state what these tell you about the current state of the country's economy.

Despite their large investments in Europe (and particularly in Britain), however, the Japanese became mistrusted by Europeans because of a wide range of concerns over their behaviour, such as:

- their targeting of strategic industries
- the low quality of their investment and jobs
- the dependence of host countries on important components made in Japan, thus turning Japanese plants in Europe into little more than 'screwdriver operations'
- lack of R & D facilities in Japanese plants in Europe
- lack of true integration by Japan into Europe
- the still closed, extremely protectionist Japanese home-market – Europe and the USA were both unhappy about Japan's propensity to import raw materials, and export high value-added manufactured goods.

It should be pointed out that Japan has received an unnecessarily bad press over some of these issues. Case 3.4 describes the setting up of the Pioneer (UK) Plant at Normanton in West Yorkshire, how Japanese methods were successfully taught to what had been an unskilled workforce, and demonstrates that the long-term plans for the company are to integrate fully with the local community. It should at the very least be recognized that in Japan, as elsewhere, there are 'good' and 'bad' attitudes towards producing added-value.

CASE 3.4

PIONEER UK

Pioneer is a successful Japanese electronics company, though much smaller than its rivals Sony and Matsushita. In 1990, it set up a direct investment company, Pioneer UK Ltd., at Normanton, West Yorkshire. It received some help from the British government to do this, because the area, once heavily dependent on mining, qualified for regional aid.

The main activity undertaken by the factory was the manufacture of high-quality compact disks (CDs). Initially, 150 people were recruited from the local workforce; this number had increased three-fold, to 450, at the end of the first eighteen months of production.

The directors and key management staff of the company, with the exception of the personnel manager, were all Japanese. However, this was conceived as a short-term policy. None of the Japanese management intended to remain in England for more than three years, and some were hoping to return to Japan sooner. They would only stay until they felt that their methods and philosophy (i.e., the distinctive competences which the company had developed in Japan in order to add value) had been learnt and could be effectively developed by a British management team.

The workforce, similarly, were encouraged to develop. Most of them were semi-skilled or unskilled workers drawn from the mining industry, and various associated commercial and warehousing organizations. On being appointed to the company, they each underwent an intensive training and socialization programme designed to make them efficient in their work, and also to foster in them an understanding of the Japanese philosophy of continuous improvement, and how they could contribute to that. In 1993, there had been an 11 per cent turnover of staff – higher than average, particularly for a depressed area in the grip of recession, but low enough for the company to feel that its recruitment drive, and indeed the entire operation, had been successful. Employees earned higher than average wages for the area, and, whilst not guaranteed a 'job for life', enjoyed greater job security than they had been used to. A tremendous pride in the company and its achievements had been fostered in staff at all levels.

Source: data collected as a result of a visit to the factory by the author in the summer of 1993.

By the early 1990s, in response to complaints from the EEC and the USA, Japan had reduced some of its tariff and quota barriers, but others still remained. It was true that Japanese investment activities in Europe alone outweighed the total foreign investment in Japan, but although Japanese investment in the EEC was regarded as an opportunity to create jobs, many businessmen feared that an increased Japanese presence in the EEC would also lead to the increase of Japanese market share. The EEC wanted to see more Japanese investment in manufacturing industries, as opposed to services. In 1987, 80 per cent of Japan's investment in Europe was in non-manufacturing activities, especially in banking and insurance. Therefore the protectionist element in the 1992 programme was largely aimed at reversing the widening trade imbalance with Japan.

See Case 3.5 for two sectors in which the Japanese were especially successful in Europe, and in which the EU has taken legislative action.

JAPAN AND THE EUROPEAN ECONOMIC COMMUNITY 1992

1 Financial services

In 1992, the EEC made an open statement that it would use reciprocity as a means of negotiating the opening up of Japan's highly regulated financial services to their European counterparts. In other words, Japan would not be able to attract more business of this nature from the EEC than it allowed back to foreign competitors in Japan.

2 Cars

An EEC White Paper stated that all national import quotas for cars would have to be replaced by a common EC quota. Because some EC countries allowed very limited Japanese car imports, it was unlikely that they would allow their national 'champions' (e.g., Fiat in Italy, Renault in France) to be suddenly subject to more liberal quotas. Their lobbying could therefore have depressed the accessibility to Japanese cars in Europe. However, Japan and the Community decided instead to negotiate a 'Voluntary Restraint Agreement' (VRA) for Japanese cars. This involved a commitment from the EC to phase out existing national quotas of car imports in return for a Japanese commitment to restrain car exports during a transitional period.

A major dispute connected with this concerned the EC's demand for a minimum 'European local content' in Japanese cars made in European plants. This was a direct attack on 'screwdriver plants' which were used as little more than assembly stations, thus ensuring that the main profits from 'adding value' were preserved in Japan. The European Commission was in a delicate position over this issue, because if they had introduced regulations that were too stringent, they could have strained foreign trade relations, and produced an adverse effect on European firms depending on foreign suppliers. However, the Japanese response was not as aggressive as it might have been; it consisted of raising the local content level of cars to be sold in the EEC, and diversifying into joint ventures and take-over.

Source: adapted from a *Financial Times* survey (1992) 'Japan and the EEC', 13 Nov.

6 **The USA APEC and NAFTA**

America has perhaps the most advanced 'pluralist' society in the world. This means that it has a tradition of listening to the views and respecting the ideological tenets of a very wide spectrum of people. In the debate about free trade versus protectionism, its governments have therefore been obliged to listen to powerful lobbies on both sides. Not surprisingly, American companies engaged in exporting have generally been in favour of free trade, whilst those largely dependent on domestic markets have been in favour of protectionism. It has been the difficult task of American governments to try to balance the needs of both sides. The USA led the world in liberalizing trade in the 1960s, but after the oil crises of the early 1970s, it became increasingly protectionist, especially after it suffered its first trade deficit since the Second World War in 1980. An important event was the passing of the Tariff and Trade Act in 1984, which continued the protectionist trend by enabling the President to negotiate bilateral free trade zones while not having to grant similar concessions to other countries enjoying Most Favoured Nation (MFN) status. However, there was a move back towards liberalization with the Omnibus Trade Act of 1988, which was designed to open up markets and improve America's overall competitiveness.

The USA traditionally looked to Europe as a major trading partner; however, the EU has often been viewed by American companies with suspicion, and both they and recent American governments have also recognized that the east – which is geographically speaking as logical an area for them to trade with as the west – is likely to provide more opportunities in the future. In recent years, therefore, the USA has been a prominent member of Asia Pacific Economic Co-operation (APEC), a group whose aim is to increase multilateral co-operation because of the eocnomic rise of Pacific nations, and growing interdependence within the Pacific region. The original APEC members were Australia, Canada, Japan, South Korea, New Zealand and the USA, and the six members of the Association of South-East Asian Nations: Brunei, Indonesia, Malaysia, the Philippines, Singapore and Thailand. In 1991, China, Hong Kong and Taiwan were also admitted, and in 1993 Papua New Guinea and Mexico were seeking to join. The USA was particularly keen to prevent moves on the part of the Asian countries to create smaller trading groups from which it would be excluded.

More controversial in America was the North American Free trade Agreement (NAFTA), which proposed to eliminate almost all trade and investment restrictions between the USA, Canada and Mexico over a 15 year period. The USA and Canada entered a free trade agreement in 1989, and a successfully concluded NAFTA pact would therefore primarily affect trade and investment with Mexico. The Canadian parliament had already approved the agreement in 1993, but the US had not. The American government, itself trying hard to promote the scheme, was being lobbied by many pressure groups against it, representing a wide range of fears associated with the plan, including an influx of cheap Mexican labour into an economy already afflicted with joblessness, and the effects on the environment, particularly on those American states closest to the Mexican border. As with the EU, it is yet to be proved whether the setting up of such a trading bloc will ultimately improve choice and enable consumers to fulfil their needs at the lowest possible cost, or whether it will constitute another form of protectionism, narrowing the range of goods available to a large body of consumers and obliging them to pay prices which do not necessarily offer the best value for money.

OTHER MOVEMENTS WORLDWIDE THAT AFFECT THE ADDING OF VALUE

So far, we have examined in some detail organizations which have been set up specifically to address the problems associated with trade. There are other bodies – some self-selected, some only quasi-official or without any specific remit, but which nevertheless have achieved power because they have been internationally acknowledged – which influence both directly and indirectly the quest for added-value. We take a brief look below at some of the most important. You will probably then be able to think of others to add to the list.

1 **The 'superpowers'**

   After the Second World War, until the mid-1980s, it was accepted throughout the world that there were two 'superpowers' – the USA and the former USSR. In the 1960s, it was generally believed in the west that the latter was the stronger of the two – indeed, the American space initiative to land a man on the moon was inspired by President Kennedy in a deliberate attempt to counteract western despondency about what was perceived to be Russian superiority in the technological and military fields. The collapse of the Communist bloc in the late 1980s finally demonstrated the error of such perceptions. Clearly, the former Soviet Union was no longer a superpower in 1995; it had in fact disintegrated, and represented no cohesive power at all. The logical assumption might therefore be that the world now had one superpower – the USA. But the America of 1995 was not without its domestic problems:
   - the low rates of domestic saving and investment were causing worries about the nation's wealth
   - consumer confidence was weak, and America was finding it hard to emerge from recession
   - debt burdens were high
   - there was a huge contraction in defence-related industries
   - there was widespread unease associated with the planned radical overhaul of healthcare facilities, which represented one seventh of the nation's total economy

- unemployment was high, and although the service sector was still recruiting, manufacturers were stadily eliminating jobs (due more to efficiency gains than industry decline, however).

There was also the shorter–term, but not insignificant, problem of the damage to the infrastructure cause by extensive flooding in several states during the summer months, and by the Los Angeles earthquake in January 1994.

Both pressure groups and individuals in the country were saying, some with great vehemence, that it could no longer afford to be the policeman and power arbiter of the world. Economists and political journalists had in fact been writing for some years that the superpowers now consisted of America, Germany and Japan (some also adding the European Union as well as or instead of Germany). Germany and Japan, however, also had domestic problems. Germany had the major problem already referred to of integrating the east and the west, which will probably take many years to resolve, and Japan had problems of recession, connected partly with appreciation of the yen, making its exports more expensive, partly due to retaliation from trading partners resentful of its protectionist policies (see above), and partly due to the 'hollowing out' of Japanese industry as companies relocated to cheaper areas in South East Asia. Neither country, moreover, could fulfil the 'superpower' role in the sense that America and the USSR formerly did, since neither had the military power base. The term 'superpower', if it continues to have any meaning, therefore seems to have shifted to refer to economic clout – though in 1995 America was still fulfilling many of its original superpower roles.

2 **The 'Group of Seven'**

In the mid-1980s the 'Group of Seven' (G7) nations – a self-selected elitist group of the world's seven most powerful industrial nations (the USA, Japan, Germany, France, Britain, Italy and Canada) which meets three times a year – agreed that an economic power base would hold more meaning in the future.

Currently, these nations have no plans for closely co-ordinated economic policies, but they exchange information about their experiences and their future plans, and annually carry out a 'mutual surveillance' of each economy's performance. The group is empowered to act to prevent one or more of its members from adopting policies that will threaten its overall economic prosperity. It aspires to become a directorate for managing the increasingly interdependent world economy. It has considerable benefits to offer:

- Decisions are taken at ministerial level, which means that some major operations take place with the minimum of delay. For instance, the G7 put together a huge aid package for Russia in April 1993 in an attempt to maintain political stability in the country.
- Meetings are often imaginative, and focus upon wide-ranging worldwide problems. For example, the 'summit' which took place

in Washington in April 1993 considered the long-term structural problems of health care costs, education and training, and the ageing of the population, all of which will have significant effects on the world's wealthiest nations in the next century.

- Also in 1993, it made arrangements for a nuclear safety programme to deal with hazards in faulty and ageing nuclear reactors in former communist states.

On the other hand, the G7 has proved to have some significant limitations:

- The seven participating nations, despite their original raison d'être of seeking to promote world trade, have failed to agree among themselves about the trade liberalization package being negotiated in the Uruguay Round of the GATT talks (see Case 3.2). The future of the group as an entity may depend on the successful resolution of these differences.
- Always elitist, (it began as an extension of the elitist 'quad' countries of the USA, Japan, the EU and Canada), it is self-oriented, and perhaps does not pay sufficient regard to the newly industrialized countries (NICs) of South East Asia, and, more particularly, to the future economic power of China.

There are, of course, many other international bodies and associations which have an impact on adding value as it is achieved by individuals and organizations. The foregoing account has tried to describe some of the more significant of these, to explain how they work, and to illustrate the complexity of the effect of governments and national and international politics on the creation of wealth by producing goods and services.

Key important issues have been raised which any student trying to place added-value should think about:

- Is any of the bodies that we have described truly foward-looking and liberationist in its approach to promoting world trade?
- How many of them are essentially carrying out ambitious, far-seeing plans for world integration in what is necessarily an incremental manner?
- Are some of them merely exchanging national protectionism for protectionism relating to wider regional areas on a cabalistic principle? How far do issues of national power intrude? Case 3.6 examines the implications of NAFTA in this context.
- Kenichi Ohmae and Peter Drucker both argue that governments are already dinosaurs which adopt outdated techniques in their efforts to promote and regulate competition. Is this really so, and if it is, how powerful do they nevertheless remain? Are they likely to become extinct?
- And – at the heart of the debate when the implications of adding value are being addressed – is it possible that some forms of interventionism, whether on a national or an international scale, can be beneficial to the consumer?

CASE 3.6

NAFTA AND ITS IMPLICATIONS FOR THE AMERICAN AND MEXICAN GOVERNMENTS

President Carlos Salinas completed the fifth of his six-year mandate as leader of Mexico at the end of 1993. Economic growth in his country was slow, and he had staked a great deal on a successful resolution to the NAFTA [North American Free Trade Agreement] talks. He was personally associated with the success of the treaty from its inception.

Although the hopes that had been set on the 'miracle cure' offered by NAFTA were undoubtedly too high, and although the President had also exhibited some sound qualities of good economic management, if the talks failed, Mexico's prospects of growth would probably be damaged in the short and medium terms, and interest rates would have to rise. The defeat of the treaty would also affect the presidential campaign of 1994, and a national backlash of opinion would damage relations with the USA.

America had other problems connected with Mexico and NAFTA. Despite the fact that President Salinas claimed to have effected significant electoral reforms, it was the view of independent international observers that there was considerable scope for the rigging of elections in the country. There was some doubt that the President had himself gained power legitimately.

One observer, former US president Jimmy Carter, said:

> 'For a democratic election to occur, all major parties in a country must accept the process and respect the results. Mexico has not yet reached the point where that is the case'.

If the United States were seen to be entering into a treaty with an administration that engaged in election-rigging, America's own position in world politics would be compromised. That alone could place the prospects of a successful outcome for NADTA in jeopardy.

Source: adapted from Fidler, Stephen (1993) 'Reform awaits its reward', *Financial Times survey of Mexico*, 10 Nov.

It is outside the scope of this work to consider the adding of value on a country-by-country basis; nevertheless, you are encouraged to find out more about individual nations in this context, and to think about such issues as the likely future impact of China's rapidly developing economy (bearing in mind that currently approximately one half of the world's population is Chinese), and, at the other end of the spectrum, whether the international community should do more to raise the competitive status of the increasingly impoverished continent of Africa.

Despite what Ohmae and Drucker say about the declining relevance of nationalism and therefore national governments, in the world of the late 1990s it is indisputable that some countries are becoming more rather than less nationalistic, even though this may have an indivious effect on their economies. Netherthess, there is an increasingly powerful group of organizations that are truly supra-national, and we conclude this chapter with a brief consideration of them.

MULTINATIONAL CORPORATIONS

Multinationals may also be described as 'global corporations' or 'international corporations'. Ketelhohn (1993), drawing on the work of Bartlett and Ghosal (1989), makes the following distinction between the three terms:

1 **Multinational corporations**. The so-called 'classic form', in which companies decentralize their assets and capabilities in order to facilitate their subsidiaries' adaptation to specific market conditions. They seek to add value by means of differentiation. Examples are Philips and Unilever. Resources are therefore dispersed and most responsibilities devolved to local-country managers.
2 **Global corporations**. Typified by the Japanese model – examples include Matsushita and Kao – they are characterized by their investment in centralized global-scale factories geared to manufacture standard products under a centralized worldwide strategy, and are driven primarily by the need to achieve worldwide cost efficiency – therefore they aspire to the low-cost value-added ideal.
3 **International corporations**. These consist of a group of corporations, such as General Electric or Proctor & Gamble, with an organizational strategy which manages to adapt the core company's know-how to foreign markets. The arrangement they adopt is a hybrid of the multinational and the global – the core maintains influence over the subsidiaries, but to a lesser extent than in a global corporation, and the subsidiaries are able to adapt products and policies coming from the core, but less than in the case of a multinational corporation. Value may be added in different cases by focusing either on low cost or on differentiation.

These definitions have been offered here because of their simplicity and clarity. Some readers may be interested in the academic debate which surrounds the description of the activities of multinational corporations. Box 3.1 offers the definitions of other writers for those who may wish to pursue the topic further.

Box 3.1: Types of multinational organizations

Fannin and Rodriguez (1988) distinguish between what they term 'multi-domestic' and 'global' organizations.

In their terms, 'mutli-domestic' organizations exhibit the following qualities:

- they pursue separate strategies in a number of markets, or
- they promote the same basic product in different markets, but
- they operate by means of national divisions which have the status of separate companies, and
- loose control only is applied by the parent over foreign units.

'Global' organizations, on the other hand, have these characteristics:

- they pursue a single integrated strategy in a number of markets
- a product of one single design is sold internationally
- components can be produced globally, and assembled near selling points
- a prerequisite is uniform product demand in all markets
- management competes on a worldwide basis
- there is an integrated span of control (i.e., links with the parent are close)

Boddewyn *et al.* (1986) have conducted research which indicates that the type of standardization that 'globalization' implies is only suitable for certain types of product:

- It is advanced in high-tech consumer durables (e.g., hi-fi equipment, cameras)
- It is difficult to achieve in 'ordinary' consumer durables, which are more influenced by local and national taste (e.g., furniture, domestic fittings)
- Standardization is very advanced in industrial goods.

Source: Fannin and Rodriquez (1988) 'National or Global? Control versus Flexibility', *Long Range Planning* Vol 19, No. 5, pp. 84–8, and Boddewyn *et al* (1986) 'Standardisation in International Marketing', *Business Horizons*, Nov–Dec pp. 69–75.

Porter seems to offer broad support to these ideas. He is an advocate for the advantages of global strategy, which he lists as follows:

- comparative advantage (see Key Concept 2.1)
- production economies of scale
- global experience
- logistical economies of scale
- marketing economies of scale

- purchasing economies of scale
- product differentiation
- proprietary product technology.

However, he also identifies a wide range of possible impediments to global strategies. Apart from the economic, managerial, institutional and perceptual or resource difficulties a firm is likely to encounter as it tries to 'go global', he also specifies:

- the impact of government policy in the parent/target nations
- relations with the host government
- the impact of systematized competition
- the difficulty of recognizing who the competitors are.

The first two of these points have been addressed at some length in the chapter. The others will be examined in more detail in Chapter 7.

Porter says that there are four main global strategic alternatives that a firm can pursue:

- broad line global
- global focus
- national focus
- protected niche.

Source: Porter, M. (1985) *Competitive Strategy*, Macmillan, Ch.13

What all such organizations have in common is that they engage in foreign direct investment (FDI). They therefore set up their plants in the countries and geographical regions which provide the most favourable conditions for their activities at a particular time. Reasons may include many of the government-related measures that we have already looked at – for example, the availability of cheap labour, a comparatively favourable national taxation system, and host-country incentives to attract them. In 1993, the stock of foreign investment per capita exceeded the Gross National Product per capita in the world.

Foreign Direct Investment classically takes place in Third World countries by companies from developed nations, and the traditional view of it, based on the tenets of neoclassical economic theory, is that it makes a benign contribution to the countries selected. Moran (1985) summarizes the reasons for this, stating that it

- brings in new, scarce resources – capital, technology, management and marketing skills
- increases competition
- improves efficiency
- adds jobs to the economy
- improves distribution of income.

However, many complex analyses of the reality of the situation have been undertaken in recent years. Discussion of them is beyond the scope of this book (further reading is offered at the end of the chapter), but they have yielded the following (highly summarized) conclusions:

- Companies engaging in FDI frequently do not bring in new capital from outside when they invest, but appropriate local capital for their own use.
- They tend to use capital intensive technology, and therefore don't create many new jobs.
- They seek protection by the government of the host country from competitive forces that might drive them to develop new (to them), least-cost, labour-intensive production methods more appropriate to a Third World locale.

As a result of the last point, the possibilities for the executives of powerful multinational companies for creating unfair economic and competitive distortions in the local environment are abundant. To quote Moran:

> 'In the extreme, foreign companies might capture the commanding heights of the host economy, soak up indigenous sources of capital as they drive local firms out of business, create a small labour elite for themselves while transferring the bulk of the workers into the ranks of the unemployed, and siphon off oligopoly profits for repatriation to corporate headquarters.'   (Moran, 1985)

What, therefore, does the host country government need to do to safeguard its national interests?

Penrose (1959) says that the foreign company should receive just enough aid from the host country government to induce it to invest in the first place, and subsequently just enough encouragement to prevent it from withdrawing afterwards and transferring the investment elsewhere. Kindleberger (1965) says that the host country government must be able to perform the more sophisticated analysis (which it may be all-equipped to carry out) of what the scarcity value is to the host country of the services which the foreign company has to offer – in other words, at what price would it rather forego those services and do without the investment? What is essentially being discussed here is the worth of the host country and its resources to the adding of value for the customer.

When it is initially negotiating with a company wishing to invest, the host country government clearly faces the choice of signing a generous investment contract and getting some benefit in return, or refusing to allow a generous investment contract and getting no benefit at all. Its bargaining power is weak. However, Vernon (1971) points out that as the company becomes 'locked in' to its investment, and as the host country moves up the learning curve of bargaining and managerial skills, the latter can, assuming that the investment has been successful, better drive a hard bargain with the company and/or threaten to replace it if the contract is not renegotiated on more favourable terms to the host. At this point, the host country demands could (or should) include imposing higher taxes, and agreeing that local input and therefore rewards will constitute a greater part of the value-added process. This might include joint marketing, more employment of nationals in managerial positions, and shared ownership.

On the other hand, full nationalization is not necessarily beneficial to the host country, as it may remove a buffer between an economically fragile state and a volatile world market – especially if the company is dealing in commodities. Also, nationalization makes the country's economy more vulnerable to the depredations of morally weak and greedy officials.

In recent years, work has also been carried out on the effects of FDI on the home countries of the investing companies. Research suggests that, although foreign investment can benefit the owners of capital, it may do so at a significant cost to the economic position of the mother country. Gilpin (1975) says it 'contributes an international redistribution of power to the disadvantage of the core'. That is to say, it results in the phenomenon that has been described as the 'hollowing out', particularly of the industrial base, of developed economies in the 1980s and 1990s, because multinationals are likely to:

- ship capital rather than goods abroad
- export jobs
- undermine the balance of the nation's industrial and service sectors, and make it poorer in essential skills.

There are considerable moral problems associated with this, which unions, particularly in the USA, have pointed out. So-called 'runaway' plants move abroad to escape the burden of higher wages and better standards that workers in the home country have fought for decades to achieve.

Both for economic reasons, and because they are under pressure from various lobbies, the governments of developed economies might therefore deem it necessary to make changes in taxation policy to make foreign operations less attractive, and/or impose direct restraints on the freedom of national companies to move abroad.

What fundamental implication does the growing power of the multinational corporations have for the adding of value, and what should the role of government be? The issues involved are so complex that, however careful the analysis of them, the answer must depend on the student's own judgment. On the one hand, it could be argued that companies that locate anywhere in the world in order to produce added-value at the lowest possible cost must benefit the consumer by doing so. On the other hand, this assumes that the benefits of low cost operations will be passed on to the consumer. It also takes no account of 'opportunity cost' – i.e., what the host country governments and the companies involved could otherwise have done with the resources committed (including the possibility of technological breakthrough in new areas) which might benefit the consumer yet more.

Let us consider this in the light of the argument put forward by Kenichi Ohmae – that the 'global corporation' represents the way forward, and national governments, which might get in the way of its progress, are outdated. As this chapter has already suggested, the power of the national government is by no means dead, but by 1995, governments were increasingly bowing to pressures put upon them by huge multinationals. From both the added-value and the ethical perspectives, an attempt should be made to assess what the future effects would be if national government power were to be superseded by the international powerbase of large companies. These are the main points that need to be addressed:

- Would it lead to an evening out of economic prosperity throughout the world, or cause a further polarization of wealthy and poor communities?
- Would it promote or jeopardize conditions of peace, which are essential for productivity and therefore prosperity?
- Would it ultimately lead to the realization of the added value 'ideal' – of producing the features that the customer requires at the lowest possible cost, with new ways continually being sought to improve upon current efforts and to innovate to meet and anticipate the customer's future needs?

SUMMARY

This chapter has continued the examination of what contribution government can make to the value-adding process, in the international context. It has considered what governments **can**, **should** and **do** do to aid productivity globally.

Specifically, the chapter has addressed:

- The principles of international trade, and explained the terms mercantilist, Liberal and Pareto-Optimal.
- After these theories have been introduced, practices actually applied by governments are considered.
- A range of government measures which affect international trade are described – tariffs, import quotas, reciprocity, exchange controls, physical controls, and rules of origin and local content – and their impact on adding value assessed.
- Some current thinking on the nature of international competition in the value-adding context is discussed, with especial reference to the work of Michael Porter and Kenichi Ohmae.
- International political movements set up to promote trade in the world are explained – viz., GATT, the EU, the former COMECON, and EFTA – and reference is made to the EU's trading relations with Japan.
- The principles involved in achieving a balance of trade are explained, and the ill effects of both trade deficits and trade surpluses discussed.

- The USA's involvement with both APEC and NAFTA is considered, as is the decline of the 'superpowers' and the influence or otherwise of the 'Group of Seven'.
- An attempt is made to offer a guide to the student on how to assess the impact of these organizations on the effective adding of value for the consumer.
- Finally, the power of multinational corporations is considered with reference to their relationship to governments, and the implications for the future of their ascendancy suggested.
- You are invited to consider whether multinationals will supersede the power of political forces in the future, and whether or not this will be beneficial to the key concern of adding value at the lowest possible cost for the customer.

REFERENCES AND FURTHER READING

Emmott, B. (1992) *Japan's Global Reach*, Century Books, London.
Goldstein, J.S. (1994) *International Relations*, HarperCollins, London.
Ketelhohn, W. (1993) *International Business Strategy*, Butterworth Heinemann, Oxford.
Moran, T.H. (1985) *Multinational Corporations: the Political Economy of Foreign Direct Investment*, Lexington Books, Massachusetts.
Ohmae, K. (1990) *The Borderless World*, HarperCollins, London.
Porter, M. (1990) *The Competitive Advantage of Nations*, Macmillan, London.
Porter, M. (1985) *Competitive Strategy*, Macmillan, London.
Williams, R. *et al.* (1992) *The World's Largest Market: a Business Guide to Europe 1992* (updated version), Amacom, New York.

Reference has been made throughout to contemporary business newspapers and journals. As with any aspect of business, but most especially when dealing with politics, students are advised to make close reference to these contemporary sources of information.

4 The economic environment and adding value

LEARNING OBJECTIVES

- To understand some of the key concepts of the discipline of 'economics', and show an awareness of the resources available to organizations, the importance of knowledge as a resource today, and of the concepts of micro- and macro-economics.
- To understand the concept of the 'circular flow of income'.
- To describe the impact upon organizations seeking to add value of the following variables: bank borrowing; raising share capital; savings; direct taxation; indirect taxation; and the notion of 'business confidence'.
- To understand output, expenditure and income measures as they are used by governments – e.g., GDP, GNP, NNP, the balance of payments, the trade balance, a trade deficit.
- To understand what is meant by the 'exchange rate' of a national currency, offer a definition of what is meant by 'inflation', and show an ability to consider its implications for organizations engaged in the adding of value.
- To explain how the Retail Price Index operates.
- To show an appreciation of the limitations of, as well as the help offered by, economic models.
- To understand and be able to appraise the differing approaches of governments when applying macroeconomic theory.

INTRODUCTION

It has already been indicated that the economic environment is closely (often inextricably) associated with the political environment. As this chapter progresses, the nature and detail of this association are explained more fully. First of all, however, in order to gain a perspective on the use which governments make of academic theory, it will be useful to examine briefly the science/art which we call 'economics'.

Definitions of economics have been offered by many of its practitioners and theorists in the 200 years since its emergence as a separate discipline. The Victorian economist Alfred Marshall described it as 'the study of mankind in the everyday business of life', which we might alter to 'the study of mankind as he adds value to goods and services by the pursuit of everyday activities.'

Economics attempts to fulfil three main functions by the way in which it takes stock of human activity:

1 It acts as a **recorder** of how things are produced and distributed, and of the factors which are likely to have an impact on this.
2 It tries to attempt an **assessment** of the picture which emerges from such an accumulation of facts.
3 It tries to **predict** future trends and developments from the accounting and deduction which has thus been undertaken.

Utility is an economic term which holds significance for the concept of adding value. It simply describes the usefulness of a product or service to someone in fulfilling a need or want; hence its importance to the organization is that it will offer a guide as to how much the customer is willing to pay for that product or service – i.e., how successfully value has truly been added.

In Chapter One, we identified that all resources are finite, and that every time an organization decides to invest resources in an activity, it forfeits the **opportunity cost** of investing those resources elsewhere. Economics is much concerned with the scarcity of resources – it was for this reason that in the nineteenth century it was dubbed 'the dismal science'. Traditionally, the resources available to organizations were divided into three by economists:

1 **Land**, i.e., all natural resources: not just agricultural land, but mineral deposits, gases, the direct produce of fields, forests and the sea and (potentially) those from other planets and space.
2 **Labour**, i.e., the physical and mental resources of human beings, including specialized skills and abilities of organization and management.
3 **Capital** – the physical assets owned by organizations. These will include such things as buildings, machinery and vehicles. Originally, they were constructed from resources of land and capital, therefore they were accumulated by the organization in an earlier period in order to take its value-adding processes forward. Accumulation of the 'right' assets is therefore a significant activity. Organizations – and nations – which accumulate the 'wrong' assets, or fail to replace and update those which they have, may find themselves locked into the position of not being able to deliver added value as well as their competitors. Arguably, this is what happened to Great Britain at the end of the nineteenth century – it relied complacently on outdated technologies and its reputation as the 'workshop of the world', and

failed to see that continual innovation and investment were needed to prevent competitor nations from overtaking it.

To these three traditional categories of resources needed by organizations for transformation into goods and services by value-adding activities, the modern economist might add a fourth:

4 **Knowledge**. It could be said that knowledge is an attribute that properly belongs to labour; and this is true of knowledge as 'know-how', a quality of individuals which can be transferred with them to tasks within an organization, or outside it, should they choose to leave or be hired out. But there are other types of knowledge important to organizations in today's world of high-tech products and fast, sometimes discontinuous progress. 'Know-how' knowledge stems from education and training; it may be augmented or restricted by the influence of culture at both the national and the organizational level. But it is 'creative knowledge' – new ways of arranging or developing the know-how – that pushes the organization forward. This evolves from a combination of the right circumstances put in place by the education/training/culture factors and the right individuals. Organizations need individual imaginations that are able to address themselves creatively towards adding value. This kind of 'capital' is the hardest of all to put in place effectively, the hardest to measure, and the most significant in terms of the organization's future success.

Organizations combine the factors of production with their adding value creativity to provide goods and services which customers consume. They then require further goods and services, which may, but probably won't, be the same as those they have just consumed – hence the value-adding process continually changes. (Economists call the consumption > > > production > > > consumption process the **cycle of production**.)

BUSINESS ECONOMICS

Business economics looks at the way organizations are run, controlled and influenced by the political environment. It can be divided into two distinct areas of study:

Microeconomics, which examines individual decisions about the production of particular goods and services within specific organizations. It is therefore concerned with the deployment of the factors of production in individual instances of adding value.

Macroeconomics, which looks at the actions within a national economy as a whole. Inputs (of commodities, people, etc.) are aggregated, and the total inputs and movements within the economy tabulated. Different factors are compared – e.g., the relationship between national wage costs and gross profits. Often they are put in context by comparison with previous years, and the performance of other nations.

It will immediately be seen that macroeconomics not only involves a series of very complex calculations, but that it is difficult, particularly in an age of intense international activity, to achieve a complete picture when the nation state is used as the relevant entity to be measured. We will return to this point.

The circular flow of income

It may seem that microeconomics is more exact than macroeconomics, and of more direct help to the organization in determining the what and how of its value-adding activities. Reflection will show that this is not so. There may be comfort in exactitude, but it is a spurious comfort which ignores the turbulence of the wider economic environment with which we are concerned. Micro- and macroeconomics set out, in fact, to provide the tools which demonstrate the interdependence of the individual business and its national economy.

Figures 4.1 and 4.2 demonstrate this interdependence. Figure 4.1 provides a simple model of how production would take place if the economy consisted entirely of households and organizations (i.e., if there were no government or other external factors to consider). Households supply organizations with the factors of production (labour in return for wages, possibly land in return for rent, or finance in the form of share capital) which they need in order to carry out their value-adding activities. The organizations supply the households with all the goods and services they require. The size of the monetary flow represents the level of the national income. The model assumes that all the goods and services which are produced are sold, and that the households spend all their income on these. Economists call this situation (were it ever really to exist) one of **neutral equilibrium**. It does not

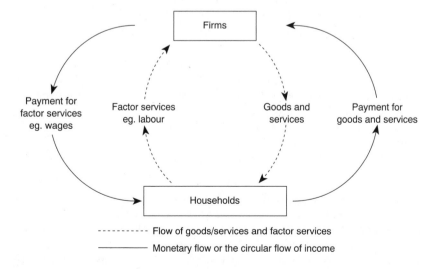

Figure 4.1 The circular flow of income.

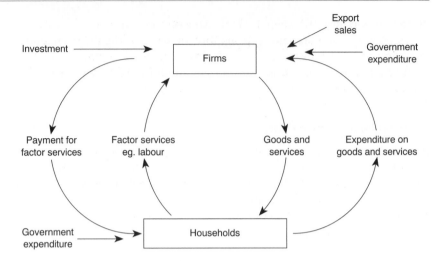

Figure 4.2 Additions to the circular flow of income.

represent an ideal situation, because (apart from the dangers inherent in any kind of stasis) it cannot assume that everyone who wants a job has one; that households are receiving **all** the goods and services which they want or need; or that the country is importing exactly the same value of goods and services as it is exporting (we return to the significance of this later).

Figure 4.2 therefore offers a revised version of the model, which illustrates how additions, often stimulated or co-ordinated by government, may be made to the circular flow of income. These additions take three main forms, as follows.

1 **Investment**. This is expenditure on more capital equipment in order to increase the organization's adding-value potential by providing it with extra resources to deliver new goods and services.
2 **Government expenditure**. For example, if the government were to build a new motorway, it would increase the adding-value potential both of organizations directly involved in the project (contractors, surveyors, etc.) and those working adjacent to the completed road, since they would be able to achieve faster deliveries, more efficient links with suppliers and so on.
3 **Exports**. These are a 'bonus' to the national circular flow of income because they are derived from adding value in return for payment from foreign individuals, organizations and governments.

Imports, conversely, are a drain on the national circular flow of income, because they contribute to the economic prosperity of another nation at the expense of domestic prosperity. Technically, they are described as **withdrawals** (or leakages) from the domestic circular flow. Sometimes, a short-term imbalance of imports can be good for the country's future prosperity, if the imports consist of raw materials to which value can then be added to generate further income; but if they are finished goods (to which value has already been added), the effect will be to reduce the number of jobs available in the national economy, and therefore depress its level of economic activity.

There are two other types of withdrawal from the flow of national income, as follows.

1 **Savings**, either in the form of income not spent by individuals, or financial profit retained by companies choosing neither to invest it in capital equipment, nor distribute it as dividend to shareholders.
2 **Taxation** by the government. Governments have two main methods of levying taxes: **direct taxation** (on individual income and profit made by commercial companies), and indirect taxation (on spending).

It will therefore be noticed that actions taken by governments have a considerable effect on the national circular flow of income. How 'interventionist' governments should be, and what constitute the most appropriate forms of intervention, is a perennial subject of political debate which is dealt with in more detail in Chapter Two.

Let us examine more closely the impact of the complicating factors which we have introduced into Figure 4.2 on the organization which is trying to add value.

Investment

1 **Bank borrowing**
   Unless they have reserve funds, organizations that operate for profit and wish to make large-scale investments often have to borrow the money they need from banks in the form of long-term loans. (Businesses may also borrow money on short-term loan for trading purposes, as there is usually a time gap between their outlay on raw materials and labour/knowledge, and the payment they receive for the value-added product they have produced; this phenomenon is known as 'cash flow'.) Banks charge interest for the money borrowed from them. This may be at different rates for long- and short-term loans, but the rate charged is ultimately dependent on the 'base rate'. This is common to all the national banks. In 1997, Chancellor Gordon Brown granted the Bank of England autonomy in setting interest rates. High interest rates are likely to discourage investment, since they make the outlay on capital expenditure more costly – a cost which the business, moreover, must be convinced that it can ultimately recoup by adding sufficient value to induce the customer to pay for it. Governments are likely to impose high interest rates to combat inflation.

   Businessmen must also be convinced that the customer is **able** to pay for the additional added value procured from investment. Therefore, they have to feel confident in the economy itself (this

Box 4.1: Share prices

The financial newspapers of developed countries carry daily information about movements within the stock market so that the performance and prospects of a company's shares can be monitored. In Britain, Monday editions of the Financial Times also include the market capitalization of the companies listed on its share pages. (This is arrived at by using Friday's closing price of the stock and multiplying it by the stated number of shares in issue for the year. The share price of the company, printed next to its stock name, is an indication only of the price at which a share is likely to be sold – usually it represents a midway point between offer and bid prices of shares traded.

Listed shares are divided into a number of sectors, as it only makes sense to compare stock market movements of companies operating within similar industries. Greek alpha, beta and gamma symbols printed against each share indicate the level of trading activity in each listed stock. Alpha shares are the most heavily traded, and are therefore often listed separately, showing the volumes traded against each share. Price movements indicate how much the rough price (i.e., before brokers' commissions) of the share has fallen or risen on the previous day's closing price. This is obviously a very short-term indicator. The Performance Record, which shows the highest and lowest prices at which the stock has been traded in the year to date, supplements this information. Further indicators are usually listed as follows:

- **Dividend**. This tells how much profit a company returned to shareholders for each share they owned at the last distribution. Dividends may be listed gross or net (before or after the deduction of tax).
- **Cover**. This is the term used for the ratio of a company's total profit to the amount of profit it distributes to shareholders in the form of dividends.
- **Gross yield**. The figure published represents the dividend paid by the company, divided by the share price and expressed as a percentage. This gives an accurate indication of how much income a share is actually yielding.
- **Price/earnings ratio**. This consists of the share price divided by the most recent year's earnings per share. It is a measure of the price an investor has to pay for a given income from his or her shares.

It will be noted that each of these indicators provides a more or less sophisticated yardstick of how well the company is adding value for the shareholder, depending on his or her interpretation of the information.

confidence may need to extend beyond the boundaries of the national economy). If they believe that the national economy, or the economies of the countries in which they are operating, will boom, and that therefore economic activity relevant to their field of operation will increase, then they will be more inclined to make capital investments to keep themselves competitive by developing the most efficient and desirable methods of adding value. The converse is also true.

2 **Raising share capital**

The other way a business can acquire funds for investment is by raising share capital. Box 4.1 contains further information about shares and how they operate. A 'private' company (one whose shares are not available on its nation's stock-market) can achieve this by flotation, or 'going public' (i.e., launching its shares on to the stock market). Companies which are already quoted on the stock market can appeal to (either/or new and existing) shareholders for cash by issuing more shares.

Such financial support is not likely to be forthcoming from shareholders unless they feel that the company is also adding value for them. Shareholders divide into two basic categories: those who are looking for income (often individuals, for instance, widows who depend on their investment income to support themselves) and those who are looking for capital growth (often institutions, such as pension funds, which are trying to obtain the best long-term return for their clients' cash). The company must be able to convince shareholders that it is capable of fulfilling at least one of these forms of adding shareholder value. Once a company is 'quoted', therefore, although it has raised the capital it requires for adding value for the customer, it has imposed upon itself the constraint of making sure that its shares 'perform'. As we discussed in Chapter One, shareholders are important stakeholders of a company. Other stakeholders who will watch the performance of its shares closely are rival companies (who might be looking for signs of weakness, and possible opportunities for takeover bids) and the government. National governments keep a close watch on the share movements of large companies to ensure not only that undue profits are not being made (i.e., that value is being added for the customer at a fair price; that he/she is not simply being 'fleeced' because of a willingness to pay), but also that the company is not likely to get into financial difficulties that might have repercussions on the economic health of the nation as a whole (by causing widespread unemployment, etc.).

Not-for-profit organizations obtain their funds for investment from other sources – often, the government itself. Clearly, the amount they receive depends not only on their successful fulfilment of value-adding activities and the political persuasion of the government, but also on

---

Box 4.2: The public sector borrowing requirement (PSBR)

The Public Sector Borrowing Requirement is the term used to define the amount of money a government requires in order to finance a budget deficit – i.e., to make up the shortfall between anticipated revenue and anticipated expenditure for the nation during a given financial period (usually one year). The government can finance the PSBR in two main ways:

1 by issuing short-dated **Treasury Bills**. These are usually purchased by discount houses and commercial banks.
2 by issuing long-dated **Government Bonds** which are purchased by institutional investors (e.g., pension funds) and by the general public.

How the borrowing is distributed between these two categories has an important effect on the level and distribution of spending in the economy. The issue of Treasury Bills increases the 'liquidity base' of the banking system (by increasing the supply of money in the economy) and therefore raises spending; the issue of bonds reduces the liquidity base (by reducing the supply of money in the economy) of the banking system as buyers of bonds run down their bank deposits to purchase the bonds.

---

the buoyancy of the national economy – driven by for-profit organizations – as a whole. One of the key annual tasks of the Chancellor of the Exchequer is to establish the **Public Sector Borrowing Requirement (PSBR)** – i.e., the amount needed to fund national services such as education and health. Box 4.2 describes the PSBR in more detail. Governments of all creeds have fewer funds to commit to social welfare in a shrinking economy. To a certain extent, the same is true of government expenditure on national investment programmes; though Keynesian economists argue that it is in times of economic recession that governments should make major investments, because they act as a generator to kick-start the economy back into life again.

Government stances on **imports** have been explained extensively in Chapters Two and Three.

Savings

There are conflicting theories about why people save, both at the individual and the organizational level. When interest rates are high there is an incentive to save, because it may be felt that wealth may be increased as successfully by retaining funds as by using them for capital to add value. However, as we have said, high interest rates are often the result of climbing inflation; therefore, the funds that are saved, even though they may be attracting the desired rate of interest, may actually be diminishing in value in real terms. If businesses choose to retain funds because they feel this is more worthwhile for their shareholders than investing in order to add value, it indicates that they have a pessimistic view of the future prospects of the economy. Also, their attitude is likely to make this a self-fulfilling prophecy, since such decisions affect all the organizations participating in the value chain. Governments consequently seek to achieve a balance between establishing interest rates at too low a rate, and encouraging inflation, and putting them at so a high a rate that investment is discouraged.

Taxation

1 **Direct taxation**

   (i) **Corporation tax**

   Corporation tax is levied on the profit of for-profit organizations. This makes a significant impact on the type of financial planning carried out by the business. Companies of any size are likely to have tax accountants who advise them of ways of making themselves most tax efficient. Some governments offer tax incentives to businesses to plough back money into investment, training, etc. If such money is carefully spent, it can boost the value-adding process. Although corporation tax is a valuable source of income for governments – and used, as we have said, in part to fund not-for-profit organizations, such as health care and education – a country which has a particularly punitive corporation tax system may deter businesses either from setting up or from staying within its boundaries. Thus, if governments are too 'greedy', their actions may detract from, rather than augment, their coffers by diminishing the country's knowledge capital and its adding-value potential.

   (ii) **Income tax**

   If a country's government levies income tax at a higher rate than that levied by the countries with which it most closely identifies (British earners, for example, would probably expect to compare their situation directly with that of other people working within the European Union), then potential customers will have less net income to spend upon a company's products. This will necessarily affect how the company decides to add value – there may be a cost/quality or cost/differentiation trade-off, particularly if its goods are aimed at attracting 'disposable income' – i.e., are not necessities.

2 **Indirect taxation**

   Indirect taxation may take a number of forms. Sometimes, a government may impose direct levies on specific products – particularly if it can justify such a measure because it is perceived as being politically or socially 'correct', for instance, taxes on alcohol and cigarettes. When companies that manufacture these products are considering how to add value, they need to bear in mind that this imposed extra cost is also going to have to be borne by the customer.

Governments have to try to adopt an overall view of the societies they are governing when they apply such taxes. Many western governments attract substantial revenues from the tobacco industry, because they know that although they are ostensibly using taxation as a deterrent, people addicted to tobacco will still buy it – therefore a certain predictable level of revenue from tax is assured. On the other hand, tobacco-related diseases are known to kill, disable or cause the repeated absence from work of so many people that they are making huge inroads into the resources of not-for-profit organizations – hospitals, doctors, counselling and support agencies – which are therefore having to scale down their value adding activities in other areas. Leaving aside the ethical considerations, from a purely pragmatic point of view it could be argued that governments should curtail the activities of organizations whose 'added value' is a source of such potential harm (see 'Trade unions as pressure groups' in Chapter Two; we consider ethics in more detail in Chapter Five). The foregoing also makes it apparent that there may be (albeit disguised) conflict between the value-adding activities of for-profit and not-for-profit organizations, and that the role of government is often to attempt to act as a regulator of the interests of the parties concerned. Case 4.1 examines various aspects of governments' relationship with the tobacco industry.

CASE 4.1

GOVERNMENTS AND THE TOBACCO INDUSTRY

It is a peculiarity of the tobacco industry that, despite the incontrovertible weight of evidence that smoking is responsible for a range of life-threatening diseases and the general impairment of good health, tobacco companies have rarely lost court cases mounted against them. Without being unduly cynical, it is possible to speculate that this is because taxes on tobacco have been a major and steady source of revenue for governments in developed countries in the twentieth century.

Now, however, governments are taking a tougher line against the tobacco companies, partly in deference to strong public feeling that their products are harmful and that therefore their activities should be curbed, and partly, perhaps, because the resulting continuous eroding of their markets means that their usefulness as a cash cow is fast drying up.

Governments are, however, bedevilled by the history of their past actions. Thus, in the USA in 1994, attempts at litigation against Brown and Williamson Tobacco, a USA subsidiary of Britain's BAT industries, for allegedly developing a genetically engineered tobacco (Y-1) that contained more than twice the normal amount of the (addictive) nicotine found in normal tobacco plants, came up against a clause in the Federal Food, Drug and Cosmetic Act of 1938. This stated that cigarettes are not a drug because they 'do not intend to affect the structure or any function of the body'.

In Australia, the tobacco company Philip Morris has also been able to use existing legislation to its advantage. In June 1994, it launched a High Court action seeking to overturn the country's ban on cigarette advertising on the grounds that it denied 'commercial freedom of speech'. Mr. David Davies, vice-president of the company, said that it was filing a statement of claim against the restrictions imposed by the Commonwealth Tobacco Advertising Prohibition Act (1992) because: 'Important issues of freedom of speech are at stake . . . the restrictions deny us the right to communicate on political, public and commercial issues'. The company was employing about 4,000 people in Australia, and paying more than A$1bn in taxes and licence fees to state and federal governments.

In Britain, earlier in the same year, newspaper and magazine publishers (dependent on advertising revenue from tobacco companies to bolster their increasingly narrow margins) united to oppose a private members' bill that would outlaw tobacco advertising for the same ostensible reason: that it would 'amount to censorship and set a dangerous precedent'. The publishers were lobbying MPs to 'reaffirm their support for the freedom of the press, the freedom of speech, and the freedom of consumer choice by rejecting any attempts to outlaw advertising of products legally and freely available in the UK'.

The Advertising Association, the umbrella group co-ordinating the bill, calculated that the publishing industry would lose about £50m a year in advertising revenue if the bill was passed.

Britain's radical alterations to the National Health Service in the early 1990s presented another complicating factor. Although the health service was still free at the point of delivery (i.e., to the patient), both hospitals and general practitioners had been given budgets. GPs who were budget holders (with finite funds at their disposal to spend on their patient-base) had to buy patient care services from hospitals for those who needed it. This might create an increasing reluctance among GPs to admit to their registers patients who smoked; alternatively (though this was a matter of deep controversy), an element of counter-selection might be introduced against patients whose illnesses were perceived as 'self-inflicted' (e.g., by smoking, when it is known that the habit constitutes a health risk). The British government's stance remained ambivalent: on the one hand, it was still gathering a hefty amount of revenue from taxing tobacco sales; on the other hand, whilst deploring smoking as a drain on the health service, it had passed on the discretion as to how to address this to the fund-holders. Apparently, if not in fact, it had minimalized its power of intervention in the value-adding activities of the health care industry. The Clinton administration in the USA, which had massive healthcare problems of its own to address, was known to be observing the outcome keenly.

Ultimately, as the pressures increase, the tobacco industry may take responsibility for its own demise. In 1993, Philip Morris cut its prices in order to win back market share. This provoked a price war with its competitors, and although it succeeded in boosting sales, the price cut contributed to a fall in after tax profits from $4.9bn in 1992 to $3.6bn in 1993 – a move which antagonized its shareholders. Such action also results in less capital being available for product development; but it is in any case difficult to see how the tobacco companies can find new ways of adding value in the present climate of opinion. Instead, they are likely to be forced to spend more on defending their industry, as they fight for an ever-smaller customer base. Most are now making strenuous attempts to diversify into other industries. Philip Morris, for example, acquired General Foods in 1985; Kraft in 1988; and Jacobs Suchard in 1990. In 1993, the food companies contributed 50 per cent of group turnover (though only 34 per cent of group operating profits). This serves to illustrate how profitable the tobacco industry has been, and indicates that its demise will probably be lengthy, and accompanied by yet more skirmishes with governments and reversals of government policy.

Source: adapted from a number of articles which appeared in the *Financial Times* and *The Economist*, Jan–Jun 1994.

Government taxation on **imports** has been considered extensively in Chapter 3. The most significant form of indirect taxation in the U.K. is probably VAT, or value-added tax. This is currently levied at a rate of 17.5 per cent on the manufacturers' selling price on all but a narrow range of goods, which may be either exempt (like food) or zero-rated (like books). Zero-rated products may be reviewed periodically and the decision to give them a zero-rating modified. Such action on the part of the government may cause an unwanted public backlash. For instance, in 1994, the UK government imposed VAT on fuels, which had previously been zero-rated, and there was an immediate public outcry. The knock-on effects of such taxes can be profound; the customer is being required to pay more, without ostensibly gaining any additional added value. However, in the long term, the company may be forced to find other ways of either cutting costs or adding value so that the requirements of both the government and the customer can be met. The situation grows even more complex in the case of privatized utilities, when the company also has to take into account the perspective of the shareholders. Case 4.2 examines the complexities of the UK government's relationship with British Gas.

THE BRITISH GOVERNMENT AND ITS RELATIONSHIP WITH BRITISH GAS

British Gas was privatized by Margaret Thatcher's second government in 1986. After privatization, in common with other privatized utilities, it enjoyed the position of a monopoly, although one which was regulated by an industry watchdog, Ofgas. It was never the intention to allow the monopoly situation to persist indefinitely, and in 1994 the government said that full competition in the supply of gas should be available to 18 million households by 1998. Independent gas suppliers had been demanding right of entry to a market whose estimated value was more than £5.6bn, and said that they would bring households savings averaging £35 – £40 per year. The government planned a 'toe in the water' exercise of opening up 5 per cent of the market in 1996–7, to ensure that the system was ready for competition. The move was consistent with the government's central commitment to the desirability of consumer choice. Michael Heseltine, the President of the Board of Trade, said: 'Choice for consumers is the best possible guarantee that they will obtain value for money'.

Competition in the supply of gas could not be a simple matter, however, as British Gas would continue to own the supply network of pipelines and storage. The sophistication and comprehensiveness of this network constituted a large part of their added value, and accounted for about half of their costs. If they were to open up the supply network to competitors, therefore, they would have to be allowed to charge fairly for this service, but at a rate which did not undermine their power to deliver the major value-adding activity of maintaining and developing the network in the future.

The Government's Monopolies and Mergers Commission made several recommendations as to how this should be done. Firstly, they said that British Gas should hive off its transportation and storage business into a separate unit; secondly, that transport and storage prices should be governed by an inflation-linked formula; and finally, that the formula should allow British Gas a return of 4 per cent to 4.5 per cent on assets, and 6.5 per cent to 7 per cent on new investments.

Industry analysts felt that this formula might be too tough, and that it would be insufficiently attractive to shareholders. Therefore, it would undermine British Gas's motivation for continued investment at the 1993 rate of £900m annually. On the other hand, the more gas – its own, or competitors' – that British Gas could pump through its system, the more it would be able to increase its profits, so there was an incentive to run the most efficient system possible.

The fuel industries generally in Britain had also acquired reflected hostility in wake of the government's decision to impose VAT on home fuel bills from 1st April 1994. Because the government, in an attempt to minimize the unpopularity of the measure, had allowed house-holders to avoid paying VAT by paying the fuel companies whatever sums they could afford (with no ceiling) in advance of its imposition, building societies reported huge withdrawals of funds. By the end of March 1994, householders had paid approximately £400m in advance, thus not only depriving the government of some £40m in tax revenues, but also creating the possibility that mortgage rates could be pushed up as building society funds shrank.

In order to deflect criticism that they were therefore excacerbating the overall national economic situation (although the decision to impose VAT was out of their hands), some of the fuel companies announced their intention to reinvest the prepayment funds in the building societies.

This case illustrates the complex relationship between the government and industry sectors, and shows how legislative measures taken to exact levies from one industry can have a (possibly unforeseen) detrimental effect on another.

Other forms of indirect taxation include road taxes and tolls. Again, these have to be added to the price which the customer pays, and are important considerations in nations which have road-based or car-based economies, particularly where the company doesn't operate close to the customer. Although they, too, are unpopular, they have the advantage of being 'politically correct' (for environ-mental reasons), and, in practice, an assured source of revenue, since those whose activities necessitate using the roads will find ways of accommodating them.

We have discussed the significance of actions by governments on the circular flow of income within a country, and the resulting impact on all kinds of organizations that add value. Let us now examine some of the indicators which governments use to measure the economies over which they have charge, and the conclusions they draw from such measurements.

OUTPUT, EXPENDITURE AND INCOME MEASURES

The total economic activity of a country may be measured in three different but equivalent ways, as follows.

1 **Gross Domestic Product (GDP)**. This represents the total of all eco-nomic activity in one country. The ownership of the capital used to add value is not taken into account – e.g., it would include the profits of a foreign car company operating in the country, even if the profits derived from the value-adding activities accrue to the foreign parent company.

2 **Gross National Product (GNP)**. This represents the total of incomes earned by a country's residents, regardless of where the capital assets

are located. Therefore it includes the profits from businesses owned by its nationals but located in other countries.

3 **Net National Product (NNP)**. This describes the GNP after allowance has been made for depreciation (the 'gross' in GDP and GNP indicates that no account has been taken of capital resources used up in the adding value process – e.g., expected wear and tear, damage, obsolescence, etc.).

The relationship between these three measures is as follows:

> GDP (gross domestic product)
> + net property income from abroad (rent, interest, property and dividends)
> = GNP (gross national product)
> − capital consumption (depreciation)
> = NNP (net national product)

Economists consider GDP to be a better measure than GNP; but in practice the choice depends on how individual governments decide to present their national accounts. Of the major industrial countries, only Germany and Japan focus on GNP; the rest use GDP. The difference between GDP and GNP is usually quite small (typically one per cent of GDP), but the economic make-up of some countries can cause it to be much larger. For example, in 1989 Kuwait's GNP was 35 per cent bigger than its GDP, due to the country's vast income from foreign assets. Key Concept 4.1 explains how GDP is calculated in more detail.

THE BALANCE OF PAYMENTS

The balance of payments of a country is an accounting record of its international financial flows. National accounting practices vary, but in general, governments produce two sets of figures relating to these external flows:

- **Overseas Trade Statistics (OTS)**, which measure imports and exports of goods and services.
- **Balance of Payments (BOP)**, which records all cross-border currency flows including movements of capital. These exclude goods passing across borders where there is no change of ownership, but include changes of ownership that take place abroad (such as ships built and delivered abroad).

KEY CONCEPT 4.1: HOW GROSS DOMESTIC PRODUCT IS CALCULATED

In order to understand what is meant by Gross Domestic Product (GDP), it is essential to understand all the elements of the terminology included in the term. As exactly as possible, the word *gross* represents *total*; the word *domestic* represents *within the country under consideration*; and the word *product* represents *all the goods and services* which are created within that country.

There are three ways of measuring GDP. These are known as the **output method**, the **income method**, and the **expenditure method**.

(i)   **Output method**. This sums the value added to a product (that is the price charged for the finished product less the cost of buying in the raw materials) by each producer.

(ii) **Income method**. This sums the value of all incomes (wages, rent, dividends and interest, plus profits) which are paid out during the production process. The argument for adopting this approach is that the total of all of these elements must equal the value of output because the value added at each stage in the production process is also an income for somebody.

(iii) **Expenditure method** (currently favoured by the UK government). This method calculates the value of output or incomes by measuring the nation's expenditure on final goods and services. The principle on which it operates is that what is bought has to be produced. Therefore, expenditure equals output.

Imports

There are two reasons why a country imports goods and services, as follows.

1 It cannot produce them itself. This inability is more accurately defined in terms of adding value. For example, India can produce cars, and so can Germany. The fact that wealthy Indians may prefer to buy German cars reflects the different way in which German car manufacturers add value to their product. Indians may not be allowed to choose freely (aside from considerations of price) the type of added value which they prefer, if their government decides to 'protect' the economy and/or gain revenue by imposing import tariffs on German cars (see Chapter Three).

2 There is comparative advantage in buying them abroad (see Chapter Two). Japan, for example, is a net importer of foodstuffs. This is because it is a country with limited spatial resources and poor agri-

cultural soil; its land capital is therefore put to better use by engaging in the production of goods (such as advanced electronic items) which achieve high added value. A conscious decision has therefore been made to rely upon imports for much of its food.

A high volume of imports of intermediate (commodities, components) and capital goods is perceived by governments as being generally beneficial where these are used to manufacture other items or to generate 'invisible earnings'. However, recorded manufacturing output declines in the short term when imports are used instead of locally-made items. The tendency is for industrial nations to import more semi-manufactured items and fewer commodities (raw materials). They therefore begin to add value at one or two stages further on in the value chain. The most common reason for this is that labour is cheaper abroad. Governments are likely to scrutinize this factor closely. Other factors which interest governments are **compressibility** – the extent to which there are non-essential goods that need not be imported in times of stress on the balance of payments; and sources, i.e., the extent of the country's reliance on one or a small number of trading partners. In the first instance, government interference would generally hinder the effective carrying out of the value-adding process, since action to discourage/ban purchase of imports would distort customer-demand (the key driver of adding value); in the second instance, government action (provided it had the power to increase the international supply pool) might benefit the value-adding process by reducing the power of suppliers.

Exports

Exports generate earnings in foreign currencies for the exporting country, and boost GDP. It should always be remembered, however, that because of the factors we have already discussed concerning imports (above), and because they raise the national level of affluence, more exports almost inevitably implies more imports. Exports and imports should always be examined together to get an accurate picture.

Companies that are successful at exporting their goods have clearly found ways of adding value – e.g., quality, reliability and price – which are attractive to customers in the nations they are targeting. The price issue is one which lies only partly within their control; it depends also on the relative rate of inflation and the exchange rate between the two countries. This is one of the reasons why governments try to control inflation levels, and devise mechanisms that will ensure a reasonable stability of exchange rates. Another reason lies in the fact that, since there is usually a time gap between delivery of and payment for goods, companies may find themselves underpaid in real terms if the exchange rate is fluctuating significantly. Such a shortfall will either have to be passed on to other customers, or leave the company with fewer funds for investment and paying shareholders' dividends; either of these will diminish its ability to continue to add value.

As with imports, the dependence of export activity on a few commodities or trade with a few countries increases the vulnerability of the country's economy as a whole. The greater the proportion of exports in relation to GDP, the bigger the boost to domestic output when overseas demand rises; similarly, a high exports/GDP ratio also implies a larger slump when foreign demand falls. Nations which have a high dependence on foreign trade are therefore more vulnerable to economic cycles, regardless of the dexterity of individual organizations within them at adding value. Countries in which there is a large internal trading market, for instance, China, and to a certain extent, the USA, are more protected.

The trade balance

The trade balance of a nation is the difference between imports and exports. It may measure visible (i.e., merchandise) trade only, or trade in both goods and services ('invisibles'). Invisibles are difficult to measure, so the published balance of trade in goods **and** services for any nation is likely to be less reliable, and probably subject to subsequent revision.

The balance of trade in goods and services measures the relationship between national savings and investment. A deficit indicates that investment exceeds savings, and that absorption of real resources exceeds output. (In developing countries, it is more usual to call this the 'resource gap', indicating that it is a reflection, not so much of economic management as of the incurrence of a necessary debt in order to make progress.)

Eliminating a trade deficit

For developed countries, a trade balance may not present difficulties. It may be a question of choice, or the presented figures may simply reflect a particular style of accounting convention. For example, since proper trading records began, Britain has always run a deficit on visible trade, but this has usually been offset by large surpluses on invisibles; conversely, countries like Japan and Germany, which have large manufacturing sectors, tend to present visible trade surpluses while also experiencing invisible deficits. The way the figures are presented for individual countries reflects both tradition and the particular gloss which governments wish to put on the figures, both at home and abroad; there is also the perennial difficulty of measuring 'invisibles'.

However, a trade deficit may be eliminated either by depressing demand in the country concerned whilst leaving the demand for its exports unaffected (if that is possible), or by effecting a change in relative prices through a change in the exchange rate or a change in domestic prices (since imports become dearer and exports cheaper if the deficit country's currency falls in value or if inflation is lower in the deficit country than in the surplus country). Both of these are most likely to be stimulated by government intervention. Clearly, they are likely to have an adverse effect on companies that have no or few foreign buyers. Case 4.3 is an example of adjusting business practice to the prevailing economic climate, while Key Concept 4.2 explains how the balance of payments is calculated in more detail.

CASE 4.3

MARKS AND SPENCER: FINDING WAYS TO ADD VALUE TO SUIT THE ECONOMIC CLIMATE

In 1994 Sir Richard Greenbury, the chairman of Marks and Spencer, the focused British retailer, described the strengths of the company as 'the three Ps' – people, property and product. He attributed the success of the company to 'giving customers the best value for money – that is 'the price paid in relation to the [quality of] the good – and the best service'.

Marks and Spencers' emphasis on product quality is one of its most distinctive core competencies – difficult for competitors to replicate, because much of it is based on strong relationships with suppliers with whom it has been dealing for decades. It specifies very stringent standards to suppliers, and set up its quality control and research laboratories in 1935.

Value for money for the customer is achieved by buying early in large quantities. M & S has a reputation for being a tough negotiator, but fairness is also a guiding principle. Its reputation for integrity is illustrated by its policy of paying all suppliers within 20 days, and food suppliers within 10 days.

Another driving principle is that of enhancing value for all stakeholders. 'Value for money' is delivered to the customer by a business strategy that creates the greatest cash value for the shareholder. As well as the features of quality and strong supplier relationships, this includes investing judiciously in freehold property, and developing and retaining talented staff.

It also involves keeping close to the mood of the economic environment. In the buoyant 1980s, the M & S range of women's clothes 'went upmarket', and competed with some of the brand names more traditionally associated with the 'power dressing' of the Thatcher era. By contrast, in 1994 it was keenly aware of the prevailing mood for practical, unostentatious clothes as Europe climbed out of the recession, and therefore introduced an 'outstanding value' sales campaign on a wide range of items. This resulted in its successfully meeting the needs of both customers and stakeholders: the campaign contributed to an increase in turnover of 10 per cent, year on year, with no reduction in margins.

KEY CONCEPT 4.2: HOW A COUNTRY'S BALANCE OF PAYMENTS IS CALCULATED

A country's Balance of Payments is a record of its trade and financial transactions with the rest of the world over a period of time, usually one year.

The account is divided into two main sections, the *current account*, and the *investment/transactions account*.

The **current account** shows the country's daily dealings in goods and services, and includes short-run income flows such as profit, interest and dividend payments, and receipts. It is split into two main components:

(i) The **Balance of Trade** in goods. Otherwise known as 'visible trade'. This records **receipts** from the export of the country's goods, and **foreign currency payments** for the imports of overseas goods.

(ii) **Receipts** from the export of the country's services, and from the repatriation of profits, dividends and interest on the country's foreign assets, and foreign currency payments for the import of services by foreign businesses and from the repatriation abroad of profits, dividends and interest on foreign-owned assets within the country. Otherwise known as 'invisible trade'.

The investment account consists of a group of capital items, including:

● the purchase of overseas physical assets (e.g., a new factory).
● the purchase of financial assets by individuals, companies, institutions and the government of the country in question.
● the purchase of the country's physical and financial assets by foreigners.
● banking and money market transactions in the country's own and foreign currencies.
● intergovernment transfers (e.g., to the EU).
● the provision of economic aid to less developed countries.

It is the ideal goal for governments to maintain a balance of payments equilibrium over a period of years, and to avoid a build-up of deficits.

The exchange rate of the national currency

The significance of this has been pointed out on several occasions. Box 4.3 describes the Bretton Woods Agreement, which sought to stimulate international prosperity after the Second World War by stabilizing exchange rates.

Box 4.3: Bretton Woods: an attempt to fulfil the perceived need for stable exchange rates

On July 1st 1944, the 'Bretton Woods' Conference began in the USA in a New Hampshire hotel, attended by delegates from 44 nations. Its objective was to frame an international monetary system for the post-war world. It gave birth to two important international institutions: the International Monetary Fund and the International Bank for Reconstruction and Development.

The philosophy underlying the meetings during the conference was rooted in earlier proposals made by the British economist John Maynard Keynes for an international organization to exchange currencies from different countries (a 'clearing union'), and others made by an equally eminent American economist named Harry White for a reserve that would help to control the fluctuation of currencies against each other (a 'stabilization fund').

The conference lasted three weeks. At the end of that period, the articles that were to support the International Monetary Fund (IMF) and the International Bank for Reconstruction and Development (IBRD) had been carved out.

The Bretton Woods agreement aimed primarily at a system of exchange rates that were to be fixed, but adjustable with the IMF's approval. Currencies were to be convertible on current account – i.e., anyone holding one currency would be allowed to exchange it freely with another currency in settlement of a current transaction.

In the event, the provision for early convertibility of currencies that Bretton Woods promoted was found to be much too optimistic. Both in Europe and Asia in the post-war aftermath, the disruption to settled life (both socially and financially) was too profound.

At the end of the war, almost every country in the world owed money to the USA, which meant that virtually no countries held reserves of dollars. Therefore, countries had to limit what they bought from America or paid for in dollars in a way that was inconsistent with the idea of convertibility; full convertibility on current account did not happen until 1961.

The Americans were keen to establish early convertibility and therefore eliminate any kind of discrimination in trading relationships. They believed that discrimination, trade restrictions and competitive depreciation were powerful causes of war.

Prior to the war, the difficulty of squaring accounts with America led to an outflow of gold from most of Europe to the USA. European countries were forced to try to stop this by means of exchange controls, import quotas and bilateral (i.e., between two or several countries) agreements. The British delegates at Bretton Woods were therefore anxious to maintain bilateral payments agreements negotiated during the war.

The Governor of the Bank of England insisted on the sovereign right of a country to fix its rate of exchange, even though this should cost the surrender of help from the IMF. The British press gave voice to fears that what was being proposed was a return to the gold standard, which was inextricably associated in people's minds with the high unemployment of the 1920s. In fact (illustrating nevertheless that the outcomes of economic measures are always a source for speculation rather than a reliable measure of control) unemployment only rose substantially after fixed rates were abandoned in March 1973.

To some extent, the developed nations have returned to a Bretton-Woods-style philosophy in the mid-1990s, with a renewed quest for exchange stability in the form of a single currency. Mass unemployment and an international imbalance similar to that of the post-war years exist again, but now the dominant economy belongs to Japan, not the USA.

However, there are significant differences in the modern world. There is a much higher volume of international trade, and convertibility of currencies and freedom of capital movement are more easily achieved.

Source: adapted from Cairncross, Sir Alec (1994), 'The buck starts here', *The Observer Business Review*, 3 July.

Bretton Woods was abandoned in 1972. In recent years, the most significant attempt to achieve exchange rate stability followed the establishment of the European Monetary System (EMS) in 1979. Countries which joined agreed to abide by a system in which there was:

- a scheme of permitted margins for exchange rates between their currencies, and permitted margins around a central artificial unit of currency called the Ecu;
- a policy of 'managed floating' (i.e., fluctuation in value only within certain bands) between the currencies of the countries operating within and outside the system.

The short-term objective of the EMS was to push inflation rates down to what was then regarded as the exemplary German level; its long-term objective was to promote economic convergence in Europe. Both objectives were massively affected by the twin impact of German reunification in 1989 and the collapse of the former Soviet bloc in the early 1990s. One of the net effects of these events was that frequent realignment of currency values undermined the stability of exchange rates. Individual currencies at the top or bottom end of permitted margins around their central rate came under strong speculative attack, and were pressured to revalue or devalue. A 'run' on the pound in the autumn of 1992, which the British government at first sought to stave off by drawing heavily on reserves, eventually led the United Kingdom to secede from the EMS. In 1993, the Danish krone and the French franc were similarly squeezed, and avoided devaluation only with difficulty. The pound now 'floats' against other currencies, including those within the EMS – i.e., it finds its own level. Its relative weakness since 1992 has made conditions more favourable for companies wishing to export, and makes imports less affordable.

INFLATION

'Inflation' is a word which we have used a great deal, and which is encountered daily in the press and other media. What, precisely, does it mean?

Inflation may be defined as a **general and sustained rise in the price level**, or a **fall in the value of money**. The net result of either means that a unit of currency will buy fewer goods. The rate of increase of inflation is as important in economic terms as the fact that prices are rising. Key Concept 4.3 gives some further information about inflation.

KEY CONCEPT 4.3: INFLATION

The term inflation is used to describe an increase in the general level of prices sustained over a period of time.

There are two main reasons why inflation occurs:

(i) **Demand-Pull Inflation**. This is caused by excess demand beyond the output capacity of the economy to supply goods and services. Prices are therefore 'pulled up' to adjust the allocation of the available resources.

(ii) **Cost-Push Inflation**. This reflects an increase in input costs – of wages, raw materials or components – which pushes up the final price charged for a product.

Inflation is harmful to certain sections of the community, particularly people living on fixed incomes. It is disliked by both governments and businesspeople because of the distorting effects it has on the nation's overall economy. It is particularly harmful to the export market, as it makes firms uncompetitive against their overseas rivals, and can also make overseas trading partners nervous of dealing with a country whose currency is, in effect, consistently becoming devalued (since there is usually a gap in time between receipt of goods and payment for them.)

Governments calculate the rate of increase of inflation by collating a complex series of variables, including oil prices, commodity price indices, wages, earnings and labour costs, and consumer or retail price indices. In Britain, one of the most frequently quoted of these indices is the **Retail Price Index (RPI)**, which has equivalents in most other developed countries.

The RPI consists of the prices of goods and services which are likely to constitute a typical family 'shopping basket', each item being weighted according to its importance to the overall household expenditure. The goods are then revalued each subsequent year at current prices, and inflation is represented by the increase in the index. Companies, as well as the government, can therefore monitor overall inflation; try to gauge what effects the prices they are charging are likely to have on sales; and try to predict the prices they are likely to be able to negotiate with suppliers.

Within its limits, the RPI is a useful tool; but its weaknesses are considerable.

- Although the goods listed are changed periodically to keep abreast of changes in expenditure patterns, the index eventually becomes outdated as the base year grows more distant in time.
- During periods of rapid inflation, the index may exaggerate the rate of inflation yet more, because consumers may substitute those goods which are rising less rapidly in price for what they would normally buy.
- Governments may alter the listed goods, not just to keep abreast of social change, but for their own reasons. e.g., mortgage repayments were removed from the British RPI in the 1980s.

Inflation and adding value

Inflation has three main results, two of which impede the value-adding process for the for-profit organization, as follows.

1 In economist-speak, it 'blurs relative price signals'. This means that it makes it hard to distinguish between changes in relative prices and changes in the general price level, thus distorting the behaviour of for-profit organizations. For example, a rise in the cost of making computers may be due to the temporary scarcity of a component or the permanent effect of pay increases which the components manufacturer was obliged to award. If it was the former, the computer manufacturer might wish to bear the cost in order to retain its competitiveness; if the latter, then it is more likely to have to accommodate the increased cost either by cutting other costs (perhaps by reducing the number of its employees) or by raising prices. The fact that it may not be able to identify the cause is likely to have a distorting effect on the company's behaviour: it might, for

example, either act too aggressively, and alienate various stake-holders, or feel paralysed into inaction by the fear of losing market share, and allow its margins to be eroded. Neither is likely to contribute to the efficient adding of value in the long term.

2 Inflation is never perfectly predictable. It therefore increases business uncertainty, which in turn is likely to discourage investment. The picture becomes more complicated when transactions are involved between businesses of different nations. For example, if the pound is 'worth' nine francs when a supplier of custom-built engines fixes his price with a French customer, but only eight francs when he delivers the finished products six months later, his final margin has clearly been seriously eroded.

The third result of inflation is more problematical in terms of its desirability for businesses, although it is disliked by governments, particularly those of a right-wing persuasion, because it is likely to alienate some of their voters. It is the fact that inflation redistributes income, from creditors to borrowers and from those on fixed incomes to wage-earners (because people on fixed incomes experience an erosion of their real wealth as a result of inflation, whilst wage earners will secure pay rises roughly in line with the rise in prices (the 'inflation spiral')). Whether or not this is a desirable outcome for the business depends on whether the company's main market lies with wage earners or those on fixed incomes, and whether there are other factors likely to influence the buying process – for example, is someone contemplating taking out the membership of a sports club more likely to invest the money in a 'home gym', because he or she thinks the club's subscription fees might rise beyond his or her means in the future?

Inflation and unemployment

In our example of the computer manufacturer, above, we said that a decision that the computer manufacturer might have to take because of inflation (caused by a supplier's raised wages) would be to trim its staff or raise prices. If it did not wish to alienate its stakeholders and weaken its skills base, it would choose the latter course of action. In due course, it would also be obliged to put up the wages of its own workforce, to keep them in line with suppliers and competitors. Throughout an entire economy in the grip of inflation, many organizations might reach the same conclusion, thus exacerbating the inflation spiral that the government was trying to control. But the alternative – unemployment – is unpopular with governments, because high unemployment makes the government itself unpopular (Chapter Two). It is also costly (in some respects, unquantifiably so) in terms of social security payments, withdrawal of skills from the national labour pool, and erosion of individual self-esteem, which in turn can lead to an increase in demand upon the resources of care and crime prevention agencies. Governments are therefore frequently obliged to juggle with two undesirable outcomes, and try to achieve the best compromise.

The trade-off between inflation and unemployment was first identified by a New Zealand economist called Phillips in the 1950s. A combination of low inflation and low unemployment is nevertheless the goal of most governments; whether or not this is achievable is less relevant than the impact of the measures taken by governments on value-adding activities. It is, incidentally, received wisdom among contemporary economists that an inflation rate of up to 3 per cent annually can be a beneficial driving force in a growing economy. Higher levels are likely to cause uncertainty – and uncertainty is the enemy of governments and businesses alike. It is almost axiomatic that, given that organizations inevitably work in a turbulent environment, the better governments can aid by managing economic turbulence, the more successful their contribution towards adding value is likely to be.

THE LIMITATIONS OF ECONOMIC MODELS

We have now discussed the major economic variables with which governments and organizations are concerned; and, in passing, touched on some of the drawbacks concerning their collation, and the conclusions which can be drawn from them. Principally, these are:

1 Data collection is based on sampling, rather than comprehensive surveys.
2 The margin of error that this is bound to introduce is aggravated by further factors:
   - a lack of common understanding by those contributing to the data (e.g., the 'category' into which some organizations fall)
   - difficulty in obtaining accurate information about (particularly) service organizations
   - some countries (for example, Italy) have significant 'black economies' (a large number of organizations that do not declare their profits to government, either to avoid taxation, or because their activities are illegal).
3 The 'lies, damned lies and statistics' syndrome. Even assuming that governments have collected data that gives a reasonably accurate picture, few governments are likely to present the conclusions which they draw from it 'neutrally'; they will find ways of adapting the 'facts' to their own political bias.
4 The actions that governments decide to take as a result of the economic information they have gathered may therefore be inappropriate, misguided, or blinkered by ideological belief. It is in any case questionable how robust are some of the models, and the received wisdom concerning the kind of actions they should suggest. We deal with this in the next section.

THE EFFECT OF GOVERNMENTS' COMMITMENT TO MACROECONOMIC THEORY ON ADDING VALUE

In Chapter Two, we examined at some length the broad types of ideological belief which informed government actions. Depending on the nature of the individual ideology, we said that governments were more or less interventionist. It should also be said that there is not a government in the developed world which does not subscribe to the tenets of macroeconomic theory.

This might be dangerous for two reasons: in the first place, commitment to an ideology, however well-intentioned, almost inevitably colours the application of rational ideas (assuming that macroeconomics can be described as 'rational'). Secondly, applied macroeconomics is built around the concept of the **nation** state: it is a way of measuring and accounting for the prosperity of individual nations. Not only might this concept be becoming rapidly outdated; but it has always, even when it was more relevant, meant that the **world** as an economic system has not been examined; instead, interacting parts of the system have been examined piecemeal, and the nature of some interconnections obscured by the arbitrary imposition of artificial boundaries based on politics and geography.

Because of these factors, it is arguable whether governments that intervene in their nation's economies are not only basing their intervention on information that might lack even a broad accuracy, but may also be either applying principles that are invalid, or seeking to 'tweak' a system that they do not understand. The international economy is a very complex system; it has **synergy** – i.e., it is more than the sum of its parts – and government intervention based on changing arbitrarily-created sub-systems, and finding patterns which may be false, is likely to fail. On the other hand, some factors which are at the moment described as 'random' or 'chance' may in reality be a vital and ordered part of the overall system that our present way of looking at the world's economy prevents us from seeing. Case 4.4 examines some of the difficulties of deducing what Japan's future economic prosperity is likely to be by using today's economic models.

CASE 4.4

JAPAN'S ECONOMIC SUCCESS AFTER THE SECOND WORLD WAR – A TRIBUTE TO THE POTENTIAL OF APPLIED ECONOMIC THEORY?

In the mid-1990s, there is a widespread feeling that if there is to be a supreme economic power in the near future, it will be Japan.

In 1951, Japan's Gross National Product was one third of the UK's and one twentieth of the USA's. In 1993, it was three times the UK's and two thirds of the USA's. It was predicted that the Japanese economy would probably grow faster than the EU's for the rest of the century.

Japan now enjoys a high capita per income society, which is the ultimate fruit of adding value. Japan's government has succeeded in reaching this point by setting up a Ministry of Trade and Industry (MITI) which works very closely with the major companies in Japan (themselves 'networked' into complexes of affiliated organizations (*keiretsu*), each of which has its own bank). MITI collects information about other national economies and global/multinational companies, identifies new product areas for its national companies, and both funds and shares in the development of scientific research on behalf of these products. It has also devised a method for quantifying the relative added value of the types of manufacture which the country's companies could potentially pursue (Table 4.1).

Table 4.1 The relative added value of manufacturers, according to MITI, 1989

Product	Added value ($/LB)
Satellite	20,000
Jet fighter	2,500
Supercomputer	1,700
Aero-engine	900
Jumbo jet	350
Videocamera	280
Mainframe computer	160
Semiconductor	100
Submarine	45
Colour television	16
NC machine tool	11
Luxury motor car	10
Standard motor car	5
Cargo ship	1

Source: 'Japanese Technology' (1989), *The Economist*, 2 December.

Apart from its own meticulous skill in sifting and evaluating economic information, there are further advantages enjoyed by Japan's economy, either because of its government's policies, or because of constraints imposed on it by other governments. After the Second World War, it was demilitarized, and in 1993 was spending a mere one per cent of GNP on defence annually (in comparison, say, with the USA's average of 5–10 per cent in the 1980s). At the same time, its economic 'clout' means that it has 'soft' or non-military influence as a world power when decisions are to be made about issues of global significance (e.g., the future role of the World Bank), which is just as effective but far less costly than 'hard' power based on tanks and aircraft (contrast the USA).

Western critics of Japan (inspired, perhaps, by envy) have said that it has paid a high price for its economic success: that it is infested at all levels with 'groupthink'; that its organizations are rigid, hierarchical and male-dominated; that it demands high sacrifices in terms of quality of life from its workers; that it is racist; and that it is likely to be hit sooner than other developed nations by the 'demographic' time bomb – in 1994 it already had the highest proportion of the elderly people in its population in the world.

Therefore, western economists have made the following predictions about the Japanese economy in the early 21st century:

- increasingly fewer workers will be supporting every retired person
- payroll taxes and social security contributions will be increased
- Japan (now the most lightly-taxed developed nation) will become the most heavily taxed
- 30m + over-65s in 2025 will draw upon the country's resources, cutting into its critically important savings rate, reducing the amount available for business investment, and weakening its capacity for growth and technological competitiveness.

These predictions confirm the status of economics as a 'dismal science'! What western economists do not know, of course (since the Japanese are very reticent about their future intentions) is how much attention and analysis they have paid to such indicators, and whether or not they have economic strategies in place to cope with them. There was already (in 1994) evidence that certain counteracting measures had been taken. For example, Japan was then allowing some (limited) immigration, women were (slowly) being allowed to join the workforce in other than menial capacities, and Japanese companies had made huge practical and psychological strides in forming strategic alliances with companies from other nations in the past 10–15 years.

It may be that the gravest threat to Japan's economic prosperity in the 21st century will be political – China, its nationals constituting almost half the world's population, is likely to emerge from its own very internalized economic arrangements to demand a place as an international trader after the handing-over of Hong Kong in 1997. It is Japan's near neighbour and ancient enemy.

Source: detail taken from Kennedy, P. (1993) *Preparing for the Twenty-First Century*, HarperCollins.

Box 4.4: The linearity of human expectations

'There is much evidence that human expectations tend to be linear. ... Wherever prosperity exists, it is natural for people to expect prosperity to continue. For this reason, much of the history of human society is a record of astonishment. Time and again, people have marginalized their affairs, rendering themselves increasingly crisis-prone. They have gone into debt, extending claims on resources to an extreme that could be supported only if current conditions were sustained uninterrupted into the future. Time and again these hopes have been disappointed'. (Davidson and Rees Mogg, 1993)

From this hypothesis, the authors go on to examine the evolution of economic theory. They point out that the quantification techniques employed by economists were developed from the sciences, especially physics: seeing that Newton's calculus could solve problems in physics, economists sought to apply the same mathematical techniques to economic problems. Therefore, to make the mathematics work, the concept of the economy itself had to be fitted into an 'unrealistic' mathematical straitjacket.

The result of this was the model of the economy existing in an imaginary state of equilibrium, a concept taken from physics. ('Equilibrium' in physics refers to a static state in which opposing forces exactly balance one another.) The artificial system thus created was a closed one made up of independent parts, all conceived as fitting together in a linear, even a mechanical, way.

The assumptions that had to be made in accepting this model were that everyone had perfect knowledge, that all expectations were identical, and that all resources were capable of being allocated to their most valued use. It implied that the goal of economies was to be continuous, ordered and stable. It offered, moreover a 'stop-frame analysis' – i.e., one which cannot capture motion.

Since economies are in reality mobile and volatile, economic theory is at its weakest when it tries to explain long-run change and discontinuity. Similarly, it is likely to be equally erratic when trying to predict the future from 'facts' extrapolated from the past.

Source: adapted from Davidson, J.D. and Rees-Mogg, W. (1993) *The Great Reckoning*, Sidgwick & Jackson.

If this thesis is accepted, then governments and economists must both be regarded as hindrances to the value-adding process for with-profit (though not necessarily for not-for-profit) organizations. In turn, if this is accepted, so is the implication that not-for-profit organizations are in fact different animals, and put in context of the wider environment, there are two fundamentally different approaches to adding value.

Davidson and Rees-Mogg (1993) contend that governments which subscribe to the 'market forces' hypothesis (aside from the fact that, to a greater or lesser degree they are also interventionist,and certainly affected by the interventionism of others) do not have a more robust philosophy. They point to the irrationality of human decision-making, and the 'linearity of human expectations' (see Box 4.4), and say that these differ in form but not in degree between societies which are and are not advanced in economic thought. Thus, considering the buying and selling opportunities offered by stock exchanges, they observe the following.

- Markets do not instantly or comprehensively reflect all the information available from the wider environment. This helps to explain the persistence of inefficient forms of saving in backward societies.
- There is a failure of people living and working in depressed conditions to see opportunities. This is matched by the equally 'irrational' failure of participants in progressive markets to anticipate 'downside discontinuities' (unforeseen slumps).
- Most investors in rich countries will overlook opportunities to make money from negative developments, hence the prevalence of the panic selling of shares of troubled companies.
- There is a dearth of buyers of shares in companies belonging to undeveloped countries because of their general instability. This 'rational' approach means that opportunities are not being capitalized upon most efficiently.

In short, Davidson and Rees-Mogg say that there is a case for advocating a 'contrarian' strategy of investment, which means waiting until market sentiment reaches an extreme and then doing the exact opposite.

If it is accepted that some of the fundamental underlying ideas of economic theory are either significantly flawed or not fully conceived, then other factors should perhaps be taken into account. Economics is based on a western picture of how things are. It is possible that this may not always be the case. For example, fundamentalist religions are in the ascendant in some parts of the world. Muslims may have different economic values and goals. (In the west, religion has largely been represented by Christianity, whose teachings gradually became less valued after Darwin's work on evolution in the early nineteenth century. However, scientists are less sure now than at any time in the last 150 years that the discoveries they are making do not indicate some overall divine plan.)

Theorists who have made broad observations of how economies work over long periods of time, without trying to explain **why** they behave in certain ways, may be getting closer to establishing robust economic laws. In 1923, a Russian called Kondratieff put forward a theory that short-term fluctuations of the business cycle (i.e., those that had been manipulated by governments) seemed to be imposed upon much larger cycles – what he termed the 'long cycles' or 'long waves', of depression and regeneration which occur about every 50 years (i.e., once a working lifetime) and seem to be largely impervious to any interventionist measures. Kondratieff included in his model over-lapping or connected sub-cycles in prices, growth rates, product innovation, agriculture, industrial production and real wages, and also identified that the economic cycle was connected with other large movements in society (cycles of power/politics, cycles of war, etc.)

If Kondratieff's ideas are accepted, then it must also be accepted that in the long run, economic 'tweaking' by governments is effectual only in a very limited way. This is, of course, of little interest to organizations whose value-adding activities, and even existence, may be dramatically influenced by government measures. It is therefore important to be aware of how governments think, what they intend by their application of economic models, and what the likely impact upon and reaction from organizations is likely to be. An attempt is not being made here to denounce the whole of western economic theory! The intention is to suggest that it should be regarded with a critical eye, and its relevance appraised, in particular, by those whose task will be to operate in organizations in what is likely to be the vastly altered economic climate of the 21st century.

Finally, it might be helpful to point out that nations and economies have thrived in the past on complicated pictures of how the world operates, which have since been discredited. To illustrate this – and for fun! – Case 4.5 describes the Elizabethan view of the world. No educated western person could swallow such ideas today, but the educated Elizabethan classes not only believed in them profoundly, but were galvanized by them to achieve extraordinary feats of exploration and scientific development. It was a question of creating a meaningful pattern, which again generated confidence.

CASE 4.5

THE ELIZABETHAN WORLD PICTURE: A 'WRONG' VALUE SYSTEM THAT WORKED

The Elizabethans believed in a chain of creation. The elements, fire, earth, air and water, as inanimate, were lower than the lowest animate creation; but the operations of the elements did not cease with the lowest living thing; nor were the higher living things compounded of the lower, but all were compounded of the four elements direct. There-fore, the elements could not be links in a simple chain: they had to be a supplementary chain connected in many places with the main one.

The entities of nature were arranged in a hierarchy, from plants and beasts to the angels. The universe was regarded as geocentric (despite wide access to the works of Copernicus). The number of spheres that the created universe consisted of was variously thought to be nine or eleven; but it was generally accepted that round a central earth revolved, with differing motions, spheres of diameters ever increasing from the moon's, through the other planets, to that of the fixed stars; and there was a sphere called the *primum mobile* outside that of the fixed stars, which dictated the correct motions to all the rest. Within this universe, there was a sharp division, consisting of the difference between mutability and constancy, which separated everything beneath the sphere of the moon from all the rest.

Angels were intermediate between God and man. They were purely intellectual beings who possessed free will, like men, but never conflicted with God's will. They could apprehend God immediately, and not through the metaphor of faith; they were arranged in orders; they were God's messengers; and they acted as the guardians of men.

The stars, through obeying God's changeless order, were responsible for sublunary vagaries of fortune. The planets were the commuting agents of eternity to mutability. The Elizabethan believed in the pervasive influence of an external fate in the world. The twelve signs of the zodiac had their own active properties. Their functions differed, with the moon accepted as the great promoter of change.

The evident havoc in nature's order did not contradict God's Providence, but was all part of his scheme: God allowed man freedom, with which man inflicted chaos on himself and the physical universe. Nevertheless, it was optimistically held that man had it in him to survive the blows of fortune, and that ultimately fortune was the tool of God and the educator of man.The extremes of virtue and vice occurred when education or evil communications fortified those whom the stars made naturally virtuous or vicious.

The earth, cold and dry, was the heaviest and lowest element. Outside the earth was the region of cold and moist, the water; and outside water the region of hot and moist, the air. Fire, hot and dry, was the noblest element, and enclosed the globe of air that girded water and earth. Though the elements were ranged in this hierarchy in their own chain of being, they were actually mixed in infinitely varying proportions, and at perpetual war with each other – e.g., fire and water were opposed, but kept by God from mutual destruction by having the element of air between them, which, having one each of their qualities, was able to act as a balancer.

In the chain of being, the position of man was of paramount interest. He was the nodal point, and his double nature (after the Fall), though a source of internal conflict to himself, had the unique function of binding together all creation, and bridging the cosmic chasm between matter and spirit.

The importance of man was at its strongest in the age of Elizabeth I. Not only did man, as man, live with uncommon intensity at that time, but he was never removed from his cosmic setting – he had a profound belief in his significance in the scheme of things. Therefore, a fertile environment was established for the extraordinary achievements of the era.

Source: adapted from Tillyard, E.M.W. (1943) *The Elizabethan World Picture*, Chatto, London.

This example of a 'flawed' value system to which almost all educated people of the time subscribed bears useful comparison with the pervasive use of modern nation-based economic theory for a number of reasons:

- It affected the way that people behaved, with far-reaching effects. The idea of fate was juxtaposed with a belief that mankind, by manipulating the sytem at various points, could influence the future course of events. Sometimes, and partly because of this belief, they did succeed; but (at least from a late 20th century point of view) the premises on which they built the system that supported their success were erroneous.
- Although the system itself was not therefore robust, some universal truths and profoundly helpful thoughts did come from it: the ideal of balance, for example. Similarly, some of the concepts that have resulted from economic theory – like the idea of comparative advantage – have helped to promote the more effective deployment of human effort.
- Mankind was celebrated and praised in the Elizabethan system. Here, there is a marked contrast with modern applied economics – the 'dismal science', which seeks to regulate human activity in a multiplicity of respects because of the ever-present need to acknowledge scarcity of resources. Interestingly enough, the era in which the application of sophisticated economic 'solutions' such as the Bretton Woods Agreement were most universally supported and seemed to work (that is, during the three decades which succeeded the Second World War) coincided with a period of post-war optimism, when continuing growth, full employment and low inflation were all considered to be realizable goals.
- Just as the idea of an earth-centred universe was appropriate to what was needed in order to pursue value-adding activities (in their broadest sense) in the period of colonial expansion, so the idea of a nation-state dominated world (the lynch-pin of applied economic theory) may have been appropriate to the consideration of value-adding activities which took place in the two centuries which followed the industrial revolution. The time may have come either to pursue another paradigm to measure, assess and predict value-adding activities, or to build upon a radically different economic theory which acknowledges that it is value-adding activities in the whole world that need such definition. No kind of clear or accurate picture can emerge from dissecting the world into a series of nation-states.

The idea of business confidence has permeated this chapter; and, in the last analysis, that is what the productive relationship between businesses and governments is about. If governments can inspire confidence in businesspeople so that they can add value effectively, then together they are on the road to achieving national and international prosperity; the difficulty, as we have seen, is that each has to take into account many other factors along the way.

SUMMARY

In this chapter:

- You have examined some of the principal theories of economics as they relate to the value-adding process. The 'factors of production' available to organizations have been listed, and it has been pointed out that today 'knowledge' is probably the most important of these. You have considered the related disciplines of micro- and macro-economics.
- You have considered in some detail the notion of the circular flow of income, and how the initially simple version of this can be made more relevant to the more complex business environment by the consideration of further variables.
- You have been encouraged to try to gauge the impact upon organizations seeking to add value of such shifting environmental variables as bank borrowing; raising share capital; savings, direct taxation; indirect taxation; and the intangible, elusive but powerful notion of 'business confidence'.
- You have examined the performance measures commonly used by governments, including Gross Domestic Product (GDP), Gross National Product (GNP), Net National Product (NNP), the Balance of Payments, the trade balance and a trade deficit.
- The concept of national currency has been discussed, and with it the notion of inflation, and how it affects both national and international business.
- You have looked at the composition of the Retail Price Index, and been encouraged to evaluate its usefulness as the key tool for measuring inflation.
- You have learned the advisability of appraising economic models carefully, and realizing that, as well as offering clarity, they each carry their limitations.
- You have been encouraged to attempt to arrive at an understanding of the differing approaches of governments when applying macroeconomic theory to their national situations. Finally, once again the importance of 'business confidence' as it is affected by the many economic variables discussed in the chapter has been emphasized.

REFERENCES AND FURTHER READING

Davidson, J.D. and Rees-Mogg, W. (1993) *The Great Reckoning: How the World will Change in the Depression of the 1990s*, Sidgwick & Jackson, London.

Kennedy, P. (1993) *Preparing for the Twenty-First Century*, HarperCollins, London.

Access to a good economics book is essential (though to dip into, not to read all the way through!)

A 'classic' is Sloman, J. (1991) *Economics*, Prentice Hall, London.

A book which readers might find more practically relevant, however, because it sets economics within an international context, is Mackintosh, M. *et al.* (1996) *Economics and Changing Economies*, The Open University/ International Thomson, London.

The Economist publishes a number of valuable annual reference works, including the *Economist Book of Vital Statistics*, which gives useful facts and figures about the wealth and industrial output of all the world's nations. Other statistical works include Central Statistics Office publications, and compilations in the 'serious' financial press. Specific works need to be tracked down by the student, as they date too quickly to be usefully referred to in a textbook.

Adding value and social issues $\boxed{5}$

LEARNING OBJECTIVES

- To appreciate both the difficulty and the necessity for the organization attempting to add value effectively of spotting long-term social trends.
- To understand that people occupy three broad roles in society – that they are consumers, citizens, and workers in/builders of organizations, and the implications of the (potentially three) different sets of standards for value-adding organizations.
- To explore and discuss the issues attendant upon people as consumers, considering
  - the implications of demographic change
  - the differing concerns of for-profit and not-for-profit organizations
  - the wider long-term global implications
  - the impact of governments and the role of chance on demographic trends
  - changes in taste and the demand for goods
  - changes in work and leisure habits, paying especial attention to a sensitive appraisal of the growing world unemployment issue.
- To explore and discuss the issues concerning people as citizens, considering
  - the importance and relevance of business ethics
  - the complications presented by and the implications of Foreign Direct Investment (FDI)
  - caring for the biospherical environment.
- To explore and discuss the issues concerning people as workers and builders of organizations, addressing particularly
  - the role of the strategic leader
  - the modern change in approach to jobs and careers
  - an appreciation of Belbin's categorization norms for management teams
  - the disadvantages as well as benefits posed by these new approaches to management

- From this, you should have developed an understanding of the wider social trends which organizations engaged in adding value collectively need to address: e.g., the polarization of society and the fragmentation of the fabric of society. You should be aware that taking responsibility for these issues will be vital if, in the 21st century, humanity is to prosper from the value-adding activities of organizations.

INTRODUCTION

The social issues facing any organization are diverse and insidious. Long-term social trends, which are likely to be of the greatest significance, are difficult to identify with clarity, and, even if they are identified, the patterns that they will take and their outcomes are yet harder to predict. Nevertheless, the most successful organizations are likely to be those that are not only able to harness their creativity to spotting social trends in their early stages and develop an intuition for those which will have a significant bearing on society in the future, but also build within themselves the manouevrability which enables them to act and capitalize on such insights, and make subsequent rapid adjustments to their activities if necessary. Thus their adding value strategy is constantly attuned and reattuned to the needs of the customer.

By definition, social issues are about people: in considering the implications that trends and shifts in society have upon the value-adding process (and which self-evidently have the most important impact on any organization's 'mission'), this chapter will examine people and adding value from three different perspectives:

1 People as consumers.
2 People as citizens.
3 People as workers and builders of organizations.

It may at first appear that there is little difference between consumers and citizens; but it will be argued that there is a fundamental difference, and one which has become much more apparent and relevant to the successful adding of value during the past 30 years. It is the difference between the customer getting what he or she wants, and getting it at an acceptable social (as distinguished from financial) cost. This difference has been described succinctly by Henry Wendt:

> 'Though corporate apologists sometimes conflate consumers and citizens, the two are not identical. As consumers, we may live in a global market, but as citizens, we live in local societies. Consumers want good products at low prices, but citizens want clean air and water, fair labour practices, good government, and ethical corporate behaviour. As consumers, we focus on our standard of living, but as citizens, we are more apt to focus on the quality of our lives.

Yes, we want the fantastic array of goods and services that global companies produce, from life-saving drugs to advanced technology to expensive toys, but do we want them at the price of neocolonialism, exploited labour, complicity with repellent political regimes, and the disappearance of regional and ethnic identities in favour of an anonymous global collectivism?'

[Wendt, p.18]

The quotation raises many complex issues of ethics, integrity and profound philosophical thinking, which we examine in the context of people as citizens. For simplicity's sake (but without forgetting that these issues have not 'gone away'), let us first explore how the organization can align its value-adding strategy to social trends driven by people as consumers.

PEOPLE AS CONSUMERS

Demographic change

Of all the variables that have an impact on how organizations deliver added value to their consumers, the most far-reaching is surely that of demographic change.

The population of the world is currently growing at a fast (many would say, far too fast) rate. In 1990, the entire world population had advanced to 5.3 billion (from four billion in 1976, and two billion in 1925). The World Bank estimates that the total population of the earth may 'stabilize' at between 10 and 11 billion people in the second half of the 21st century, but other calculations predict that the total may reach 14.5 billion.

This population growth is not uniformly spread across the countries of the globe; indeed, the populations of the 'developed' nations have stabilized or are declining. The increases in population are taking place almost entirely in developing countries, and this is a new phenomenon. For example, in 1950, Africa's population was half that of Europe; by 1985 it had drawn level (at about 480 million each); and by 2025 it is expected to be three times Europe's (1.58 billion as against 512 million).

These rather bewildering statistics contain two major implications:

1. In the countries of both the developed and the developing world, there is a radical and opposite shift in balance between the proportions of young and old. For example, in Kenya in 1993, 52 per cent of the population was less than fifteen, and only 2.8 per cent over 65; while in France at the same time, 10 million of a population of 55 million were aged over sixty – a figure predicted (on a scientifically calculated basis) to rise to 15 million by 2020.
2. Leading on from this, both the relative balance of young and old and its likely future overall power in terms of sheer numbers and earning capability means that the developing world holds the key to

the way in which the big multi-national and transnational organizations will add value in the 21st century.

Let us look at the likely effects of these trends at both the local (national) and global (international) level.

Local

1 'Not-for-profit': the health service network

In almost every developed country, the statistics referred to above suggest that health care services will need to concentrate increasingly on the types of care needed by ageing and progressively longer-lived populations. Further considerations will include how to overcome the manpower problems which will be the future legacy of a declining birthrate – can these be partially overcome by the use of new technologies, for example? – and the vexed question of who is going to pay for such services, and how, as the total proportion of the population able to work diminishes. Conversely, in a country like Indonesia, where the birthrate is rising very fast, but where life expectancy still has not attained the level enjoyed by the developed nations, it would clearly be a mistake to concentrate resources on developing geriatric care: the (frequently less complex) requirements of children and a young working population would take priority. Furthermore, decisions about expending resources on costly labour-saving equipment would be influenced by comparing their long-term cost-efficiency with the ready availability of cheap labour.

2 'For-profit': the alcohol industry in Britain

Research conducted by alcohol manufacturers in Britain concluded that the generation of consumers which patronized public houses in the 1970s (the so-called 'bulge babies', or 'baby boomers' born after the Second World War) were also the chief buyers of their products in the 1980s – with the difference that, by the later period, most had family ties, and were therefore more likely to consume alcohol at home. Furthermore, women, as they became more emancipated, had emerged as the main buyers of some alcoholic products, in particular wines and 'composite' drinks. The manufacturers altered their approach both to marketing their products, and to new product development, accordingly.

Global

The effect of demographic trends on organizations currently or intending in the future to operate on a global or international level depends on how far the shift in balance of population and power throughout the world will dictate consumer tastes. There is a vigorous academic debate on whether, strategically speaking, it is better for companies to aim for a 'global' approach, in which they are supplying what is more or less the same product to different markets around the world, or for a differentiated, or 'multinational' approach, in which the tastes of local customers are consulted and different products made for different geographical regions. In the former case, the company may be fulfilling the low-cost imperative, but at the expense of not adding the value that the customer really wants; in the latter case the issue becomes one of ensuring that the customer is able and willing to pay for the additional costs incurred by adding value in this way.

It should be pointed out, however, that proponents of both sides of this debate are considering it from what might be described as a western approach to adding value. It may be that this is both correct and reasonable, given that both capitalist and industrialized societies – responsible for developing corporate value-adding activities as we know them today – evolved in the west, and that there is every chance that sophisticated and affluent consumers in other countries, as they develop, will be 'educated' into accepting this western model. On the other hand, there are nations, such as China, which may both build industries with vast future potential for adding value in the 21st century, and offer (because of their population – in 1994, China's represented one-fifth of the world's total) huge new marketplaces, that use quite different criteria from what are currently accepted. Even the biggest of the international companies may have to embrace new philosophies if they are to continue to add value in the way the consumer really wants.

Governments, the role of chance, and demographic trends

Governments may try to alter demographic trends. Generally, unless they operate totalitarian regimes, their measures are unlikely to prove very effective. For example, in recent years both France and Sweden have offered financial and tax incentives to encourage people to have more children, but these have not resulted in any significant alteration in the balance of their respective populations. In countries like China, where governments have the power to enforce policies designed to alter the size of the population – in the 1990s, China has a (very unpopular) one child per family policy in an effort to achieve zero population growth by the year 2,000 – the long-term demographic effect is likely to prove to be more disastrous than non-intervention. If the Chinese government is successful in its policy, China's population in 2035 will contain 'twice as many persons in their sixties as in their twenties, an age composition that even the most enthusiastic supporter of the virtues of the elderly could scarcely favour' (Kennedy, p.168). China's trends in consumer demand may also be distorted by this policy. Case 5.1 examines China's attempts at population control in more detail.

CASE 5.1

CHINA'S POPULATION CONTROL POLICY AND ITS LIKELY EFFECTS

China began to operate a stringent population control policy in 1979, consisting of a 'one child per family' mandate which, if broken, incurred severe penalties for both the disobedient parents and their relatives, sometimes including imprisonment in labour camps.

The Chinese government introduced the policy because it hoped that China, which contains one fifth of the world's population (virtually all of whom are ethnic Chinese), would thereby be able to stave off predictable future economic and social difficulties. However, the policy was oversimplistic in its approach, and 'China-watchers' in the West and elsewhere foresaw complications which, in 1994, were beginning to materialize, and could only be expected to grow worse. Not least among these was the cultural imperative that each family should have a male heir. Girl children were therefore hidden, abandoned, or even put to death – sometimes, quite openly on the streets of big cities, as a kind of macabre protest against the government's policy.

The government did not waver from this policy, however, because it saw it as the only potential salvation from the following problems associated with sustaining such a massive population:

1 **Unemployment**. In 1994, the Chinese labour force was projected to reach 1.1 billion, if growth continued at the current rate. The danger of both acknowledged and 'hidden' unemployment was apparent, and would undoubtedly have the effect of retarding China's economic development. Research undertaken in the west suggested that one third of the workers employed in Chinese SOEs [the economic units into which the country is divided] were unproductive. This was partly due to overmanning, but also because the SOEs were not just about economic output – they were responsible for social services for employees and their families throughout their lives, including food and housing.

2 The **dependency ratio** (of working to non-working) population was likely to increase. The prediction was that it would be 3/4 productive people: 6+ unproductive people by the year 2020. What the government did not take into account, however, was that in the long term the population policy would exacerbate this situation, as the number of people able to work (i.e., of the right age, and fit) would be immensely reduced in the next generation.

3 **Political instability**. The dramatically swift decline of communist power in eastern Europe, following the dismantling of the Berlin Wall in 1989, had placed China's 'post-communist regime' in even greater isolation than that in which it had existed previously (Chinese communism was historically of a different 'brand' from Soviet communism). The Chinese economy in the mid-1990s

appeared to be in a transitional stage. Economic investment and productivity appeared to be making impressive progress, but there was no political liberation of the individual. This could have implications for China's aspiration to become a major world trading nation, if other nations were to impose sanctions for its poor record on civil rights. China was ruled by a nonagenarian dictator, Deng Xiaoping, and his death, in 1997, may precipitate 'struggles for power, and possibly widespread social conflict' (*Economist*, 27 August 1994).

4   **Loss of 'finite resources'.** There had been a loss of arable land – particularly significant to an economy heavily dependent on agriculture – through increased industrial requirements and over-intensive farming. Accelerating deforestation was an attendant problem.

It would be hard to defend the government's population policy as an effective measure against these problems. Aside from the other problems that it was casting up in its wake, it appeared not even to have had the desired effect on population growth. In 1994, China had 20 million more women citizens (123m altogether) than in 1983. Nevertheless, the policy was making a deep social impact. As well as the rejection or killing of girl babies, there was an upsurge in the abortion of female foetuses – China owned 100,000 sex-deducing ultrasound scanners in 1994. Families lucky enough to gain the permitted only boy frequently pampered him to an unhealthy extent. 'Little mandarins' was the term coined for these only boys, often grossly overweight, whose every material whim was indulged.

The future social implications could be grotesque. When the present generation of Chinese children reaches adulthood, it will be predominantly male – causing social imbalance and a dearth of heterosexual partners – and, probably, anti-socially self-obsessed.

From the adding-value point of view, questions arise concerning the kind of society that is likely to be built by such a population, the kind of ethical and cultural values that are likely to be observed by it, and the types of products and services that its members are likely to require. Within the global context, it is also necessary to consider whether China will, within one generation, have achieved such economic significance in the world that the answers to these questions will also provide guides to how value is added in world industries as a whole.

Chance, on the other hand, may have very profound effects indeed. The Aids epidemic currently sweeping Africa may reverse the population explosion there. It will certainly have major implications for the economies (both in Africa and other countries) most afflicted by it, as the main Aids casualties are young adults of working age whose significant contribution to their countries' economies will be removed by their premature deaths. Epidemics like Aids offer value-adding opportunities for for-profit organizations such as pharmaceutical companies (though they are taking the risk of perhaps never recouping the millions of pounds of investment that they have to sink into researching and developing effective drugs); they offer value-adding challenges to not-for-profit organizations which have to channel their finite resources into coping with such a catastrophe; and they present all currently or potentially involved organizations with the necessity of trying to predict what the long-term effects will be on their value-adding activities. War is another chance phenomenon which simultaneously offers opportunities for some organizations and stretches the resources of others in a similar way, while making demands upon the imaginative and predictive powers of all.

Changes in taste and demand for goods

Generally speaking, in today's world, societies are continually becoming better informed and more sophisticated. It therefore follows that, over a period of time, broad consumer tastes change, as people become better educated, more affluent, or simply more blasé (or less naive)! There is a tendency, therefore, particularly in developed nations, for retailing chains to become progressively more 'up-market'. Case 4.3 describes how Marks & Spencer, the British clothes and food retailer, became one of the first in the field to follow this course; and explains how, within this broader strategy, it also developed ways of responding to shorter-term trends caused by more temporary influences upon society, such as the recession of the late 1980s/early 1990s. Tesco, one of the four leading U.K. supermarket chains, consciously altered its value-adding strategy during the 1980s from 'pile 'em high and sell 'em cheap' to offering consumers a wider range of more expensive, but still competitively priced, health-conscious food products, to which further value had been added by describing their precise nutritional content clearly on the labels. This move was backed up by free literature, distributed in the stores, about healthy eating and healthy lifestyles. It proved to be successful – the company was adding value which the customer wanted, and for which s/he was prepared to pay.

Whilst customers are prepared to pay for this type of quality, however, increasing sophistication also often means that people become sceptical of the value added by 'reliable' brand names. Even the mighty Coca Cola label has been hit by 'own label' competition – for example, Sainsbury's, the leading British food retailing group, successfully launched its 'Classic Cola' own-brand cola drink in the spring of 1994. They charged approximately two-thirds of the price charged by Coca Cola for its product, and, in a widespread advertising campaign invited people to test the two products by tasting them blindfold. Most could not distinguish between the two, or – even better for Sainsbury's – preferred the Sainsbury's product.

Other companies have tapped into changing consumer ideas about brand names by extending or 'reconfiguring' the value chain. Normann and Raminez examine the case of Ikea, a no-frills American furniture-kit company which not only produces well-made furniture-kit packs at competitive prices, but enlists the help of the customer in contributing to its low-cost strategy. Thus, the customer who visits an Ikea show-room is actively engaged in packing up his or her purchase, and 'delivering' it as well. Ikea maintains that it has built the customer into its value-adding strategy in such a way that customers view their own contribution to the service in a very positive light, and find it enjoyable too.

Similar shifts in consumer taste have been tapped by other industries. Travelodge, the British motel chain set up by the Forte group, was conceived of and prospered by recognizing the demand for cheap, clean, basic hotel accommodation with none of the additional services which make conventional British hotels so costly. In 1996, a Travelodge room cost £36.50 per night (however many people were to occupy it), and included sleeping accommodation for four, an en suite bathroom, and tea- and coffee-making facilities. A three or four star British hotel room might typically be charged at anything from £55 to £90 per person.

By no means all such shifts in demand reflect a desire to add value by reducing costs or moving 'down-market'. When Richard Branson set up Virgin Airways, he tried to find ways of competing by differentiation rather than low cost, and, after undertaking extensive market research, came up with a range of innovative ideas, including more space, better quality food, and more imaginative in-flight entertainment, which added value for customers by making flying a more enjoyable experience. Swissair, which particularly targets business travellers, realized that businesspeople did not necessarily want the endless in-flight meals which have become part of the routine service for all air companies. They therefore devised a range of lighter snacks for those who preferred them, and also made travelling time more productive for businesspeople, again by offering them more space, and also by introducing special airport lounges for business class passengers where they could work quietly, have the use of telephone and fax facilities, and, if they wished, take a shower.

Changes in work and leisure habits

In the 1960s, there was widespread belief in the western world that as a result of the development of all types of electronic gadgets and labour-saving devices, and the advent of the computer, society would become much more leisured. It was thought that the three-day week would become commonplace, and that people would have so much leisure time on their hands that they would need training in how to use it. The implications for how to add value in such a society would be far-reaching: people would become well-versed in a range of leisure activities, and want both expert tuition and all the necessary paraphernalia for their chosen pursuits, whilst all organizations would rely increasingly on advanced technology such as robotics for carrying out their operations.

At the beginning of this chapter, we considered the difficulty of interpreting the future outcomes of changes in society correctly. The misplaced optimism of 1960s social scenario builders offers a classic example, and today we view their projections with some incredulity. What has in fact happened is that there has been a polarization of workers and non-workers. The reasons for this are complex, and only partly due to the increasing part that high-tech plays in organizations. (What the idealistic society-watchers of the 1960s did not realize was that people would not be happy with the modest, relatively egalitarian distribution of wealth that a shorter working week would offer; nor that in a society where manual skills were becoming increasingly less relevant, some people ('knowledge workers') would be sought after, whilst others would find it near impossible to gain work.) In the 1990s, people who do have jobs are often working much longer hours than their parents did – partly because the 'restructuring' of organizations in the wake of recession has meant fewer people doing the same work, and extensively because the rise of the 'knowledge worker' has led to the type of employment that does not fit neatly with the traditional nine-to-five working day.

As a consequence of these shifts in the pattern and nature of employment, most western economies now have a large mass (between 10 per cent and 20 per cent of those employable) who have plenty of 'leisure time' on their hands, but no money to add value to it; a larger group of employed people, who represent the powerhouse of the economy, and have the cash, but not much time for leisure products; and a further, and quickly-growing group of 'retired' people, some of whom are very affluent because of their handsome pension provisions, but whose tastes in leisure are frequently conditioned by their physical limitations.

Clearly the recognition of this profile of modern western society has a profound effect upon how the organization can add value successfully. For example, companies producing sports gear, who might have believed in the 1960s that they were targeting large market segments consisting of individuals who each had several 'hobbies', might now be aiming at a much smaller, more exclusive group, consisting of individuals with not much time at their disposal who want to pursue perhaps just one sport 'seriously'. Such people are likely to be very discerning buyers, prepared to pay for expensive equipment, but extremely fastidious about its quality and performance. There is potential for a very high added-value mark-up; but companies operating in the area are targeting very small market segments and simultaneously facing intense competition. Continually improving and developing the products is essential, and likely to demand costly investment.

An example is provided by the small, successful Berghaus company. This was a family firm which produced high-quality outdoor clothing for walkers and skiers, and had developed garments of man-made fibres with high insulating capabilities. Although the company was very profitable, the family eventually decided that they would have to sell it (and it fetched a premium price), because the amount of investment needed to keep pace with the necessary product developments was more than they could raise.

Saga Holidays is a company which has targeted the needs of the affluent elderly in order to add value to package holidays for this segment of the market. Saga couriers are specially trained to look after older people by planning less taxing days for them, arranging accommodation which they find pleasant and relaxing, and making sure that special requirements (of diet, mobility, etc.) are taken care of. Within these constraints, they nevertheless succeed in taking the elderly to exotic places which they have not had time or money to see before, and which they would perhaps be afraid to visit if the company did not take away all the potential worries. It has flourished by adding value in this way. Different ways of adding value to products to cope with demographic change is not, of course, confined to the leisure industry: for example, cereals manufacturers have been trying to target the elderly as well as the young for their products, by modifying them to have greater appeal for those more interested in their nutritional qualities than their taste and appearance.

How to add value for those who are not employed, or have low incomes, has not until the present greatly preoccupied the rest of society. This is understandable, particularly where for-profit organizations are concerned, because there is little financial incentive for them to seek creative solutions for this problem. However, as the number of people who genuinely cannot find work grows, governments are beginning to see their condition as a threat to the existing fabric of society; the more enlightened are even beginning to realize that the premises (the 'work ethic', the 'American dream', the 'acceptable face of capitalism') upon which modern society is built may have to be challenged. It cannot be claimed that this constitutes more than a very small part of organizational activity at the moment; and it remains to be seen whether the activity that is taking place heralds a significant social trend (cf. the question of the influences on adding value of developing nations). Case 5.2 describes the 'LETS' system which has been devised to add value for people with low incomes by the west London council of Hounslow.

CASE 5.2

LETS: ADDING VALUE FOR THOSE WITH LOW INCOMES

'LETS' is an acronym for 'local exchange and bartering system'. In 1994, there were 200 LETS systems operating in the United Kingdom, particularly in 'financially disadvantaged' areas. Each scheme consists of mutual self-help groups of 15 to 400 people who have united to form alternative economies.

The first LETS was set up in Norwich in 1985; in 1990, LETSLINK, a national co-ordinator of all the local schemes, was initiated by members in Wiltshire and Gloucestershire. In the autumn of 1994, Hounslow Council appointed a full-time development officer, with a budget of £30,000, to start a LETS scheme.

Each LETS group produces a directory of services which its members are able to offer. This may be charged at an hourly rate, or be calculated on a varying scale according to the degree of skill involved. In Hounslow, the scheme operates in terms of 10-minute units, each of which is called a 'beak'. A shiatsu massage costs 15 beaks; redecoration of a flat 80 beaks (materials not included).

Members of the schemes are given cheque books, and a central record-keeper debits or credits their accounts after each transaction. Interest is not attracted, and there is no set payment schedule, so a member can start at zero and go into debt immediately. The system – a modern variant of barter – simply requires all of its members to be capable of and prepared to offer services or goods.

Increasingly, people with professional skills are taking part in the schemes, and some businesses will accept barter units for goods. The primary purpose of the schemes is to provide goods and services for those who are unable to afford to pay cash for them, but the fact that all participants are directly involved in adding value themselves has, it is claimed, strengthened local community ties as well.

Interestingly enough, there are few defaulters on their debts; the people who obstruct the system are those with large credits, who cannot think of goods or services that they themselves wish to receive. This illustrates in microcosm the economics of all trade, and an essential truth about adding value – that it must be consumed as well as produced effectively. Anne-Marie Mayer, a participant in the Hounslow scheme, explained it thus:

> 'If people do a lot of work for other people but cannot think of anything they want, it creates a lot of people with large negative balances who then become disinclined to trade'.

Keynes would have approved!

Source: taken from material collected by Mokoto Rich for the *Financial Times*.

PEOPLE AS CITIZENS

Over the past 30 years, and at a much accelerated rate during the last 10 of these, consumers have not only been interested *per se* in the value-added properties of the goods and services which they buy, as we have discussed in the various examples above, but also in how the organization which produced them operated in behavioural terms in both its external and its internal environment. In short, with the rise of the well-informed consumer, a corresponding interest in **business ethics** has developed. To cite again part of the quotation from Henry Wendt given at the beginning of this chapter, customers as citizens are ever more likely to reject products made 'at the price of neocolonialism, exploited labour, complicity with repellent political regimes, and the disappearance of regional and ethnic identities in favour of an anonymous global collectivism'.

We have already considered the last issue from a purely economical point of view, in the standardization/ differentiation debate. It now becomes relevant to ask, not only whether people from different ethnic backgrounds are **willing** to buy standardized products, but whether it is **right** to encourage them to do so. For some products, the question does not arise: because of the later advent of industrialization in newly industrialized and 'under-developed' countries, there are no 'ethnic' refrigerators or vacuum cleaners. There is, however, still the implicit erosion of a lifestyle which did not need them – but it could equally be argued that to dwell on this is to romanticize a way of life that may have been harsh and undignified as well as simple. Other products, such as western-style clothes, oust styles of clothing that have been worn for generations, and are not inherently superior in quality or design to more traditional garments. Is the introduction and vigorous marketing of western styles therefore comparable in moral terms to the proselytizing of the Victorian missionaries, who arrogantly sought to replace ancient and sophisticated religions with their own, or is it equally arrogant to assume that people from the countries being targeted to buy western products do not have the intelligence and independence to make their own purchasing decisions?

This brings us to the notion of 'neocolonialism', also raised by Wendt. We established in Chapter One that, in order to be successful in the long term, organizations had to find ways of adding value for all their **stakeholders**, not just shareholders; it has also to be acknowledged that **shareholders** are a very powerful group. In order to satisfy their demands for return on their investment, most companies accept the concept that growth is an imperative. As successful companies grow larger, they are likely to look to underdeveloped countries, not only in their search for new markets, but also as places in which to invest. This is known as **Foreign Direct Investment (FDI)**. The traditional ('neoclassical') economic argument is that this is a good thing, because it brings new, scarce resources – capital, technology, management and marketing skills – to the host country, and adds jobs to the economy, and improves distribution of income. However, recent research (reinforced by dissent from the host countries themselves) suggests that companies engaged in FDI are more interested in exploitation than investment. Moran (1985) writes:

> 'In the extreme, foreign companies might capture the commanding heights of the host economy, soak up indigenous sources of capital as they drive local firms out of business, create a small labour elite for themselves while transferring the bulk of the workers into the ranks of the unemployed, and siphon off oligopoly profits for repatriation to corporate headquarters.'

People who are employed from the indigenous workforce commonly receive a fraction of the remuneration that the equivalent job would command in the west – though with the ethically complicating factor that it might afford a higher-than-average standard of living in the country concerned.

Moreover, FDI companies might 'add value' for consumers unversed in the sophistication of western advertising techniques in a spurious way. A notorious example is provided by the marketing of dried baby milk in poor African countries in the 1970s and early 1980s. Mothers were deluded into thinking that the milk was better for their infants, but they did not have the hygienic facilities at their disposal to be able to administer it safely; furthermore, when they were no longer able to afford it (as was often the case), their supplies of natural milk had ceased, and they were unable to nourish the children at all. Many babies died.

Organizations which are associated with 'repellent regimes' are likely to have their goods or services banned by governments, as well as boycotted by individuals. Sometimes, the consumer has no choice – the government puts an absolute embargo on the product, so the consumer is unable to apply his or her ethical judgement as to whether to buy it. An instance is offered by the ban in the west on imported Iraqi oil in the aftermath of the Gulf War of 1990–1. Other bans are less comprehensive. Britain frowned on the apartheid activities of South Africa until apartheid was dismantled in 1993, and operated some trading sanctions, but these were never absolute, South African fruit, for example, was usually available in the UK. It was therefore up to the consumer to decide whether he or she wished to purchase the product, in the knowledge of the conditions under which it had been produced – a type of 'negative added value' which he or she must weigh up against the 'positive added value' of being able to buy very superior quality fruit all the year round.

Perhaps the most publicized, and therefore the most influential, ethical issue of all concerns the biospherical environment. Heightened by the campaigning of determined pressure groups, there is now widespread concern about what organizational activity is doing to the planet, and what its likely impact will be upon our descendants. During the past two decades, there has been an ever-accelerating interest in a company's credentials in 'environmental friendliness' and 'environmentally ethical behaviour'. Bebbington and Gray (1993), extending the economist's notion of 'factors of production', suggest that the 'capital' available to humanity can be divided into three categories, as follows.

1 Critical natural capital (those elements of the biosphere which are essential for life, and must remain inviolable) – e.g., the ozone layer, a critical mass of trees.
2 Other (sustainable, substitutable or renewable) natural capital (those elements of the biosphere which are renewable) – e.g., non-extinct species, woodlands – or for which substitutes can be found.
3 Man-made capital (elements created from the biosphere which are no longer part of the natural ecology) – e.g., machines, buildings, roads, products, wastes, etc.

The point that they make is that man-made capital is generally increased at the expense of the other two types of capital, and it is this capital that is almost universally measured by humanity to establish successfulness and profitability. Organizations of the future will have to find ways of creating 'profit' without undermining the supply of natural capital. **Case 5.3** illustrates the dangers of failure to realize this.

CASE 5.3

ETHICS AND SUSTAINABILITY: THE QUESTION OF PLANT EXTINCTION

The media exposure throughout the world of the dangers caused by mankind to large animals such as whales, elephants and condors has resulted in the successful halting of the threat of extinction to these creatures. Plants have not enjoyed such a high profile: approximately 400 species of plants are lost from the earth each year (as compared with about 200 animal species in total since the year 1500). Often this is due to the effects of short-term opportunism by entrepreneurs unable or unwilling to realize the irresponsibility of their actions.

The case of the Turkish sow-bread cyclamen offers a typical example. Wild cyclamen, unlike their cultivated counterparts, are small and delicate. There are more than 20 species to be found in the countries bordering the Mediterranean, almost all over-collected because of the popularity that they have found as rock garden plants, particularly in North European countries, in the twentieth century. The most popular of all these species has the botanical name *cyclamen hederifolium*, and for decades it was offered to gardeners worldwide by peasants in the Middle East and Turkey, who gained extra income from selling the flowers. Though the flower stocks were not being harvested systematically, they eventually became so depleted that further sale of the entire genus was forbidden by international treaty.

Despite the international ruling, an English firm placed a large order for the wild-collected tubers of *cyclamen hederifolium* from Turkey during the 1980s. When the 10,000 tubers arrived in England, the importers noticed that the plants had an unfamiliar look about them. Examination carried out at Kew Gardens, England's botanical research centre, revealed that what had arrived from Turkey was not *cyclamen hederifolium*, but an extremely rare species called *cyclamen mirabile*. Not only were these plants known to only exist in two locations in Turkey, but, unlike *cyclamen hederifolium*, they were unsuitable for cultivation in English gardens, and did not survive the winter. The whole consignment died. The entire species was thus put in jeopardy by one profiteering action, and *cyclamen mirabile* is now believed to be on the verge of extinction.

The catalogue of greed and irresponsibility extends beyond the English importers and the peasants with whom they were dealing (the latter of whom may or may not have understood that their transactions were illegal). It is difficult to explain why the Turkish authorities allowed protected plants to be exported in express contravention of both an international treaty and their own internal laws, or, equally, how the plants got past British customs. On the face of it, it is also inexplicable why the British trader insisted on importing plants that were known to be protected, and for which (if his claim that his original order was for *cyclamen hederifolium* is accepted) there was a readily available source of cultivated material in his own country. It is probable that his illegal action was designed to add value for a particular type of 'purist' horticulturist, who is willing to pay a premium price for 'genuine' wild flowers. The story illustrates that the organization's quest to add value that the customer requires at a price which he or she is willing to pay cannot be used as an explanation for breaking the law or acting without integrity. The organization's ethical values may have to supersede the customer's own.

It should be added that the crime in this case does not end with flouting the law. Although it is true that species of flora and fauna have flourished and then become extinct since the beginning of the world, human activity is now accelerating the process at an alarming rate. What this means to posterity is incalculable, for the following reasons: firstly, any action which either threatens a species globally, or removes a species which formerly had a significant presence in a particular geographical area, has an effect on global and local ecology which is difficult to quantify, but is potentially catastrophic; secondly, scientists are only just beginning to discover the properties of many plants. Plants have a major contribution to make to future value-adding activities in areas as diverse as medicine, pharmaceuticals, space exploration, mineralogy, the food industry and textiles – if they are not destroyed before their full capabilities are realized.

Organizations can be induced by the law, by pressure groups, and by their regard for their own reputation into adopting a responsible attitude; but it is unlikely that depredations to the plant world caused by mavericks out to 'make a fast buck' will ever be stamped out.

Source: details taken from Koopowitz, H. and Kaye, H. (1990), *Plant Extinction: a Global Crisis*, (2nd edn.), Croom Helm, Bromley.

We have now touched on some of the many ethical issues that organizations are having to address; we are ready to look at the implications which ethics has for adding value in more detail.

A professed and demonstrable commitment to high ethical values has become a way of adding value that can gain powerful competitive advantage for the organization. 'Demonstrable' is the key word here: organizations cannot get away with claiming to observe ethical principles for long unless they are actually doing so. Customers and shareholders will find them out – and there is an increasing number of shareholders seeking to put together 'green' portfolios. Companies which either intentionally or inadvertently break international environmental laws (for example, Exxon in the Exxon Valdez oil spill catastrophe) both incur large fines and suffer immense damage to their reputations, which is reflected in their share price and, ultimately, their market share.

Reidenbach and Robin (1994) have identified five basic stages to corporate attitudes to ethics. These are 'Amoral', 'Legalistic', 'Responsive', 'Emerging Ethical' and 'Ethical'. Box 5.1 explains them in more detail. 'Ethical' represents the highest stage, and a number of significant international companies have flourished by publicizing themselves as ethically sensitive over a broad range of issues. The Body Shop, the international cosmetics retailing chain, provides a famous example. When Anita Roddick was asked how environmental issues affected her strategic approach, she replied

'Well, it's neither the first nor the last, it just is. It's like breathing. Every decision is made, every new act or every new movement or whatever we do has an environmental consciousness. The most important thing is environmental management. On the company's board, we have a member who is absolutely responsible for the environmental education and management of the company. Then we have an environmental department manned by very strong environmental scientists and workers who have come out of the environmental movement. Then each department within our company has a representative for the environment who is responsible for an environmental audit every six months'.

Box 5.1: The Reidenbach and Robin way of measuring organizational ethics

Figure 5.1 illustrates a 'moral pyramid' devised by American professors Eric Reidenbach and Donald Robin (Reidenbach and Robin, 1995) to describe the current range of corporate ethical attitudes.

At the base of the pyramid are **amoral** or 'ethically challenged' companies. They tend to have short lifespans, demand high levels of employee loyalty (infrequently reciprocated), and subsist on a here-today, gone-tomorrow philosophy of winning in the short term at whatever the moral cost.

Stage 2 represents **legalistic** organizations. These set out to obey the law, but strictly to the letter, not in spirit. They are not squeamish about ethical loopholes either overlooked by the law, or which it finds difficult to address. Ethics does not worry them unless it presents a problem for the organization – which it is increasingly likely to do, as customers, shareholders and employees become more ethically conscious.

The **responsive** companies of Stage 3 have reached the level where it is understood that value can be added by not merely adhering strictly to the law, even though to do so would not necessarily mean trouble. The attitude reflects a sense of balance between ethics and profits, on the premise that such a stance adds more value and therefore more profit for the future. A cynic might say that the prevailing philosophy is one of 'we'll be ethical, because it pays'.

Emerging ethical companies (Stage 4). These companies include ethical values in their culture. Employees are aware of their company's stance on ethics. All corporate issues – new product development, relationships with customers, suppliers and employees, advertising, etc. – are approached with an awareness of the ethical consequences of actions, as well as their potential profitability.

Stage 5 companies are the only ones to which Reidenbach and Robin will accord the label **ethical**. In such companies, ethics is a seamless part of the coporate profile. This is reflected in carefully selected core values, as well as the company's approach to hiring, training, firing and rewarding employees.

Even in Stage 5 companies, however, Reidenbach and Robin say that the answer is not to try to attempt to turn staff and companies into saints, but rather to ensure that the correct ethical stance is taken so that reputation is not put at risk. Therefore, even at this level, attention to ethics is a matter of expediency, rather than altruism, but whether or not altruism can ever be said to exist constitutes a profound philosophical debate; we cannot do more than raise the question here.

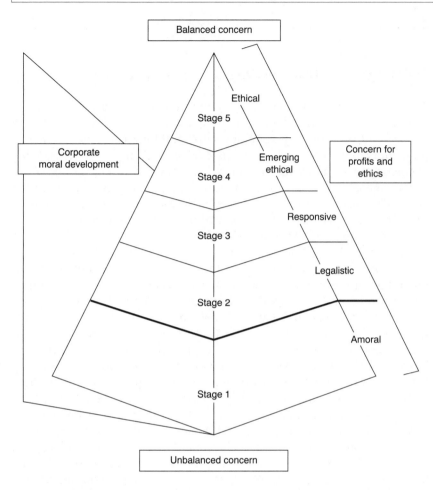

Figure 5.1 The stages of ethical concern (Reidenbach and Robin, 1995).

Since its foundation in 1976, The Body Shop has succeeded in commanding premium prices by adding value in this way, as well as by producing high quality products. However, there are pitfalls associated with taking the moral high ground in the quest to add value. In 1994, an investigative report suggested that The Body Shop did not observe the high ethical standards that it had always claimed; this undermined one of the two major thrusts of its value-adding strategy, and its share prices fell swiftly. City analysts predicted that it would be forced to lower prices in order to retain its high market share. By (apparently) defaulting on its added-value strategy for customers, it had therefore simultaneously failed to add value for its shareholders. Case 5.4 examines the alleged case against the The Body Shop in more detail.

CASE 5.4

BODY SHOP INTERNATIONAL AND ETHICS, 1994

Body Shop International, a cosmetics company started by Anita Roddick in 1976 and floated with great success on the Stock Exchange in 1984, added value by simultaneously fulfilling consumer demands for beauty products made from natural ingredients, and recognizing and acting in harmony with the increasing public awareness of environmental issues. Value was also added by the personality of its founder. Anita Roddick represented the face of Body Shop. She added value to the company's primary activity of selling cosmetics by giving frequent newspaper interviews in which she revealed her own beauty tips, how she furnished her house, and her various thoughts on life – all 'free' advertising, at no cost to the company; Body Shop publicised its second great concern of observing strict ethical codes by, for example, having Anita Roddick filmed in underdeveloped countries dealing with producers of herbs and fruits as part of her 'Trade not Aid' programme. The latter was designed to ensure that trading with 'Third World' countries was carried out on a non-exploitative contractual basis, and that 'fair' prices were always paid. The Body Shop group also encouraged customers to recycle plastic bottles by returning them to the shops for refills; it campaigned against testing beauty products on animals, and urged customers to fight to preserve endangered species; allowed every employee half a day of paid time off each month to do voluntary work; campaigned for child care in the work place; and donated £230,000 to launch the Big Issue, a magazine sold by the homeless. On the basis of all these ways of adding value linked to a high ethical profile, the company attracted many shareholders interested in holding 'green' porfolios, and, post-flotation, it expanded rapidly.

In 1994, however, its shining reputation was damaged considerably by investigative research undertaken by an American journalist, Jon Entine. Among the things which he questioned was the originality of the name 'Body Shop' itself, the composition of the ingredients in its products, its record on quality control, animal testing, relations with franchisees (Body Shop's rapid growth has partly been enabled by the fact that it operates by franchise), charitable donations, environmental policy, and staff working conditions. Entine's work encouraged other critics of the Body Shop to make public their views. Richard Adams, the founder of 'Traidcraft', a company which had long established 'fair' trading relations with Third World countries, claimed that Body Shop's much-publicized 'Trade, not Aid' programme represented less than 0.1 per cent of its actual supplies commitment. Body Shop replied that it could not quantify the amount, but that it was 'more than one per cent, but less than ten per cent'.

The vagueness of this reply in itself offered an indication of why Body Shop's good reputation was being called into doubt by interested parties. Many of its self-promoted ethical values had been taken on trust; when scrutinized more carefully, they appeared, at the least, to have been exaggerated, and sometimes not to have been observed at all. Jon Entine's allegations included the claim that there had been a leakage from Body Shop's bottling and warehousing plant in New Jersey. Gordon Roddick (Anita Roddick's husband), the chairman of the company, confirmed that there had been two spills of 30 gallons of shampoo in 1992, and said that the company had taken the appropriate action of informing the authorities immediately. This was contradicted by the Hanover Sewage Authority (whose evidence might be assumed to be 'neutral'), which said that it traced three spills caused by Body Shop in 1992–3, totalling at least 62 gallons. In each case, it had been the authority which had detected the leaks and informed the company.

An immediate outcome of the damage inflicted on Body Shop's reputation as a result of these allegations was that the Franklin Research and Development Corporation, a US investment adviser which specializes in building 'ethical' portfolios, sold its 50,000 Body Shop shares and advised its clients to follow suit. Other American and British funds were also considering whether to sell. At the end of August, 1994, the company's shares dropped during the space of one week from 242p to 218p on the London Stock Exchange. Franklin said that its advice to sell also took into consideration the fact that Body Shop shares were priced too high for its sector at a time of increasing competition – in other words, that the company had over-capitalized on its 'environmentally friendly' strategy, to the point where it was trying to use it to add value at a price which the customer would no longer pay.

It was nevertheless true that Body Shop had tried much harder to be 'ethical' than other companies in its sector; and some city analysts doubted whether the majority of its customers were as influenced by the ethical considerations as by the high quality of its products – its other way of adding value. The outcome was likely to be that the company would retain the loyalty of its customer base, but that it would perhaps not be able to charge as highly in the future for its particular methods of adding value.

This case demonstrates the pitfalls as well as the advantages that may be obtained by giving ethics a prominent part in the value-added strategy. One of the problems with dealing with ethics is that companies are addressing moving targets – values change, tending to get more stringent, all the time. This was certainly the case with Body Shop – observers of the company had turned a blind eye to some of its failings in the past, because of the good which Anita Roddick herself was doing in the promotion of business ethics generally. Commenting on this, Richard Adams said:

'One of the problems is the desire of the ethical movement to seek champions. . . . It was a role that Anita was eminently fitted for. But you need a balance between champions and the development of systems'.

(The importance of systems to adding value is considered in Chapter 7). Body Shop's fall from grace illustrates that while business ethics must be addressed by all organizations, and can be exploited very profitably, the higher the aspiration (cf. the Reidenbach and Robin pyramid, where for some years Body Shop undoubtedly occupied a place at the top) the harder it is to maintain successfully as part of a value-adding strategy.

PEOPLE AS WORKERS AND BUILDERS OF ORGANIZATIONS

It is a truism that adding value activities are performed by people for people: the same people who take advantage of the products and services offered by organizations are themselves likely to be contributing to a product or service. As Chapter One outlined, the ways in which people within organizations seek to do this have changed radically in recent years. Top-down autocratic management systems have been replaced by participative management ('empowerment') and team-working; quality inspection has been replaced by total quality management; the hierarchical, functional organization has been challenged by business process re-engineering; and keeping close to and caring for the customer has become the paramount concern of all forward-thinking organizations.

The strategic leader and adding value

This does not mean that the role of the strategic leader has become easier; in fact, his/her role has increased in difficulty as the parameters have become blurred. On the one hand, most strategic leaders now recognize the need to involve their staff at every level in the value-adding process; on the other hand, they have to motivate them in the face of flattened hierarchies, fewer promotional prospects, and the spectre of redundancy. At the end of the day, it is still the strategic leader who carries the responsibility of performing acceptably for shareholders; and as both shareholder and consumer interest in corporate ethics has grown, the personal values of strategic leaders – which, research strongly suggests, give the lead to the ethical and cultural values of the entire organization – have come under fierce scrutiny. Particularly in America and Britain (the two nations which have led the field in trying to establish corporate ethical codes), powerful strate-

gic leaders have been criticized in recent years for the following practices: paying themselves too highly in relation to their employees and
to the profits of their organization; radically 'restructuring' their organizations, sometimes in a panic-inspired manner, with the resultant
laying-off of many hundreds of employees; excessive borrowing undertaken to acquire other companies ('leveraged buyouts') in order to
make their empires grow more quickly; and blatant law-breaking – for
example, 'insider trading' on the stock exchange (i.e., using internal
knowledge of the company's activities to buy and sell its shares at
propitious moments), bribery, and the appropriation of funds which do
not belong to the company in order to bolster its share price (most
famously exemplified by the late Robert Maxwell's seizure of the
Mirror News Group pension funds to pay the interest on debts
acquired in setting up the Maxwell Communications Corporation).

With the exception of the last – and law-breaking is difficult to justify
– key executives have defended such behaviour as a necessary part of
the value-adding process, on the grounds that senior staff deserve to be
rewarded for undertaking taxing workloads and responsibilities, and
for their sheer talent and vision; that growth is an inescapable imperative (as we have already discussed) for organizations which seek
future significance; and that 'restructuring' becomes inevitable in times
of recession, and therefore that hard choices have to be made if the
organization is to continue to add value that the customer will pay for
at the lowest possible cost – the necessary prerequisite for its future
survival. Despite the criticism they engender, many controversial key
executives continue to lead, and often to lead effectively. Case 5.5
considers the case of 'Tiny' Rowland of Lonrho, who successfully if
controversially led his company, though running the gauntlet of hostility and disapproval from shareholders and fellow board members for
more than 20 years until he was finally ousted from power, and it has
to be acknowledged that their personal charisma is often an unquanti-
fiable but very real part of the added-value supplied by their respective
organizations. (This is not to assert that some do not fall by the
wayside by antagonizing their shareholders too much, nor that all
organizations need 'colourful' leaders; there are quieter ways of
running companies successfully, but flamboyance appears to be a
necessary ingredient for some.)

Jobs and careers: the modern change in norms

Whatever their personal style, what do today's executives have to consider when trying to build and maintain a workforce which can add
value effectively? Rosabeth Moss Kanter (1994) has identified six
important shifts in emphasis that have affected corporate jobs and
careers:

CASE 5.5

TINY ROWLAND

In the autumn of 1994, Mr. Dieter Bock, the joint chief executive of Lonrho, the international trading and mining group set up by Mr. Tiny Rowland in 1961, made a strenuous effort to have Mr. Rowland, the other joint chief executive, removed from the board for his unethical practices.

Ostensibly, the particular practices that were objected to concerned Mr. Rowland's decision to sell, for £200,000, a film on the alleged Libyan terrorist bombing of Pan Am Flight 103 over Lockerbie in 1988 (in which all the passengers and crew and several people in Lockerbie lost their lives), to an Egyptian company connected to Lafico, Libya's trading arm. Mr. Bock argued that this was possibly a breach of United Nations sanctions, and would certainly result in damage to the company's reputation.

However, it appeared that in reality Mr. Rowland's sale of the film provided a convenient excuse: the main reason that Mr. Bock and his fellow directors wished to eject him was connected with the enormous amounts in salary, expenses and other forms of emolument that Mr. Rowland cost the company.

In 1994, an informed breakdown of these went as follows:

- A salary of more than £1.2m.
- Almost £500,000 paid annually in contribution to the costs of his two homes in London and Buckinghamshire.
- A Gulfstream private jet, entirely paid for by the company, and costing about £2m annually in running and financial provision.
- £200,000 for the education of dependants of African politicians and agents who were protegées of Mr. Rowland.
- Approximately £1m of personal business expenses claimed against the winning of international business.

If it were accepted that the issue over the film provided a smokescreen for the directors' real grievances against Mr. Rowland, then these bore a striking resemblance to the reasons why eight directors, the so-called 'straight eight', led by the then deputy chairman, Sir Basil Smallpeice, tried to get rid of him in 1973. At that time, a similar combined catalogue of inflated salary and lavish spending items prompted the prime minister of the day, Sir Edward Heath, to describe Mr. Rowland's methods of business and of conducting himself as a captain of industry as 'an unpleasant and unacceptable face of capitalism'.

In 1973, Mr. Rowland sought to justify the costs that he incurred on the grounds that the company's links with the African continent were most effectively maintained in this way. He managed to persuade shareholders of this, and was therefore able to gain their support despite his fellow directors' attempt to oust him. In 1994, however,

Africa was not seen as the most important trading area for the company's future. In addition to this, Dieter Bock was a more formidable adversary than Basil Smallpeice. Mr. Bock owned 18.8 per cent of the company's shares – as against Mr. Rowland's (reduced) 1994 shareholding of 6.5 per cent – and the latter needed a 10 per cent shareholding in order to be entitled to call an Extraordinary General Meeting of the shareholders of the type that had gained him victory in the past.

Despite the apparently insurmountable odds stacked against him, at the end of August 1994 Mr. Rowland did succeed in keeping his position on the Lonrho board. A company spokesman explained this by saying that it would be 'too damaging to the company's image' to expel him. This phrase, in fact, offered a cryptic acknowledgement of a very complex situation – one in which a charismatic and controversial, yet unpopular and allegedly unethical, business leader had become so much part of the identity of his organization that to dismiss him would be to take too risky a step into the unknown. That he was, in fact, finally expelled some months later was more as a result of a personal feud rather than the conviction of the shareholders. At the time of writing, the effect upon the company of his departure is still not clear.

- **The shift from 'fat' to 'lean' organizations**. The new staffing principle is to do more with fewer, but better skilled, multi-skilled workforces. The benefit of this for adding value is that the organization becomes more flexible – and hence more responsive to new changes in the environment – and more cost efficient. The trade-off in terms of human cost is that such an approach strains people's endurance, and undermines their sense of security. It is the task of the strategic leader and senior management to try to reconcile these opposing pressures.
- **The 'shape' of organizations is moving from the vertical to the horizontal**. As we have already said, this means fewer promotional opportunities; therefore, other ways of motivating staff have to be found. 'Delayering' also has its structural problems. Since Peters and Waterman wrote *In Search of Excellence* in 1984, many writers have glibly extolled the virtues of the 'flat' organization. As Hoopes (1994) points out,

  '... in a small organization, it is easy to understand flatness. As the organization grows larger and more complex, it becomes hard to conceive of [as] totally process orientated ... If a large organization is to be totally flat, who will co-ordinate the relations among the organization's diverse processes?'

- **The make-up of the workforce is shifting from the homogeneous to the diverse**. People are being recruited from widely-diversified social and cultural mixes – in contrast to the 'like choosing like' or 'old school tie' approach which prevailed after the Second World War to the 1960s and 1970s, and beyond. Women, people from ethnic minorities, and people with 'alternative' lifestyles are occupying key positions within organizations. At the same time, teamwork has become the foremost way of pressing forward with value-adding activities. This means that managers building teams have a richer diversity of talents to draw from, but also trickier problems of matching personalities and outlooks so that effective co-operation can take place. Key Concept 5.1 describes Meredith Belbin's categorization of the key roles in management teams; Case 5.6 illustrates how some American companies are trying to offer equal benefits to homosexuals as to their conventionally married staff.

- **There is a shift from status and command rights to expertise and relationships**. The new power source in organizations does not derive from who you are, but what you can do, and how well you can mesh your skills with those of others. Therefore formal authority derived from a hierarchical chain of command (even if this is still nominally in place) is less important than professional expertise in gaining respect, because it is the latter which gives the lifeblood of the organization, by providing both the inspiration and the know-how for adding value. (This is another way of endorsing Drucker's identification of the importance of the 'knowledge worker'.)

- **The new loyalty is not to the organization, but to the project**. Value is therefore added in the most direct, relevant, and, in all probability, cost-efficient way. This shift in loyalty also has ethical implications – staff are less likely to behave unethically as a result of a misplaced allegiance to 'the company'. Loyalty to the project is also a result of the new human resource 'shape' of organizations, which are increasingly building outsourced and contracted activities around an organizational 'core' manned by relatively few staff.

- **In terms of the individual's working career, there is a shift from organizational capital to reputational capital**. In other words, people increasingly rely on having added value to one project successfully in order to gain the credence to be engaged for another project – very probably, by a different organization. Therefore, it is at the heart of their interests to add value successfully, and thus build on their 'portable' career assets – i.e., skills and reputation that can be applied anywhere.

KEY CONCEPT 5.1: MEREDITH BELBIN'S THEORY OF TEAM ROLES

Table 5.1 Meredith Belbin's nine team roles

Roles and descriptions – team-role contribution	Allowable weaknesses
Plant: Creative, imaginative, unorthodox. Solves difficult problems	Ignores details. Too pre-occupied to communicate effectively.
Resource investigator: Extrovert, enthusiastic, communicative. Explores opportunities. Develops contacts.	Over-optimistic. Loses interest once initial enthusiasm has passed.
Co-ordinator: Mature, confident, a good chairperson. Clarifies goals, promotes decision-making, delegates well.	Can be seen as manipulative. Delegates personal work.
Shaper: Challenging, dynamic, thrives on pressure. Has the drive and courage to overcome obstacles.	Can provoke others. Hurts people's feelings.
Monitor evaluator: Sober strategic and discerning. Sees all options. Judges accurately.	Lacks drive and ability to inspire others. Overtly critical.
Teamworker: Co-operative, mild, perceptive and diplomatic. Listens, builds, averts friction, calms the waters.	Indecisive in crunch situations. Can be easily influenced.
Implementer: Disciplined, reliable, conservative and efficient. Turns ideas into practical actions.	Somewhat inflexible. Slow to respond to new possibilities.
Completer: Painstaking, conscientious, anxious. Searches out errors and omissions. Delivers on time.	Inclined to worry unduly. Reluctant to delegate. Can be a nit-picker.
Specialist: Single-minded, self-starting, dedicated. Provides knowledge and skills in rare supply.	Contributes on only a narrow front. Dwells on technicalities. Overlooks the 'big picture'.

In 1993, Meredith Belbin, a well-known management guru who specializes in anatomizing the various characteristic 'types' which make up successful teams, revised his famous *Management Teams – Why They Succeed or Fail*, which identified seven basic team types, and decided, in the light of his extensive practical experience, that these should be altered, and expanded in number to nine. Belbin's work is particularly relevant to today's 'participative' management environment, in which teamwork is recognized as perhaps the most significant method of carrying out the value-added process.

One of the most valuable features that Belbin's research suggests is that a person strong in the characteristics of any one of the roles is likely also to have correspondingly marked attendant 'weaknesses' (see Table 5.1). These are called 'allowable' weaknesses, in that they may be regarded as a trade-off for the person's positive team-building qualities, but they might be damaging if the other members of the team were not aware of their nature. Executives may embody several of the team roles, but are seldom strong in all nine of them.

A practical difficulty when trying to set up a team to address a value-adding process is that there may not be an 'optimum' or even a good balance of the necessary traits available, combined with the practical skills needed for the particular organization. Like all academic contributions to practising organizations, Belbin's work can therefore only offer a guide, or an insight – but one of particular worth if it is used in an intelligent way.

Source: the table is taken from Belbin, Meredith (1993) *Team Roles at Work*, Butterworth-Heinemann.

CASE 5.6

ADDING VALUE FOR EMPLOYEES: EQUAL TREATMENT FOR GAY STAFF

In 1992 Lotus, the Boston-based American software company, began to offer the same health insurance benefits to the partners of gay and lesbian employees as were enjoyed by the spouses of heterosexual employees. In the following two years, almost 200 other American organizations followed suit – especially those operating in the entertainment, education and computing industries.

The main reason for adopting this practice was that it offered a good way of attracting and keeping valuable homosexual employees – by adding value to their contracts, not only in intrinsic terms, but psychologically, by indicating to them that their lifestyles and home commitments were as respected and important to the organization as those of heterosexuals. The move was also influenced by pressure from gay and lesbian advocacy groups, which had complained that homosexuals were not being treated equally.

Organizations which had introduced the equal insurance benefits were able to use them as a marketing tool to attract the custom of gay consumers; conversely, serious consumer boycotting was taking place against organizations that did not offer them, particularly in the Fortune 500 and food and retail groups.

The insurance benefits were a very cost-effective way of adding value both for employees and customers, because not many employees took up the offer. This was attributed mainly to the fact that both partners of a homosexual couple usually like to work, and therefore both are likely to have health insurance cover through their own jobs. Other reasons included the desire to keep their private lives private, and the fact that companies might require individuals taking advantage of the benefit to register legally as domestic partners – which, under U.S. law, carries property rights implications.

All in all, the main benefit both to the organization and the employee seemed to be an improvement in their mutual relationships which far outstripped the financial cost of the measure, and was bound to make a significant difference to the value-adding activities of the former. However, in 1994, some organizations were beginning to experience adverse effects from other quarters concerning the policy. Some local governments were being criticized for not extending the benefits to the unmarried partners of heterosexuals – which they declined on the grounds that such people could choose to marry; and Apple Computer was prevented from setting up an office in the deeply conservative Williamson County, Texas, because of the company's encouragement of gay and lesbian employees.

Source: Griffith, Victoria (1994) 'Equal Treatment for Gay Staff', *Financial Times*, 31 August.

The above points identify that new organizational approaches to adding value, despite their complexity, have a considerable 'up-side'; the 'down-side' consists of the following – in each case, linked to wider social issues. First, self-reliance and personal excellence only provide effective goals to strive for when there is sufficient work to be found to soak up the pool of talent available – which again raises the question of whether society has not lost its way in trying to find the optimum blend of work and leisure for each individual. Second, the unit of society which provides its most significant building brick – the family – has come under increasing strain. Households where there are children in which both parents work, in which neither parent works, in which one parent works long hours while the other stays at home, one-parent families of either sex, households where the total income is inadequate (often despite strenuous attempts to find employment, or in which people have consented to some form of sweated labour) and in some cases, households (with or without children) where the woman is the major earner, all suffer significant pressures. These are reflected in most western countries by an increase in the rate of divorce, of psychiatric and stress-related illnesses, steep declines in the birth rate (storing up problems of an ageing society for later on), a rising crime-rate, a polarization between 'haves' and 'have-nots', and an anxiety-induced propensity for people to put themselves first and 'get on' whatever the cost. Newly-developed and 'Third World' countries are either beginning to acknowledge a similar range of issues or will find the need to face them in the future.

These broader issues have become the specific problems which the organization and its leaders have to address if their power-house of adding value – human energy – is not to be significantly depleted. As Willmott (1994) points out, people are unlikely to engage whole-heartedly in value-adding activities, however effectively they are able to fulfil the organization's short-term projects, if ultimately they are destroying their own futures (either in the personal or the career sense). There must be a sense of wholeness about organizational objectives – they must have been thought through to address the spectrum of society's needs – if they are really to add value. In other words, the demands of **all** the stakeholders must be reconciled as far as possible. To quote Meredith Belbin (1993):

> 'It is in the interests of society as a whole that each fit and able adult member becomes ... both a contributor and a beneficiary; a contributor as a provider of goods, services or money, as well as a beneficiary of the wealth that economic synergy produces.'

Elsewhere in the same work, he writes in a starker vein:

> 'It will take all our energies to enrol the roleless; to create and restore personal and work identities in those on the fringes of society. That will be the coming challenge awaiting the twenty-first century'.

To accept this is not to imply that our original definition of adding value as 'providing what the customer wants at the lowest possible cost' has been over-simplified; but it does involve the recognition of exactly what is included in the concept of 'cost'.

SUMMARY

In this chapter we have considered the elusiveness of social trends and the difficulty of identifying them accurately, whilst at the same time pointing out the necessity for attempting this if the value-adding process is to be carried out effectively.

We have divided the social roles of people with regard to organizations into three categories:

- people as consumers
- people as citizens
- people as workers and the builders of organizations.

In looking at people as consumers, we have considered the issues raised by

- demographic change, and its impact on for-profit and not-for-profit organizations; the global implications of demographic change, and the differing effects upon developing and developed nations
- the effect of governments and the role of chance upon demographic trends
- changes brought about by social shifts reflected in an altered demand for various types of goods and services
- the impact on consumers of changes in work and leisure habits
- the question of unemployment as it affects the way organizations add value.

In the section on people as citizens, we have explored:

- the questions raised by business ethics
- the issue of Foreign Direct Investment and its impact on both consumers and the host countries involved
- environmental issues and their connection to competitive advantage.

Finally, the chapter concludes with a section on people as workers in and builders of organizations. It examines the role of the strategic leader in the modern organization, and goes on to discuss in detail Rosabeth Moss Kanter's work on the changing patterns of jobs and careers in today's organizations. It continues with reference to the work of Meredith Belbin on the importance of building balanced teams within organizations; and finally tries to provoke throught on the disadvantages as well as the benefits which the 'new organization' brings. An attempt is made to place the specific issues discussed in the chapter within the widest context of society as a whole. The question of unemployment is returned to, and the reader is asked to consider whether a new approach is needed if mankind is to prosper in the next century.

REFERENCES AND FURTHER READING

Belbin, M. (1993) *Team Roles at Work*, Butterworth Heinemann, Oxford.

Bennett, L. (1995) 'Ethics and Strategy', *CIMA Handbook of Strategic Management* (ed. J.L. Thompson), Butterworth Heinemann, Oxford.

Davidson, J.D. and Rees-Mogg, W. (1993) *The Great Reckoning: How the World Will Change in the Depression of the 1990s*, Sidgwick & Jackson, London.

Kanter, R.M. (1993) *Men and Women of the Corporation* (2nd edn.) Basic Books, New York.

Kennedy, P. (1993) *Preparing for the Twenty-First Century*, Harper-Collins, London.

Peters, T. (1992) *Liberation Management*, Macmillan, London.

Schein, E.H. (ed.) (1987) *The Art of Managing Human Resources*, Oxford University Press, New York.

Wendt, H. (1993) *Global Embrace: Corporate Challenges in a Trans-national World*, HarperCollins, London.

Technology and adding value

LEARNING OBJECTIVES

- To make a distinction between adding value through **technology** and **information technology**, and point out the importance of each.
- To understand in simple terms the nature of **Information Technology** (IT), and the six main elements which constitute it.
- To discuss how information technology may be deployed to **add value**, and the opportunities and problems related to this.
- To evaluate what computers **do** to add value. It is suggested, for example, that they can aid **productivity**; they can aid **competitive advantage**; they can aid corporate **responsiveness** to customer requirements.
- To appreciate that using IT can also lead to transforming the nature of the **product** (as in the case of multimedia); change how the business **operates** (as in the case of car manufacturing); change the **shape** of the industry and the way it operates (the example of crime and criminal apprehension is given); and **make the world a smaller place** (as technological products and communications systems are developed that 'shrink' distances).
- To consider the **MIT in the '90s Research Program** and its findings about the impact of IT on the future of organizations.
- From this, to develop views about processes and consider what constitutes a **process** in the management context, and the implications that this has when IT is being developed by organizations.
- Thinking about processes will lead you to an examination of what is meant by **IT-induced business reconfiguration**, explained, particularly, by the work of Venkatramen.

The chapter concludes with a survey of what progress in IT means in relation to the **globalization** of businesses. Finally, it emphasizes the importance of people (the 'human resource') in the intelligent, progressive and cost-effective use of IT – i.e., in making it truly add value.

INTRODUCTION: TECHNOLOGY AND INFORMATION TECHNOLOGY

Birds building nests may be said to have developed a particular technological expertise: lower down in the animal kingdom, the caddis larva building its shell from the grit it collects in streams makes use of the things around it by a kind of reflex, or instinct; whilst at the highest level of non-human animal intelligence, chimpanzees can learn to use sticks and other simple objects to perform tasks. But the continual evolution and development of technological skills is peculiar to mankind.

These have been major factors in the adding of value ever since humans created civilizations sufficiently sophisticated to divide labour, so that individuals perfected specialisms rather than just producing for their own households. The potter's skill, to give one instance, evolved in certain prehistorical societies from the capability to fashion rude utilitarian artefacts such as earthenware bowls and platters, to the highly ornate painted and glazed vases which have been left, for example, by the Greeks, the Minoans and the Romans. To define technological change, therefore, involves an awareness of historical progress, as well as the anticipation of futuristic issues.

There have been technological watersheds in history, and technological development has accelerated at an amazing pace since the Industrial Revolution, when the invention of machinery that could be harnessed to steam power saw the beginnings of mass production as we know it. Historians, sociologists, and, latterly, management gurus have characterized recent eras of technological development as, variously, the industrial age, the post-industrial age, the atomic age, the information age, and the age of the knowledge worker. The last two of these we have already touched upon during the course of this book, and we explore them more thoroughly in this chapter.

Adding value by means of technology does not mean adding value by means of information technology only, although IT is likely to play a major, if not key, part in technological development today. This is true not only in the new, 'sunrise' industries (such as computer science itself), which are predicted to hold the key to the world's future prosperity, but also in that of the more traditional 'smokestack' industries (steel, mining, manufacturing) as they evolve.

In Chapter One, Box 1.1 describes the technological breakthrough of growing plastic on trees. This fledgeling industry is adding value by developing a technique which both breaks new ground in terms of the flexibility and sophistication of the textiles that may be created from the product, and by producing them in an 'environmentally friendly' fashion; these primary value-adding capabilities are, however, facilitated by an information base, accessed by computer, which makes the achievement possible.

The importance of information technology to technological development is so great, so complex, and increasingly such an integral part of adding value in all industries throughout the globe that it forms the main subject of this chapter. However, the reader is encouraged to be aware of the fact that a 'technological development' can also be something as simple as designing a special catch for a zipper so that it can be secured, or turning a mistake into a competitive advantage by creating a use for a new glue which does not stick properly (the 'Post-it' note). Case 6.1 describes how technology has altered the mining processes employed in South African gold mines, and thus added value for the shareholders, and made the product more competitive for customers in a difficult market by reducing cost. This is an example of a more complex technological breakthrough which is not specifically dependent on IT.

CASE 6.1

TECHNOLOGY: THE PROCESS

Technological advances in the mining industry

In the early 1990s, a combination of steadily declining real gold prices, double-digit inflation and the deteriorating quality of ore reserves sent the South African gold industry into a spiral of decline. Two big gold mines closed. What the industry needed was a breakthrough that would transform the mines' productivity underground.

In the present decade, such a breakthrough seemed to have been achieved with the development of two new techniques. These were diamond wire cutting, pioneered by Gencor and Anglo-American, the country's biggest gold producer; and the impact ripper, developed by an industry research project that had been taken over by Gold Fields, the mining house.

The first of these methods involved the application of the established method of quarrying granite and other hard stones to underground mining. A synthetic-covered steel cable, less than a centimetre thick and studded with industrial diamonds, sawed through the rock face, cutting away the ore in large chunks. The impact ripper was an hydraulically-powered chisel, mounted on rails, which attacked the rockface with an accuracy which blasting lacked.

Kobus Olivier, chief consulting engineer at the Gencor group's gold division, said that the potential benefits were huge, because either technique could transform the cost structure of the industry and underground productivity. Diamond wire cutters could operate 24 hours a day, require less labour, and minimize the amount of waste rock mined. Diamond wire was expensive – the first material Gencor ordered cost R1,000 ($290) per metre – but greater demand would reduce its cost and eliminate much of the need for explosives used for the 900,000 blasts made by the gold mines each day. The technique would lead to the redesign of underground mining plans, save tunnelling, timber and explosives costs, and shave 60 per cent off transport costs.

Underground safety would also improve, because the narrower stopewidths and minimal use of explosives would do less to aggravate the rock pressure underground. (In recent years, rockfalls have killed about 270 workers a year underground.)

Similar benefits could be experienced with the impact ripper. Len Gibbs, the consulting engineer at Gold Fields, which had introduced a number of the machines at its Kloof mine, said: 'The possibilities have to be exciting. The deeper you go, the more you need mechanized mining methods and less reliance on manpower'.

This has been true since the early days of gold mining. The geological challenges of extracting the precious metal at deeper and more dangerous levels have forced producers to refine their techniques. Much gold output now comes from mines sunk to below sea level, or more than 3,000 metres underground.

Despite the excitement about the new methods, there were some teething problems. Gencor temporarily abandoned its experiment with diamond wire cutting in 1993. Olivier commented that the group 'knew it worked', but found that the wire tended to get pinched as the rock face closed once it had been cut. Gencor had therefore decided to wait and see what progress Anglo could make, since the group's mining equipment and industrial diamond businesses had a keen interest in the technology's success.

Len Gibbs said that the main drawback with the impact ripper had been the excessive wear and tear on the expensive equipment, but stressed that it was 'early days'. Gold Fields found that the first orebody on which it tried the impact ripper proved more susceptible to the technique than the orebody at Kloof, where the equipment would most probably be used.

However, it was maintained that the problems were unlikely to be insurmountable. Whilst one technology might not transform gold mining, a combination of the new technologies, with further refinements being developed all the time, still promised the mining breakthrough which the industry needed.

Source: adapted from Curtin, Matthew (1994) 'Gold Rush', *Financial Times*, 22 March.

WHAT IS INFORMATION TECHNOLOGY?

Information technology consists of six main factors:

- **Computers** (from personal computers to microcomputers, minicomputers and mainframes).
- **Software** – i.e., the programs on which computers run. Traditionally, these address quantitative issues, but newer techniques are continu-

ally being developed to deal with more qualitative and verbal information.

- **Communications networks**. These enable computers to 'talk' to each other. They may be relatively simple links between computers on the same site, or complex feats of technological engineering that span continents.
- **Professional workstations**.
- **Robotics** – i.e., machines which have been built and programmed to perform (currently, only manual) tasks otherwise carried out by humans.
- **Silicon chips** – tiny information packages embedded in 'smart' products, from state-of-the-art washing machines to ballistic missiles.

INFORMATION TECHNOLOGY AND ADDING VALUE

It has become evident that information technology, from having been initially devised as a business resource, has grown into an integral part of the business environment. This is not to say that it comes packaged without drawbacks, that it is 'easy' to use, or that it replaces people at any but the most mundane levels in the value-adding process.

The potential and the problems associated with the exploitation of information technology were eloquently described in an Amdahl management report in 1991:

> 'Information is assuming increasing importance as the main commodity of business exchange. This allied with the ability to transfer vast amounts of information immediately anywhere in the world, are major factors driving the globalization of the world's markets ... [but] ... information technology, like the original solver of the Gordian knot, Alexander's sword, is in itself only a tool, albeit one endowed with tremendous potential. The extent of its productive application is entirely dependent on the uses, and choices, made of it by its corporate owners'. (*Amdahl Research Report*, 'Applications in the 1990s: Reducing Complexity and Enabling Change', Amdahl Executive Institute, 1991.)

This quotation raises a number of key issues, as follows.

- A computer system is only as good as the imaginations and ingenuity of the people who design it – the data which is stored and recalled only becomes information when it is so organized that it presents the user with an intelligent and manageable output. It follows from this that the system is only as good as the applications software which has been devised to run it. To put these two variables into perspective, it could be said that the system is only as good as its developers x the skills of its users.

- The expenditure of large sums of money on computer systems will not be rewarded with an acceptable level of return on the investment if they are used only to automate systems which were previously operated manually. As computers were rapidly improved in the 1950s, 60s and 70s, it was the almost ubiquitous objective of corporations to use them to automate existing systems, to control costs, and to reduce staffing levels. It was only in the 1980s, and then only by some enlightened companies, that the realization dawned that the key role of the computer was to 'informate', not to automate: i.e., that its value adding role was not to replace that of the human.

- Computers, nevertheless, are not intelligent. The comment may seem obvious to the point of being fatuous, but is one which needs emphasizing, because even in the minds of sophisticated users, the machine, or the system, sometimes seems to take on a life of its own, which at once surrounds it with a mystique, and apparently absolves its users from responsibility for what it 'does'. A very simple example can be offered from the author's own experience: visiting a brasserie in London just before Christmas 1994, my companion and I waited almost one hour for two salads. The waitress explained: 'The food is ready, but the computer won't let me have your bill, so I can't serve you.' No computer is responsible for causing such bottlenecks: only the people who design the systems which operate it. The point is summed up by a sign which was said to hang in IBM's Tokyo office:

  'IBM: FAST, ACCURATE, STUPID
  MAN: SLOW, SLOVENLY, SMART'

- Despite all of these caveats, intelligent and innovative use of information technology can transform markets and industries, and give companies a competitive edge in their quest to add value.

We now consider the different ways in which the development of the computer and information technology has affected the adding of value in today's organizational environment. The question that intelligent managers have to ask is not 'What can the computer do?', but 'What do we want it to do?' For our purpose, however, we must first ascertain what the computer is used for.

WHAT CAN COMPUTERS DO?

Computers can aid **productivity**. They can replace people in the carrying out of mundane tasks, and save wages bills; they can carry out precision work, though it will still be subject to human error – and in each case, if the transition is not made with very careful forethought, it can cost the organization money, rather than saving it. Some enlightened companies are taking advantage of automation, not to reduce staff, but to use their existing staff more productively. However, the (sometimes intricate) cost implications of this need working out carefully – are they really adding enough more to the premium to cover their own keep? Research suggests that computers have frequently added to overhead, by requiring more expensive staff. (N.B. this is the fault of the organization of the information technology within a company, not of the information technology itself. For example, on a car assembly line, it is possible to remove operations and replace the work with robotic equipment; but this equipment requires the employment of a maintenance worker, who must be skilled in preventative and reactive maintenance.)

Computers can aid **competitive advantage**. Companies can, for example, 'lock in' their customers with technological links. It is debateable, however, whether competitive advantage derived from information technology can be sustained in the long term. It can be rapidly copied by competitors, and sometimes competitors can demand access to it on the grounds that it constitutes an unfair advantage.

For example, in the early 1980s, American Airlines developed a seat-reservation system which made it at once easier and more profitable for travel agents to buy seats with the company than any other, by creating innovative and complex fare structures (aimed at filling every seat). All the information regarding seats on American Airlines 'planes, and the facility to reserve them could be accessed direct by the travel agent via a simple keyboard routine. The system was called 'Sabre'. However, in 1984, eleven rival airlines brought an antitrust suit against American Airlines on the grounds that 'Sabre' had become an 'essential facility' to the industry to which they were unfairly denied equal access. Thereafter, American Airlines generated some more income from 'Sabre' by running it as a general travel-reservations service, with equal access to anyone willing to pay the appropriate fee – but the competitive advantage aspect of the facility had been lost.

New kinds of competitive advantage derived from information technology also bring new kinds of threat to established players in an industry. For example, during the last decade, banks have made huge strides in technological progress, first by introducing automatic teller machines (ATMs), and then by developing a range of services which can be accessed by corporate and private customers via Electronic Data Interchange (EDI) – in other words, two-way communication links between their respective computers. Such data interchange has become so important to the financial services industry that the question might be whether the business is essentially about software development for financial services (among other industries), and not about financial services *per se*. In other words, does the core competence lie in the dissemination of financial knowledge, or in developing the software? If the latter is, or is perceived to be, the case there is a threat to the financial services sector from non-traditional competitors, such as, for example, the huge and cash-rich Microsoft empire, which could develop the software itself, and buy in the financial knowledge (a possibility made more likely by the increasing deregularization of financial services throughout the world). The example serves to illustrate that in the field of information technology competitive advantage is at best a two-edged sword.

Computers can aid organizational **responsiveness to customer needs/ requirements**. They can enable companies to deliver a customized product (i.e., one tailored to the customer's needs) more rapidly and more cheaply. The McGraw-Hill publishing company has developed a computer programme which enables university lecturers to 'create' their own textbooks by choosing individual chapters on related topics from a database.

Several forward-thinking architectural companies now have the facility to allow customers to play with a computer package which helps them to create their 'ideal' building. This provides them with the capability of seeing what the logistical implications will be of creating buildings of a given set of dimensions; the projected elevations also allow town planners to assess the impact of new buildings in terms of their effect on existing structures and road systems.

Changing the Product

It will be seen that both of the examples given above involve changing the nature of the product itself, and the way in which it is traditionally perceived by the customer. Such changes in perception can be far-reaching in their implications – some of which have yet to be fully realized.

Multimedia is a case in point. In Chapter One, we detailed the many activities which go towards adding value to the book. With the advent of multimedia, the nature of some of these activities are radically changed, whilst others are rendered obsolescent. Multimedia products consist of an electronic document, produced on a CD-ROM (compact disk-read-only memory) which uses at least three forms of media – typically, text, sound and video applications – and which does not exist in conventional 'book' format. Instead, the user accesses the material 'interactively', retrieving information to suit his or her needs of the moment, rather than absorbing it in a linear, passive way (as with traditional reading). The manufacturer may also offer 'routes' through the package for those who prefer to have some guidance.

Not only does the invention give a new meaning to the word 'publication', but it radically alters the relationship of the author and the editor to the reader. New questions are raised. For example, in an interactive world, whose is the copyright – since the reader adds his or her own value by devising a particular combination of text – and who safeguards the format which has traditionally been the publisher's preserve? Who should have a financial stake in 'jackdaw' productions which amalgamate parts of the work of many authors, artists, film producers and technicians? These questions are especially pertinent when the issue of a printed version arises; for, contrary to what one might expect, the rise of multimedia does not herald the demise of the printed word – partly because people like to have a 'hard copy' and partly because the screen has yet to be invented that is as easy on the eyes as traditional print. Instead, electronic print corporations are making large sums from on-demand printing of the sections which the customer requires (rarely the whole work); they have found a lucrative new way of adding value. The author and the publisher, however (whose contribution in terms of creative input was arguably much greater) are being cheated of their dues in many cases.

Case 6.2 further explores the idea of the 'virtual' book and its implications.

CASE 6.2

TECHNOLOGY: THE PRODUCT

The 'virtual' book

The Pontifical Libraries in Rome contain books that have been used by students and scholars of the city's Gregorian Library for centuries. Academics were competing to have access to them. Not only could waiting for such access be protracted, but the books themselves were becoming increasingly fragile.

At the beginning of 1994, however, an alternative method of reading these rare books was devised. They were turned into packets of digital signals which were sent out on the Internet data network. They could then be perused at will, and, if the reader so wished, be printed out at a low cost, in the same format as the original. Enthusiasts and those with associated business interests claimed that 'the document super-highway' would reconstruct the book publishing industry, and revolutionize the way in which books are bought.

Their vision of the 'virtual library' included slashing the prices of specialist editions, and bringing whole libraries of rare tomes into the home at will, via computer networks. All books, from the Bible to the latest thriller, could be published from digital formats, and entities 'called down' to be printed or sold only when there was a demand for them. Giant corporations embraced the idea; a New Document Alliance was brokered in New York by the Xerox Corporation with its industry partners, including AT&T, Sun Microsystems, and Microsoft.

This group anticipated that there would soon be a $93 bn market in offset printing. Their expectation rested on the belief that the 'paperless office' concept propounded with such enthusiasm in the 1980s was unlikely to take place in the forseeable future – that people still had not found ways of dispensing with the modern, paper-ridden office, and that huge profits could therefore still be generated from the need to print annual reports, documents and forms, as well as from publishing books for general readers and academics.

Paul Allaire, chairman of the Xerox Corporation, explained the strategy of the Alliance:

> 'We are going to transform this industry by avoiding printing reports and books in advance of their need and by storing them in a costly warehouse until copies are needed. ... That is expensive and wasteful. In future we will store books globally and electronically and print locally only when there is demand'.

Books of the future, therefore, may exist as ghostly electronic entities on the Internet, or another 'superhighway' network, until they are summoned and turned into solid paper and ink at a local print shop. Potential readers will be able to browse through the 'superhighway' and not necessarily select whole books, but just the few pages which they wish to have printed. At Duke University in the USA, business studies students were in 1994 already selecting their courses from material stored in the network and only printed on request.

What has made such a facility possible has been the technological development of powerful printers, scanners, binding equipment and fibre optic cables. A change in attitude has also been a great enabler. The growing awareness of the ability to create open systems, and to develop devices that are compatible, has made an impact on users previously locked into the mindset of using the machinery of a sole supplier.

There are drawbacks, however. The protection of copyright is one issue. Another concerns the difficulty of ensuring that academically correct 'manuscripts' are not interfered with while they travel the ether.

The solution of Xerox and its partners was to claim that they would be able to keep their 'electronic' documents in secure optical storage machines which would only release material on demand. However, such a system would not allow users to 'browse' books before having them printed up – one of the great advantages of the superhighway. Nor would it solve the copyright problem of customizing material, such as lecture notes, for individual users.

A third drawback is the relative user-unfriendliness of even browsing electronically, as opposed to reading hard copy. It has been calculated that it could take 50 years to produce a computer screen which is as congenial to read from as the printed book.

However, this is not to minimize the extent of the revolution. The concept of reading, learning and publishing is undoubtedly changing rapidly and irrevocably. Watch this space!

Source: adapted from McKie, Robin (1994) 'Ghost books haunt the superhighway', *The Observer*, 24 April.

Changing how the business operates

We have said that information technology can change the shape and nature of an industry, or create a new industry, and we explore this in more detail later. Even where the core activity of the industry stays the same, however, information technology can radically change the way in which the businesses within it operate.

An example is offered by Computer-Integrated Manufacturing (CIM) in the mass production car industry. This makes car plants instantly responsive to the requirements of the enterprise of which they form a part. Computer-aided management processes enable the following innovations to take place, which together add up to an industry radically different from the traditional assembly-line giants which represented the car industry until the mid 1980s:

- The **flexibility** of computer-aided design systems has meant that production can take place within much smaller, customized manufacturing units.
- **Increased automation** means fewer employees. Therefore, where a plant is situated is no longer such a burning issue. (International car manufacturers have increasingly operated in Second or Third World countries since the Second World War to minimize staffing costs.)
- **Centralized engineering** has become a feature of high-tech manufacturing. There is no need for designers to leave head office (or their own computer terminals at home, for that matter). Product blueprints, drawn using computer-aided design, can be transmitted via long-distance telephone lines to computer-aided manufacturing plants in the company's main markets.
  Note. It will be evident from this, and from the first point above (concerning flexibility) that computers allow either decentralization or centralization to take place effectively: whichever the company requires. A further spin-off from this may be a growth in 'industrial boutiques' – small independent companies with the latest computer-aided and CIM techniques who act as suppliers of tailor-made products to the bigger companies, who can then reduce further the number of their own manufacturing units.
- **Manufacturing flexibility** rises significantly as a result of applying the new techniques to machine tools, permitting a wider variety of products to be produced with raising costs. It also allows CIM plants to break even at 30–35 per cent of capacity (compared with 65–70 per cent for conventional plants).
- **Plug-in service facilities** enable the detection of faults. Faults in products made by computer-aided design techniques can usually be diagnosed by plugging them into a programmed computer. In the late 1980s, General Motors installed computerised diagnostics in repair centres across America.

Exercise. In Chapter One, we described in diagrammatic form how the motor industry adds value, and students were invited to draw a 'value chain' reflecting this. The exercise should now be undertaken again in the light of the above information, and the results compared, to demonstrate the impact of information technology on adding value.

CASE 6.3

TECHNOLOGY: THE INDUSTRY

Crime and technology: from both sides of the fence

In 1993, the World Trade Centre in New York was damaged, many people were injured and several killed, by a terrorist bombing. The criminal who carried out the attack was eventually apprehended and convicted. His name was Ramzi Yousef. Federal criminal investigators said that he was planning a further bombing campaign against US jetliners. He had used a commercially available encryption (code-protecting) programme to safeguard the hard drive of his lap-top computer, the main tool that he had employed in the planning of his bombing campaign. He also had a suitcase containing explosive gel, a powerful substance invisible to most airport X-ray machines. In his search for potential targets, he could easily have downloaded airline schedules from the Internet. He could be described as the first star of 'cyberterrorism'.

In the international battle between high-class criminals and the various agencies whose task it is to outwit them, both sides are scrambling for the technological edge. Counterterrorists now have the use of laser microphones, which can pick up conversations hundreds of yards away, even if they are taking place inside a different building. The mid-1990s has seen the invention of a series of tapping (or 'bugging') devices that have as yet proved completely undetectable. Highly refined electromagnetic transmitters have been developed, which can bombard an area with waves that prematurely detonate remote-controlled bombs. Information gathered from listening devices, fed through a specialized computer analysis, can pinpoint with precision terrorists' exact locations – a facility whch allowed French commandos to storm a hi-jacked plane in Marseilles in December 1994.

Terrorists have not lagged behind in developing technologies of similar sophistication. In south Lebanon, guerrillas used timing devices to switch on remote-controlled detonators after airborne electromagnetic transmitters had passed. Militants have devoted much of their time, ingenuity and financial resources to perfecting high-tech bombs. Brian Jenkins, a terrorism expert, commented: 'The small, concealable device that still gives you a powerful explosive force – that's where there's the most innovation'.

There is a downside, however, to technology-orientated late 20th century crime and its prevention. Yousef thought that the encryption programme was adequate protection, but once investigators had taken possession of his computer, they quickly cracked his code, found alleged 'terror plans', and located the names of his accomplices.

Criminals may therefore be lulled into a false sense of security; a parallel situation exists for counter-terrorists, who may be too inclined to believe that state-of-the-art surveillance equipment can provide all the answers. The 'wisest' terrorists have now turned full circle, and taken the easy and cheap solution of going 'low-tech or no-tech'. They communicate, not over the Internet, but face to face. For destruction, fanatics use a detonator which is horrifying in its implications, and has so far proved unstoppable – a bomb-laden volunteer, prepared to give his or her life for whatever 'cause' they are defending. In Israel, for example, it is not unknown for terrorists to dress up as rabbis and drive Israeli-registered cars. Two suicide bombers killed 19 people waiting at an Israeli bus stop in January 1995. Just one month later, an Israeli soldier was killed when he picked up a booby-trapped canteen. Maurice Botbot, a terrorism expert in France, explained: 'While technology has been getting more and more sophisticated, the terrorists' methods have been getting simpler and simpler. The very simplicity tends to cause them to be overlooked by the detection agencies.

There is a widening disparity between wealthy societies which are increasingly being run on high-tech products and systems, and the 'third world' or non-tech backgrounds of many of their fiercest adversaries. The end result may actually add shock value to crude acts of violence. The televised image of a single dead GI being dragged through the streets of Mogadishu rendered superfluous America's high-tech search for a fugitive clan leader. Therefore it is likely that the war against terrorism will only ever be pursuable in part on the technological front.

Source: adapted from Masland, Tom *et al.* (1995) 'Terrorism: a battle on high – and on low', *Newsweek*, 27 February.

Changing the shape of the industry, and the way it operates

We have considered how technology might alter the shape of the financial services industry. A further example is given in Case 6.3. which details how crime and its prevention have been changed by technology. The case is interesting because it demonstrates that in some areas technological development can be too 'clever' – that in the constant pitting of wits between criminals and those whose task it is to apprehend them, methods can turn full circle to return to the simplest (and therefore least predictable) pre-high-tech ploys.

Making the world a smaller place

It is almost 30 years since an American named Marshall McLuhan made popular the concept of the 'global village' – i.e., the idea that combined communications and information technology would mean that people throughout the world could 'talk' to each other as if they were in the same street, with the effect that communication difficulties would be minimized and cultures gradually homogenized. As we examine further in the last section of this chapter, the reality is a good deal more complex, and is hedged around with difficulties at present. Nevertheless, information technology is making rapid strides all the time to minimize the effects of distance. This has implications for the nature and structure of the workforce; for it means that knowledge work can take place anywhere. For example, British Airways flight bookings are now routinely performed in India.

Videoconferencing – where people from different organizations in different places talk to each other and are able also to see each other on a 'live' television screen – offers another example. Case 6.4 describes the development of the pan-European telephone, another advance in making long-distance communication 'easy'.

CASE 6.4

TECHNOLOGY: MAKING THE WORLD SMALLER

Pan-European mobile telephones

It is still a matter for debate whether pan-European mobile telephones are a business necessity, or merely the ultimate executive toy. The manufacturers of course promulgate the former view. Vodafone promoted its EuroDigital service heavily during the early summer of 1994, and Cellnet launched a rival service in July 1994.

Friedman Wagner-Dobler, a computer consultant at Clasma Software, explained the reason for his Vodafone purchase: 'Our marketplace is Europe, so it's useful to be contactable on the numerous occasions I escape to Sweden or Germany'. Vodafone's GSM (Global System for Mobile) is a digital cellular technology, which is becoming the standard for new European digital mobile telephone services.

Also in 1994, British Nuclear Fuels bought a number of Cellnet GSM telephones from Securicor Cellular Services to comply with European regulations for the transportation of hazardous goods. They used the telephones to keep in touch with trucks carrying fuel rods and to inform the authorities of the whereabouts of their vehicles.

Consumer choice for telephones that work on the European mainland was both limited and expensive in 1994. In Britain, only Vodafone and Cellnet offered GSM cellular services which could be used by UK customers in continental Europe through 'roaming' agreements with national service providers. The GSM services were separate from the analogue (nation-specific) services offered by these companies. GSM users had to invest £200–£500 in handsets (the analogue equivalent cost £50–£100). However, it was possible to shop around on the continent for other makes. Prices varied considerably from country to country, and were dependent in part on whether the phone was bought with or without airtime. Switzerland and Sweden both operated competitive price scales.

In addition to the GSM options, two UK mobile services, Mercury's One-2-One and Hutchison Microtel's Orange, were signing roaming agreements with other European operators whose services were also based on PCN (Personal Communications Network) digital technology, a variant of GSM.

Whichever service was chosen, a pan-European mobile telephone was unlikely to be cheap. This was not due to high registration or monthly subscription charges: a Vodafone or Cellnet GSM user paid about the same for UK calls and for registration and subscription as a business customer of its analogue services; but the mark-up on calls between countries could be very high. Despite this, most customers felt satisfied that they were getting value for money; they were prepared to pay the going rate for the facility.

One way of avoiding the expense was to make use of a facility offered by Vodafone. Their phones could be pre-programmed 'call forward unconditional' before the owner left the UK. All calls then went straight to Vodafone Recall, and could still be checked from abroad.

However, GSM coverage in Europe was still patchy in 1994. A Vodafone spokesman said that it was very good in Germany and Scandinavia, good in Italy and the UK, but virtually non-existent in Spain. There was a limited service in France.

The GSM network was user-friendly. The subscriber was issued with a credit-card-sized Subscriber-Identity-Module Card (with built-in computer chip) which, when inserted into the telephone, would select a local GSM network automatically. The local GSM network would also notify the home network where the subscriber was, so that it could transfer calls. Call quality was better in some countries than in others, with mountainous areas causing particular difficulties.

Such teething problems were likely to be ironed out as the technology was improved; but, as Friedman Wagner Dobler said, 'It's a miracle that this kind of thing works at all'.

Source: adapted from Shillingford, Joia (1994) 'On the move, but still in touch', *Financial Times*, 12 July.

THE MIT IN THE 90S RESEARCH PROGRAMME

While reading this chapter, the reader may have become increasingly aware that in order to use information technology effectively to add value, the organization has to address complex issues of how IT interacts with its structure, strategy, management processes, and individuals (both within the organization and outside it), and also with the external environment – in short, with all the variables that we have been examining in this book. Figure 6.1 illustrates this interaction in diagrammatic form. The model, which is dynamic, shows clearly the complexity and all-embracing nature of the issues involved. It was developed as a result of the findings of the MIT Sloan School of Management at the Massachusetts Institute of Technology research project entitled the 'Management in the 1990s Research Program', which set out to investigate:

- what role information technology could play in response to the increasingly turbulent business environment, and
- whether IT had a part in causing such turbulence.

The 'MIT in the 90s' model was developed from research undertaken in the 1950s on change in turbulent business environments by Alfred Chandler, a historian, and Hal Leavitt, an organizational behaviour expert. Chandler's research concluded that changes in an organization's strategy caused changes to its structure. (This has since become received opinion in management circles, but it broke new ground at the time.) Chandler pointed out that the relationship between strategy and structure was interdependent, and that therefore unforeseen consequences could result if both were not considered when one was being changed.

Leavitt arrived at a similar conclusion by a different route. He proposed that an organization can be viewed as a set of four forces, which together account for a large proportion of what propels it: organization structure and the corporate culture; corporate strategy; individuals and the roles they play at work; and technology.

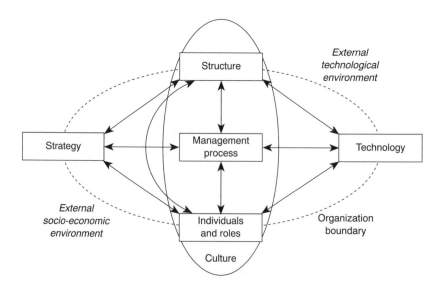

Figure 6.1 The MIT in the 1990s: explanation of how IT interacts with the internal and external organizational environment.

The Management in the 1990s team (which carried out research into more than 50 organizations) developed the model illustrated in Figure 6.1 to combine the ideas of Chandler and Leavitt in the context of a future turbulent business and technological environment. The most significant innovative feature of the MIT model is that it identifies management **processes** as a separate element. These include the planning, budgeting and reward systems needed to keep the other forces of the model in balance and moving towards common objectives. The area contained within the oval in the centre of the model is crucial – alignment of these features is essential if the ability to rethink and transform structures and people is to be achieved. The fundamental conclusion of the MIT research was that organizations are not getting the most from information technology because they have not broken through the barriers erected within this vital area in order to think about and apply information technology creatively, effectively and economically.

Box 6.1: The key findings of the MIT in the 90s research project

Finding 1: Turbulence in the business environment will continue

There is no reason to believe that there will be a reduction in the rate of change of various technologies. If anything, the rate of change of these, and factors such as economic systems, new business methods, and growth of new competitors is likely to increase.

Finding 2: Improvements in IT capability will continue

There is no evidence that the rate of technical progress in the IT industry will slow down; IT contributes not only to personal and organizational productivity, but to changes in the way business is done and how the organization performs its tasks. BUT IT alone does not provide sustainable competitive advantage – systems are easily copied. The real benefits derive from the combination of IT, the organization's structure, and people capable of exploiting the information/new functionality of IT.

Finding 3: It is necessary to rethink the core of the businesses

IT provides new ways of performing many of the basic processes of traditional businesses – and new entrants may be more effective because they are not cluttered with outworn methods. Therefore, it is essential to use IT to develop new effective business processes, rather than just to increase the efficiency of existing business processes.

Finding 4: Integration provides the main opportunities for improving business effectiveness

Integration is vital both within an organization and across organizational boundaries. It means achieving close and effective working relationships between parts of an organization and with other organizations in terms of, for example, structure, common or inter-linked processes and shared information.

Finding 5: Flexible networked organizations need to be created

New forms and styles of organization will make extensive use of electronic integration: workers will have terminals and workstations that are linked together, making people informed and flexible in their approach to tasks. Team-working across internal and external organizational boundaries will be common, assisted by IT.

Finding 6: Data and information will be a major problem area

An informed workforce, using information and IT fluently, is a key attribute of a flexible, networked organization. But much of the information in many organizations is dispersed, inconsistent, incompatible and inaccessible – i.e., it is data waiting to be transformed into information. This is a difficult problem to face, and some of the solutions may at first be inflexible and incomplete. What is important is that organizations are aware of the major technical and business problems that result until the information transformation has happened, and devote adequate resources to solving them.

Finding 7: The nature of work is changing

There will be many basic changes in the way in which work is done. Machines will take on some of the traditional human tasks, and require new skills and services to support them. Organizations will therefore need to consider education, training, and, most importantly, work design. Getting these right is central to establishing the rate of change that the organization can achieve.

Finding 8: Managers must be agents of change

Change must be exploited (proactively) rather than managed (generally a reactive response). Managers need to predict and intercept change before pressure from outside (from, for example, customers; suppliers; competitors; regulators) becomes irresistible. It is the task of top management to stimulate transformation, rather than to wait until uncontrollable change is forced upon the organization.

Senior managers should provide disconfirmation, that is, start to alter established beliefs and values in advance of generally recognized requirements for change. Not all eventualities in a turbulent environment can be predicted, but preparing staff to cope with them is essential.

Finding 9: There are new roles for organization leadership

The first priority for business leaders is to predict requirements for change; the second, to plan and implement it.

The key attribute of leadership is being able to achieve regular (even continuous) refocusing of the organization, without traumatic interruption of its operations. This requires the leadership style of the missionary (encourager and persuader) rather than the corporate general (who makes decisions and gives orders).

Finding 10: Line managers must take up the roles of leadership

Leadership of a large organization is too big a task to be the role of one person. Top management must delegate to line managers, who must accept:

- the obligation to work in the same way and under the same principles as the organization leader
- responsibility for new functions and for protecting the overall interests of the organization, rather than just their own parochial interests as subordinate managers.

Source: adapted from ICL (1992) *A Window on the Future: an ICL briefing for Management on the Findings of the Management in the 1990s Research Program.*

Box 6.1 describes the ten main findings of the MIT in the 90s research project. All these findings are important, but the ones that seem to be the most significant for future organizational development are that:

- the impact of IT can enable the creation of substantially different kinds of organization suited to the dynamics of the 1990s

- IT has industry-wide impacts and is a competitive necessity but provides no sustainable competitive advantage
- IT can be an enabler only when the organization invests in people before technology.

The following example, about the Ford Motor Company, serves to illustrate these points.

The Ford example

During the 1980s, the Ford Motor Company embarked on an efficiency drive to try to reduce the amount of paper which was being generated by its administrators. (The 'paperless office' was a much-celebrated predicted result of the advent of information technology, which in fact has yet to happen in most organizations.) What seemed to be a relatively mundane efficiency campaign was eventually to challenge Ford's long-established ways of doing business. Ford employed about 500 people to order components, receive the parts, and pay suppliers. Ford also had a strategic alliance with Mazda, the Japanese carmaker, and through this discovered that Mazda carried out the same administrative tasks with fewer than 100 employees. Ford developed an elaborate automated system (based on its existing manual procedures), but this still only cut the administrative force to 400. Ford then discovered that Mazda used fewer computers than themselves; but it streamlined its operation by not waiting for invoices from its suppliers. When goods arrived at the Mazda loading dock, a warehouseman waved a bar-code reader over each box. This single action entered the parts into inventory, updated production schedules as necessary, and sent electronic payment to the supplier.

The technique (known as a 'shared database facility') was simple, and, technologically speaking, not advanced at that period. Once Ford had seen it in operation, the opportunity of boosting efficiency by eliminating the time-consuming tasks of matching parts and invoices seemed obvious. The biggest hurdle which had to be overcome was one of mindset: understanding the change and picking up the issues associated with it. Ford had viewed invoices as essential. When they realized that they were not, they had to develop new ways of operating: closer relations with their suppliers, a warehouse that could 'talk' directly to the finance department, and workers who were comfortable with the new way of doing things.

Note: once Ford had mastered the 'secret', it no longer constituted a competitive advantage for Mazda; and getting acceptance from their own staff was a key factor.

Creating such change is not easy – it can be seen that culture is a crucial issue – and creating such change with IT often makes the task harder. Computers can be expensive and complicated, and the potential for introducing the wrong system, based on the wrong ideas of what the organization 'does', i.e., its core processes – is great.

WHAT IS A PROCESS?

The MIT model demonstrates that management processes constitute the most important link between business strategy and IT. If an organization does not have clear management processes, therefore, it will not be able to align its strategies with its IT. It follows that, in order to establish this alignment, organizations need to view IT as a strategic resource, and achieve a balance between it and other elements of the model. They also have to be clear about what a process is, and the exact nature of the processes that make up their adding-value activities. Adding value is key here: and it is for this reason that an organization's or an industry's processes may not be captured by automating manual systems. (Most manual systems have accumulated 'waste' or pockets of inefficiency over the years, or they perform functions which have become obsolete – i.e., they do not add value for the customer.)

KEY CONCEPT 6.1: BUSINESS PROCESSES: WHAT THEY ARE, AND HOW TO SELECT THEM

Thomas Davenport says that the following questions help to define the boundaries of a process:

- When should the process owner's concern with the process begin and end?
- When should the process customer's involvement with the process begin and end?
- Where do sub-processes begin and end?
- Is the process fully embedded within another process?
- Are performance benefits likely to result from combining the process with other processes or sub-processes?

Davenport emphasizes that this is an iterative activity – i.e., that subsequent innovation in one process might give rise to a need to reinnovate or to modify others.

He offers a further four criteria that might guide process selection:

- The process should be central to the execution of the firm's business strategy.
- The process should be 'healthy' – i.e., lean, fit, necessary, forward-looking.
- The process should be qualifiable – i.e. able to be conceptualized and 'bought into'.
- The scope of the process should be manageable – i.e., not so vast that its boundaries are lost sight of. There should not, however, be too many processes within any one organization.

Davenport says that the appropriate number is between 10 and 20. Other writers have limited the number to 5 or 6.

> 'The fewer and broader the processes, the greater the possibility of innovation through process integration, and the greater [the number, the greater] the problems of understanding, measuring and changing the process'. (Thomas Davenport)

Source: ideas adapted from Davenport, Thomas (1993) *Process Innovation: Re-Engineering Work Through Information Technology*, HBS Press.

Box 6.2: Further detail about processes

Table 6.1 The impact of information technology on process innovation

Impact	Explanation
Automational	Eliminating human labour from a process
Informational	Capturing process information for purposes of understanding
Sequential	Changing process sequence, or enabling parallelism
Tracking	Closely monitoring process status and objects
Analytical	Improving analysis of information and decision-making
Geographical	Co-ordinating processes across distances
Integrative	Co-ordination between tasks and processes
Intellectual	Capturing and distributing intellectual assets
Disintermediating	Eliminating intermediaries from a process

Davenport also points out that information technology can act as a constraint when processes are being developed. When an IT system informing those processes is being built, the following questions need to be asked:

- Who are the intended users of the system? (Account needs to be taken of **all** stakeholders).
- What are its inputs and outputs?
- What process tasks is the system designed to support?
- How difficult is it to add task functionality to the system?
- What interfaces to other systems are possible?
- What processes do other firms use with the system?

Source: Davenport, Thomas (1993) *Process Innovation: Re-Engineering Work Through Information Technology*, HBS Press.

There is currently fierce academic debate concerning the finer points of what constitutes a business process, but this need not concern us here (further reading suggestions are included at the end of the chapter for those who wish to become embroiled. Key Concept 6.1 and Box 6.2 also go into further detail). A good working definition of a business process is that it is ' a sequence of interdependent tasks and functions, which together produce outcomes that contribute to the (business) success of an organization' (from the *ICL Report* (MIT), p.7). Within the terms of this book, it could therefore be described as adding the value the customer requires in the most efficient and effective way, in order to achieve a product for which he or she is prepared to pay at a price which will sustain the company into the future. A research report prepared by Butler Cox gives the following extended explanation of what a process is, though this should not be taken as definitive:

'A business process is a set of work activities that is independent of the traditional functional structure of an organization. Business processes are oriented to results, rather than tasks. They satisfy business objectives, such as supplying a customer order or receiving and paying for a supplier's services. The activities of any business can be viewed as the aggregation of a relatively small number of basic business processes. At the highest level of aggregation, business processes accord with ... four principal value activities (planning and developing new products and services; operations or production; marketing, sales and customer service; financial management and control)'. (Butler Cox, 1991)

Figure 6.2 illustrates how business processes cut across traditional functional organizational boundaries.

A typical business process might therefore be the development of a new product, or the definition of production requirements and consequent placing of orders with suppliers. The overall activity of an organization is a high level process, which can be divided into a number of component processes.

Note. 'Process' does not equate with 'procedure'. A business procedure gives a clear directive to workers that they should act/take decisions in a certain way in a given set of circumstances. Procedures are designed in detail, and leave no scope for individual discretion. Processes leave the detailed execution of certain tasks to the workers, though they may also include some tasks that require very precise and consistent standards of output, and which thus have to be defined with procedures. For example, a team of people building a light aircraft may choose a variety of methods to arrive at the end result (they are exercising discretion over the process), but each of the parts of the aircraft must conform to standard and the aircraft must also be assembled to a strict specification (this involves procedures).

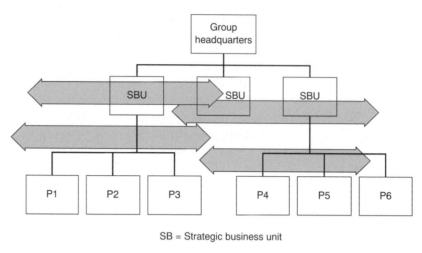

SB = Strategic business unit

P = Product (or service)

Figure 6.2 How business processes cut across the conventional functional organizational boundaries.

Thomas Davenport (Davenport, 1993) identifies five key activities which an organization needs to undertake in order to identify its 'true' processes, so that it can innovate in order to gain competitive edge:

- enumerate the major processes
- determine the process boundaries
- assess the strategic relevance of each process
- render high-level judgments of the 'health' of each process (i.e., is it necessary – does it add value?)
- qualify the culture and politics of each process.

KEY CONCEPT 6.2: THE INTERNET

A new computer network (networking was in itself a new concept) was developed in the late 1960s in America, with the objective of keeping the U.S. communications structure functioning in the event of an atomic war. Known originally as the ARPAnet, it connected four computers – three in California, and one in Utah. By 1971, there were 23 'hosts' (information providers) on the network; by 1980, there were more than 200 hosts, including the first international connections. This rapidly increased to 5,000 hosts in 1986, and 700,000 by the early 1990s.

The Internet is not owned or operated by any single authority. In order to standardize Internet protocols, and bring organizations to the Internet, the Internet Society was chartered in 1992.

A variety of Internet directory and information services was provided. By 1994, the Internet was growing at a massive rate, due to the media attention that it received, and the commercial opportunities it provided. In July 1994, there were more than 2.2 million registered hosts on the Internet, and about 25 million users.

The Internet is the supreme example of what can be achieved with electronic mail. Throughout the world, groups with special interests on virtually every conceivable subject carry out 'conversations' with each other which defy distance and time zones.

In 1994, publishers and entertainment providers were rapidly establishing themselves as on-line content providers. Digital convergence – the integration of the television, the telephone and the computer on the 'Net' – was moving beyond its early stages of development.

The Internet is poised to add value to business, government, education, entertainment and social interaction (though critics say that it is an anti-social device, because it encourages people to talk electronically, rather than face to face).

It still has some bridges to cross, however. Increasingly, special interest groups have been inundated with junk mail; and there are growing concerns that the Internet is being used as a vehicle for pornography and other types of crime. Security is another issue that needs addressing: although it is possible, for example, to conduct credit card transactions on the Internet, it is unwise, since details of the cardholder's number, credit limit, etc., can then be accessed by other people.

On the plus side, however, new technologies are continually being developed to address these problems; and the value-adding potential of the Internet is almost without limit. It is possible, for example, to select a holiday, buy the groceries, and even get married in 'Cyberspace'!

Source: details taken from *Internet World*, September 1994 issue.

It will be seen that in addressing these questions, the MIT in the 90s paradigm (Figure 6.1) provides a relevant framework for analysis. Key Concept 6.1 gives more detail about processes. Box 6.2 offers Davenport's views on the impact of information technology on process innovation.

INFORMATION TECHNOLOGY-INDUCED BUSINESS RECONFIGURATION

If organizations really concentrate on defining and developing their processes, rather than sticking to the old functional ways in which they have always operated, it follows that the shape and nature of the organizations themselves will change. They will become 'reconfigured'. The study of how such reconfiguration might take place, and the resulting benefits to the way in which value is added, has become well known as the work of N.Venkatramen (Mortow, 1991), an American academic also associated with the MIT in the 90s project.

Figure 6.3 illustrates the five levels of IT-induced reconfiguration which Venkatramen identifies. Venkatramen points out that the challenge to organization leaders is how best to reconceptualize the role of IT in business (i.e., to get away from thinking of it as merely fulfilling a technical or administrative function), how to identify the applications relevant to the industry's or organization's particular environment, and how to reconfigure the business so that the IT capabilities are not only fully exploited, but also in such a way that the business can be differentiated from its competitors.

The following offers an explanation of the 'levels' of Venkatramen's model:

Level One: localized exploitation. By this, Venkatramen means the exploitation of IT within business functions (manufacturing, marketing, or even isolated business activities within the functions). It is the first step on the ladder of using IT – the 'traditional' deployment of IT applications that improve the task efficiency of operations. Therefore, there are improvements in the way that the business operates, but these are very localized.

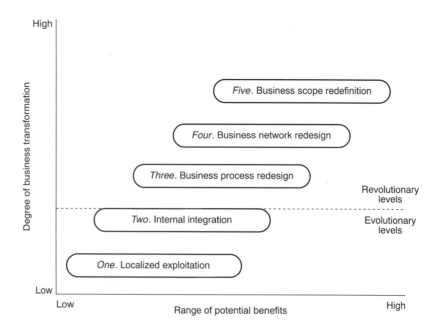

Figure 6.3 Venkatramen's five levels of IT-induced business reconfiguration.

Level Two: internal integration. This is a logical extension of Level One, in that IT capabilities are exploited in all possible areas of the existing business operations. In order to achieve this, the business needs to have a common IT platform – i.e., the computers of all the personnel need to be integrated into a system, so that they can 'talk' to each other. It is likely that Level Two capability leads to improvements in the organization's efficiency and effectiveness.

Note. Venkatramen characterizes Levels One and Two as 'evolutionary' – i.e., they require only steady and gradual changes in the existing organizational processes.

Level Three: business process redesign. This involves an initial attempt at reconfiguration of the business environment, using IT as the driving force. This means that, instead of accepting the status quo of 'how things are done' within the organization, and trying to fit an IT infrastructure around it, the business process itself is redesigned in order to be able to exploit to maximum effect the available IT capabilities. (Venkatramen's note: 'If we believe that the capabilities of IT signal a major departure from the capabilities offered by the Industrial Revolution, then the distinction between Levels Two and Three can be better understood'.)

Level Four: business network redesign. This is concerned with the reconfiguration of the scope and tasks of the business network involved in the creation and delivery of products and services. It includes business tasks both within and outside the organization as it is traditionally understood. Consequently, it introduces the idea of a 'virtual business network', or 'virtual organization' through the use of IT capabilities. This means that electronic integration of the key partners in the network becomes the main strategic issue. The potential of 'doing more with less' and setting up *ad hoc* groups working within different organizations to carry out specific projects can be seen to be tremendous.

Level Five: business scope redefinition. When the organization has reached this 'highest' level, it is engaged in a profound examination of its own *raison d'être*. What is it about? What are its true core competences? What is its 'ideal' relationship with partners and competitors? What is its business scope? Are there opportunities for developing that scope through producing related products and services (e.g., should Bill Gates of Microsoft be considering going into banking?). At this point, the traditional capabilities of the business have been substituted with IT-enabled skills.

Note. Levels Three, Four and Five are 'revolutionary' in their deployment of IT and the degree of business change that can be attained, and require that fundamental changes are carried out within the organization and beyond.

GLOBALIZATION AND INFORMATION TECHNOLOGY

We have already considered briefly how information technology helps to 'shrink' the world; we have also said that arranging and co-ordinating IT systems across geographical and cultural boundaries is not as easy as was once hoped.

International organizations now generate more wealth than the gross domestic product of individual nations. It is therefore vital to the future prosperity of the world that they exploit the value-adding potential of IT in the best possible way.

In an extensive research project, the Amdahl Institute (Amdahl Institute, 1991) has identified four basic types of global operator, each of which has a distinct style of systems management . They are the exporter (centralized system); the national adaptor (autonomous system); the centralized co-ordinator (replicated system) and the global co-ordinator (integrated system).

The **exporter** is characterized by concentrating heavily on operating key functions (financial management and control, planning and operations) at the home base. Marketing, sales and customer services are dispersed (typically, through agency agreements or subsidiaries), with little or no co-ordination between them.

National adaptors also concentrate financial management, control and planning, and disperse sales and customer service. In addition, they disperse manufacturing and retail operations, with little or no co-ordination.

Central co-ordinators have a high degree of co-ordination of operations and marketing, sales and customer service between dispersed countries; but financial management and control, and planning are kept centralized in the country of origin, and the products often reflect that origin.

Global co-ordinators configure all the principal value-adding activities to take advantage of local factor endowments, but endeavour also to get the added benefits of concentration by co-ordinating all the activities internationally. The arrangement is essentially country-neutral.

Figure 6.4 illustrates their typical configurations for managing systems activities.

It will be apparent that only global co-ordinators have reached Levels Four or Five on Venkatramen's model. Many have therefore a long way to go in order to achieve the 'mindset' which will help them to exploit IT to its maximum potential. All the companies in the Amdahl survey were successful, however, in 1992, and each of the companies participated in identifying the benefits they gained, and the difficulties they experienced, from using IT across national boundaries, and sometimes across continents. Key Concept 6.3 describes some of the main IT capabilities they employed.

Activity	Global strategy			
	Exporter[1]	National adaptor[2]	Central coordinator[3]	Global coordinator[4]
Financial management and control	►◄	►◄	►◄	◄►
Planning and development	►◄	►◄	►◄	◄►
Operations (or production)	►◄	►◄	◄►	◄►
Marketing, sales and customer service	◄►	◄►	◄►	◄►

►◄ Concentrated

◄► Dispersed

◄► Coordinated

[1] Also referred to as imperialist
[2] Also referred to as multi-domestic, country-centred or multinational
[3] Also referred to as franchiser or clone
[4] Also referred to as integrated decentralizer

Figure 6.4 The four main global strategies.

KEY CONCEPT 6.3: KEY TECHNICAL TERMS IN INFORMATION SYSTEMS MANAGEMENT

1 **Advanced system-building tools**
   (i) **Integrated computer-aided software engineering (I-CASE) tools**. These provide a comprehensive package of aids covering all the conventional system-building tasks, from systems analysis to testing and maintenance. The main difficulty with these applications is that there is still a lack of consistency in standards.
   (ii) **Re-engineering tools**. These convert existing computer systems so that they can be maintained and enhanced using I-CASE, thus enabling companies to break away from outdated computer languages such as COBOL without losing all the work that has been done. There are three types of re-engineering tools: redocumentation tools document the application; restructuring or renovating tools restructure the application; and inverse-engineering tools redevelop the application.
   (iii) **Object-oriented tools** allow applications to be constructed from software 'objects' that represent objects in the real world and the way they relate to each other. Objects are

arranged in a hierarchy, with each building on the attributes of the others. Constructing applications in this way has four main advantages: the application is easily understood by people who are not computer experts, but have some knowledge of the business area; changes in business requirements are easy to implement because only those objects directly affected need to be changed; the hierarchical arrangement of objects means that the amount of coding required is radically reduced; and objects can be stored in a 'library' and re-used in other applications.

(iv) **Rule-based tools** integrate the techniques of expert systems with existing facilities to improve their performance. Expert systems capture human expertise for the purpose of solving problems that cannot readily be resolved by more traditional methods.

2 **Workstation networks**

These are becoming an essential element of the IT infrastructure, because they are the part closest to the user, and they provide a very cost-effective form of computing.

Figure 6.2 illustrates the configuration of a workstation network. The workstations are linked over a local area network. Resource-sharing servers provide the workstations with access to printers, discs and files. Information servers provide access to resources, such as databases and applications, that are inherently shared.

Workstations in the network can support graphics and images as well as data and text. They can run multiple applications, with access via a graphical user interface. High-capacity local area networks may interconnect several workstation networks on a single large site. In turn, several sites may be interconnected through a growing range of wide-area networking alternatives. Workstation networks can now be linked into mainframe computers, often remotely located. These are called client-server systems. By dividing applications between personal workstations, mainframes and other specialized machines, client-server systems enable organizations to take advantage of the technologies that can handle the different parts of their applications most effectively; they are therefore likely to become the most important part of many organizations' IT structures.

3 **Technologies to support group-working**

These co-operative working technologies are of rapidly growing importance to global companies.

(i) **Electronic mail** transmits messages over telecommunications networks between sender and receiver. The messages may be in the form of text, graphics or documents (sometimes with illustrations). Normally, no 'hard copy' is generated.

Electronic mail systems do not require the attention of the receiver at the same time as the message is sent. The message can be stored until the receiver is free to access it.

(ii) **Electronic Data Interchange (EDI)** connects suppliers and customers in a value system with the purpose of exhanging orders, invoices and information electronically. It establishes a direct link between suppliers and customers, thus obviating the need either for 'hard copy' or for re-keying.

(iii) **Conferencing systems** put several people in touch simultaneously through telephone, data or video links. Telephone conference systems are widely available, both through private voice networks and through digital exchanges in public telephone networks. Computer conferencing connects three or more remote terminal users. Video-conferencing is a TV-like service that enables conferers to see as well as hear each other. Its principal purpose is to substitute for travelling (perhaps long distances) to face-to-face meetings.

(iv) **Groupware systems** manage the details of group collaboration. For example, they help co-authorship by facilitating the preparation and review of documents between several users. Procedure processors provide facilities for personal computer and host-based systems that make it possible to automate routine and semi-routine office procedures for moving documents between people. Examples include dealing with customer complaints, handling budget requests, and processing engineering change orders.

Source: adapted from *Globalisation: the IT Challenge*, published by the Amdahl Executive Institute, 1992.

The main benefits derived from international systems capabilities were identified as follows.

1 **Improved business co-ordination of worldwide activities**. These included:
- shortening the planning-cycle time for new products
- speeding up feedback into the design and manufacture of a product by incorporating improvements based on nation-by-nation operating experience
- reacting to shifts in customer preferences (email and EDI were widely used to help achieve this).

2 **Superior marketing to customers**, including:
  - improved customer contact, focus and responsiveness
  - achieving a more consistent worldwide image
  - the ability to increase added value on a local or regional basis (by targeted product differentiation).

3 **Better supply-chain efficiency** (i.e., improved contact and interaction with suppliers).

4 **The ability to measure and compare performance** within the company on a site-by-site basis (not just financial performance, but also in the areas of planning and development, administration, sales and marketing and customer services activities).

5 **Cost-saving in the systems function itself** (in some cases only – though in theory, international systems should be cheaper to develop than piecemeal national systems).

Case 6.5 shows how Trafalgar House, the construction conglomerate, has been able to add value with its global Information Systems strategy. The case also demonstrates the importance of standards, and of the 'buying in' of staff to direct and utilize systems effectively.

CASE 6.5

TECHNOLOGY: GLOBAL INFORMATION SYSTEMS STRATEGY

Trafalgar House

Trafalgar House is a group of companies primarily engaged in developing commercial and residential properties. It owns the Ritz Hotel, and also the 'luxury' liner, the QE2. Trafalgar House's blend of businesses, combined with its expansion into foreign markets, has created difficult challenges for its Information Systems professionals.

The group's global IS strategy seeks to balance the tactics of decentralization with the control of centralization. John Blagden, IT planning director for Trafalgar House Information Systems, attempted in 1989 to explain the philosophy:

> 'The company believes in diversity and decentralisation ... but divisional IT directors can't go tramping off to do anything they wish'.

In 1988, the Trafalgar construction and engineering division was responsible for more than half the conglomerate's turnover. The construction companies are 'vertically integrated' – i.e., together they form a series of continuous links in the supply chain – and this allows Trafalgar House to build residential property virtually from mortar to finished building, and to develop industrial facilities from Computer-

Aided Design (CAD) drawings to completion. Because Trafalgar House is involved in every stage, it can keep track of projects better than its competitors; nevertheless, such a large conglomerate wouldn't be able to do so effectively without advanced global information systems.

A technological concept that helped Trafalgar to maintain its competitive edge in the late 1980s was Electronic Data Interchange (EDI). The company's first use of this technology was to streamline its maritime operation, Cunard Ellerman Cargo – indeed it was one of the first companies to be able to see the value of the concept to shipping. The Data Interchange in Shipping (DISH) rules for maritime documents developed by Trafalgar House were to become the industry standard.

The company decided to build on its success in shipping by taking EDI into the property business; but other divisions in the group would be persuaded, rather than ordered, to use it The group understands the value of encouraging its staff to 'buy in' to new ideas. John Blagden explained:

> 'For the most part, Trafalgar House Information Systems has an advisory status. Our planning consultants serve two functions – they handle all IT issues and they centralise information'.

He estimated that approximately one per cent of Trafalgar House's revenue (i.e., between $40m and $50m) was spent on Information Systems. The figure could only be a rough guess, because the group maintained a loose federation of IS departments, and didn't add up budgets across the companies.

There was no grand strategy dictated from above. Systems people from the operating companies worked together with group IS directors to set overall strategy for one- and two-year periods. Trafalgar divisions could plan from three to five years ahead if they chose.

The ultimate goal for the company was what Blagden called a 'seamless, integrated, distributed, co-operative processing' (SIDCP), which would place an emphasis on such technologies as EDI for its property operations. SIDCP would be based on the UNIX and Open System Interconnection (OSI) standards that were being developed in the late 1980s.

Trafalgar House hoped that if this venture was as successful as DISH had been, they would gain the accolade of having it accepted as the standard for vendors throughout the construction industry.

Source: adapted from Runyan, Linda (1989) 'Global IS Strategies', *Datamation Magazine*, 1 December.

Not surprisingly, the Amdahl research found that the power of computer systems to help give the benefits of flexibility were strongest in businesses where information was the product – e.g., in on-line information service companies.

The hurdles yet to be overcome by international systems were perceived to be:

- **Cost** (despite the theoretical savings to be made on international systems). Many companies were now appraising systems on a value-for-money basis, and had cut back their systems budgets in real terms since the mid-1980s. Nevertheless, it was felt that systems spending was still running at a level which most business executives found uncomfortable.
- **Standardization**. Total international standardization of systems has yet to happen. When it does, it should help to cut costs by making IT provision for a shared base of international users.
- **Communication across time zones** was still difficult even when sophisticated technology was used – even if you have the power to communicate, it is not always possible to achieve an instant response if it is 4 am in the country you are calling. Account also has to be taken of the fact that the 'communication circumstances' of people do not change substantially. Although the workplace has become more mobile, humans still need sleep, rest periods, holidays, etc.
- **Management structure** from country to country was perceived to be the greatest problem. This included people and systems issues, cultural differences from country to country, legal complications (different countries have different rules about trans-border data flow), and ensuring adequate security when information passed from one country to another.

    People-specific difficulties included agreeing on common user requirements, gaining user acceptance, and co-ordinating applications developments between plants.

In the words of one of the survey respondents (a systems director): 'The greatest problems are those relating to people. ... In a business offering the same services globally, the prerequisite is strong, clear management direction. Then, the systems issues fall into place. Otherwise, all you get is conflicting views.'

This returns us to the interconnected elements of strategy, structure, culture and information technology expressed in the MIT in the 90s model It should also suggest one of the main tenets of SWOT analysis – that every problem or threat is also an opportunity. For companies that recognize the 'people' issues, address them successfully, and so get their strategy (seamlessly incorporating Information Technology) right, the future could indeed be bright. The point is summed up by Niederman *et al.*:

> 'Without the right people – smart, educated, properly trained, empowered – almost nothing we can do is likely to bring great success; with the right people, it is difficult to fail.' (Niederman *et al.*, 1991)

SUMMARY

Now that you have read this chapter, you are able to do the following:

- Make a distinction between how value is added through information technology and other types of technology.
- Explain what the term 'information technology' means, and describe briefly the six main elements that it includes.
- Discuss how information technology may add value; and the problems and advantages that might contribute to this.
- Identify some of the key capabilities that computers offer in the quest to add value.
- Explain the far-reaching effects of IT in the following areas: changing the nature of products; changing how businesses operate; changing the shape of the industry; 'shrinking' geographical distances.
- Explain in some detail the rationale behind the *MIT in the '90s Research Program*, and its main findings. The significance of the MIT model should be well understood.
- Have an understanding of the nature of processes, and their relevance to the management of organizations, particularly in the context of IT development. You should be able to describe what a process is.
- Explain the ideas of Venkatramen, especially the five levels of IT-induced business reconfiguration. Venkatramen's model should be well understood.
- Understand the significance of IT to the globalization of industries. You should know the main types of IT applications that enable increased networking over large distances.
- Finally, and perhaps most importantly of all, you should have a clear idea of the importance of people in the complex interrelated processes of IT, change, and turbulence in the external environment.

REFERENCES AND FURTHER READING

It is difficult to be prescriptive about further reading for this chapter, because the information itself changes so rapidly, and is, furthermore, ubiquitous – some of the best insights can be gained from quality contemporary newspapers and specialist journals.

For an 'easy' overview of IT capabilities and the significance of IT generally, a survey entitled 'Information Technology' which appeared in the 16 June 1990 issue of *The Economist* magazine is still a very good guide.

Amdahl publications are excellent on the subject. The ones referred to in the text are:

Amdahl Institute (1991) *Applications in the 1990s: reducing complexity and enabling change*, Amdahl Executive.

Amdahl Institute (1991) *Globalization: the I.T. Challenge*, report prepared by Butler Cox, Amdahl Executive.

Amdahl Institute (1990) *Innovation through Information Technology: Proceedings of the Third Amdahl Executive Conference*, Amdahl Executive.

The following are essential for an understanding of the MIT in the '90s Research Program and IT-Induced Business Reconfiguration:

ICL (1991) *A Window on the Future: an ICL Briefing for Management on the Findings of the Management in the 1990s Research Program*. (This is an excellent resume; alternatively, more detailed information can be gained from *Management in the 1990s* Working Papers, Room E40-294, MIT, Cambridge, Massachusetts 02139, USA).

Morton, M.S. (ed.) (1991) *The Corporation of the 1990s: IT and Organisational Transformation*, Open University Press, Oxford. Especially Chapter 5 ('IT-Induced Business Reconfiguration', by N.Venkatramen), and Chapter 7 ('The Networked Organisation and the Management of Interdependence', by J.F. Rockart and J.E. Short).

The following is important for a detailed understanding of processes:

Davenport, T.H. (1993) *Process Innovation: Re-Engineering Work Through Information Technology*, HBS Press.

Niederman, F. *et al.* (1991) 'Information Systems Management Issues for the 1990s', *MIS Quarterly*, December, p.474.

For those interested in globalization and the development of IT systems:

Ciborra, C. and Jelassi, T. (eds.) (1994) *Strategic Information Systems: a European Perspective*, Wiley, Chichester. Excellent guide, but may be too in-depth for some readers.

Strategies for adding value 7

LEARNING OBJECTIVES

After reading this chapter, you will see how all the preceding chapters, which consider the interdependent variables of the business environment, can lead you to an informed consideration of the strategies the organization should adopt; you will have an initial awareness of the types of strategy that can be pursued; and you will be ready to embark upon a detailed course of instruction in strategic management. Specifically, you will have:

- considered the importance of getting and staying **close to the customer**, and how this can be achieved
- gained an understanding of the nature and strategic importance of the 'traditional' organizational functions of **marketing**, **operations**, **finance**, **personnel** and **information technology**
- reconsidered the concept of **architecture** as a means of exploring the relevance and interrelatedness of these functions when developing a strategy
- developed an understanding of **why** and **how** organizations grow
- understood the interrelationship between **strategy** and **structure**.
- recognized the importance of **people** to all strategic dynamics.

INTRODUCTION

The preceding six chapters of this book have examined how the wider external environment affects organizations that are seeking to add value, and have reinforced and emphasized our initial premise, which is that adding value at a price which the customer is willing to pay, and which will also sustain the organization into the future, is the organization's sole valid claim to existence. We have argued that this premise is equally relevant to not-for-profit organizations, although the yardsticks by which they measure their effectiveness may be a little harder to define.

We have examined at length the turbulence, as well as the complicated variables of the external environment. For example, we have seen how the changing laws of the European Union might affect businesses; we have seen how changing attitudes to and among the workforce might affect the ways in which products and services are created and delivered; we have observed the massive impacts that increasingly sophisticated information provision has, not only upon how organizations operate, but upon how they think and how they create and reform themselves.

Operating, as most organizations in the 1990s do (and, we would argue, as all **should** do), with limited resources and streamlined workforces, it is all too easy for them to be so overwhelmed by this complexity that they fall into the trap of forgetting that it is the customer who drives the whole process. Therefore, in this chapter, which suggests strategies for adding value, the first and most important point to make is that in order to remain healthy and to thrive, every organization must ensure that it is at all times close to the customer. Peter Drucker was making this point two decades ago, when he wrote:

> 'Marketing is not a specialised activity, but rather the whole business seen from the point of view of its final result, that is, from the customer's point of view.'

Later writers have added to this, observing that successful strategic leaders have urged their employees to focus everything on the customer, and to take the customer's measures as their yardsticks and sources of inspiration. The fact that these ultimately have to marry with the organization's budget measures should always be a point of reference within the organization, but not obtrusive outside it: thus, reconciling the customer's needs with the exigencies of the balance-sheet should constitute a seamless and invisible process.

GETTING CLOSE TO THE CUSTOMER

Stages of customer care have been identified as threefold within most organizations:

Stage 1: Bliss (in the 'ignorance is bliss' sense). The organization goes on doing what it thinks fit, not listening to the customer (or, perhaps more accurately, not instituting an adequate listening mechanism), and assumes that the customer approves of the approach that is being taken.

Stage 2: Awareness The organization becomes aware that the customer has views about the goods and services being provided, and their delivery and after-care arrangements, and that these do not necessarily coincide with what the organization is doing. This process will most probably have been started by 'happenstance' – by conclusions drawn by a new and more sensitive sales representative, for example, or by losing a valued customer to a competitor; or, less frequently and less cataclysmically, by the organization's taking steps to introduce new, more effective channels of communication with customers before an external impetus prompts it to do so.

Stage 3: Commitment The organization and the customer find ways of working together in order to fulfil the latter's needs. The relationship becomes a truly symbiotic partnership. Often, especially in high-tech industries, such a partnership can help to accelerate new product development and push back the frontiers of technology rapidly and relatively economically.

The Malcolm Baldridge Quality Award is awarded to companies annually on the basis of the degree of customer satisfaction achieved. These are assessed from four basic points of reference, each of which represents a fundamental consideration for organizations wishing to ensure their future relevance by working properly with their customers. The four points of reference are:

1 The company's knowledge of the customer
2 The overall customer service systems that the company has developed
3 The company's responsiveness, both to customer requirements, and to the types of external change that have formed the bulk of the subject-matter of this book, particularly as they are addressed by and communicated to the customer with his/her needs in mind
4 The ability of the company to meet the customer's requirements and expectations.

Once these principles have been grasped, the company (or organization) should be able to identify its own value delivery sequence, which should overlay and determine the format of the value chain it has developed, and which should influence the value system within which it operates. This might involve some complex research, thinking and evaluation, but the bedrock processes can be explained simply:

1 **Choose the value**. The organization has to work out a way of meeting the customer's demands in terms of the product and the price charged. This will almost inevitably mean a trade-off between low cost and added-value features (Key Concept 1.5 in Chapter One), though it does not imply that the eventual product will be inferior or superior: simply, that it will fulfil the customer's requirements.

2 **Provide the value**. The organization, having identified what it needs to do, then has to develop the product and service package that creates superior value by focusing on service quality (in the sense of relevance to what the customer wants). Clearly, for this to be effective, operations strategy (which addresses what the organization does internally) and marketing strategy (which looks outward to the customer/ competitor environment) need at least to work harmoniously together. In the most effective organizations, they are inextricably inter-twined.

3 **Promote the value**. This is a two-part exercise: first, it means promoting the outstanding product/service package that the company has developed, so that it reaches as wide a potential customer base as possible; second, it means continually adjusting the package (often in small rather than major ways) as a result of listening to the people who make up that customer base.

Note. It has already been stated throughout this book, and several times within this chapter, that customer satisfaction is a function of the whole organization which everyone (if they have a valid role within the organization) contributes towards in some way. (It is also the principal tenet of business re-engineering.) No organization which fails to grasp this point is likely to succeed in the long term.

The work which Peters and Waterman undertook in the 1980s to identify what makes companies 'excellent' has been partially discredited: follow-up researchers discovered that many of their original excellent companies had subsequently failed to flourish, or had even closed down. However, it could be argued that the tenets which Peters and Waterman put forward hold good: it was the companies themselves who were at fault, for not continuing to put them into practice.

Sets of guidelines are just that: neither more nor less than a guide. But for strategic leaders who seek a more concrete prop than chaos theory, the identification of what high-performing companies do can help them formulate their own successful value-adding strategies. Once again, the processes are complex, but the broad practices themselves may be expressed in simple terms:

● High-performing organizations emphasize customer expectations.
● High-performing organizations research customer needs.
● High-performing organizations use customer-based performance measures.
● High-performing organizations formulate quality control objectives for all functions.

Organizations that pursue these practices, and which are therefore armed with a Janus-headed internal/external monitoring mechanism, have positioned themselves to deal most effectively with opportunities and threats which arise within their environment (the reader is invited to remember that each opportunity is also a potential threat; each strength is also a potential weakness). As we have already pointed out in earlier chapters, such opportunities and threats may not be industry-specific. For example, professional tennis has become a huge and lucrative entertainment industry, with the stars themselves providing the main ingredient of high added value in the form of glamour and virtuoso performance. Therefore there was considerable concern when in 1995 a dearth of world-class female tennis players led American researchers to conclude that promising potential female tennis stars were not simply being lost to other athletic pursuits, but that the wide range of attractive choices of career now open to young women meant that many were electing not to develop their sporting prowess at all. American tennis associations were consequently planning to launch a recruitment drive, spearheaded by some of the world's most famous female tennis stars, to highlight the attractions of professional tennis.

Yet more difficult to identify are threats and opportunites which challenge accepted ideas of industry boundaries. Such challenges are proliferating as innovative ways of using information technology supersede the preservation of received ways of carrying out almost every organizational activity. For example, Lacerte Software was set up in 1978 on $25,000 capital to provide tax software for small to mid-range accounting practices. In 1995, it had become a multi-million dollar business, providing software to large companies so that they could dispense with the services of tax accountants by carrying out the same range of activities in-house. What had begun as a service to a specific industry had developed into a new industry that threatened the traditional industry's existence, as the high added-value of the service itself eroded the mystique of the accountancy industry's 'expertise', and deregulation meant that large company finance departments no longer needed to defer to 'experts'. It will be seen that there were a number of environmental factors at work in this example.

In order to address the organization's threats and opportunities effectively, it needs to build consistently upon its competitive advantage. If this is not continually developed, it perishes with time, as competitors develop similar skills, practices and products. Therefore, the organization needs to develop both the physical and mental capability for continuous innovation. For almost all organizations today, innovation means relying on the skills of the knowledge worker. Knowledge workers can belong to the core workforce of the organization itself (in which case, in this context, they are known as 'intrapreneurs'), or they can be bought in (or 'outsourced') from other organizations, partnerships or sole traders and their skills commissioned for particular tasks or projects. They might, for example, be members of the 'professions', designers, craftsmen, or computer experts.

Whether 'intrapreneurs', or external 'experts' or 'entrepreneurs', such knowledge workers are collectively seeking to innovate within the organization at every level, and within the following major areas:

- in new products and services
- in the way the organization operates
- in the organization's view of itself, as it is transmitted both externally and internally
- in the organization's mechanisms and its use of resources.

The innovations themselves can be large or small – they do not have to be of earth-shattering magnitude to be effective. They may consist of something as mundane, but nevertheless vital, as setting up a more effective internal reporting system, or the fitting of rubber feet to a laptop computer so that it does not scratch the worksurface.

Whether or not innovation is effectively promoted and sustained within the organization depends largely on the skills of the executive leader. He or she has to make sure that the right climate for creativity is fostered, without allowing too much scope for chasing 'red herrings', or allowing some individuals to dominate, and therefore intimidate or thwart the ideas of others. Kanter says that what is needed is a 'balancing act' between discipline and creative flow. Thus it is the task of the leader to:

- keep everyone's mind on the shared vision
- set explicit boundaries to areas for discussion and place constraints on decisions
- watch for uneven participation/group pressure
- keep time bounded and managed.

How can the organization set about developing itself to achieve these things, and, having developed, keep itself continually poised to sustain its competitiveness? First of all, it needs to make sure that its own internal arrangements are as effective and efficient as possible. Traditionally, companies consisted of **functions** – typically, **marketing**, **operations**, **finance**, **personnel**, and, in recent years, **information technology**. In a large organization, each of these functions would come under the aegis of a director. Shortly, we examine an alternative way of looking at how an organization might be arranged; but let us concentrate first of all on these functions, as they have been conceived almost since the beginning of the study of management.

MARKETING

Marketing is perhaps best defined by explaining what it is not. It is **not** hard-selling; it is **not** advertising; and it is **not** market research (though effective market research might lead to better marketing). Marketing could be more accurately described as a **philosophy**, in the sense of being a way of thinking about or approaching customers. At the heart of the concept of marketing is the wish that the company should provide the products that the customer wishes to buy. This is in contradistinction to the company's (or not-for-profit organization's) offering the customer the goods or services it wishes to produce. It will be seen, therefore, that the basic philosophy that underpins marketing is the same as the creed that we have identified as underpinning the concept of adding value.

A moment's thought will make it apparent that not all customers want the same goods or services. From this, it logically follows that the marketer's true objective is to locate and identify a group of consumers with unsatisfied needs that could be met by his/her company. This group of consumers is known as a **market segment**, and the process is called **market segmentation**.

There are both **strategic** and **tactical** processes involved in identifying what product or service the organization should then produce:

Strategic processes

- identify a group with a strategic need
- sketch out an idea for a new product
- undertake strategic research into the idea
- plan new product development
- gather information – test the market
- make sure the organization is doing the right things.

Tactical processes

- match the organization's needs with the needs of the target segment
- look at existing products
- undertake tactical research – how can the product or service be improved?
- **add value**, having assessed the result of these activities
- persuade/remind customers what the organization has to offer
- make sure that the organization is doing things right.

Some companies will conclude that they want to produce a low-cost, value-for-money product that appeals to the widest possible market. (Not-for-profit organizations may in many cases be obliged to adopt this view also.) These companies will be seeking to gain **high market share**. Others will decide that they are best suited to providing a costly or unusual product or service for a relatively small but loyal and appreciative group of customers. They are then said to be operating in a **niche market**.

In either case, if the marketing function has been carried out properly, the organization will have been looking at itself as a business **through the customer's eyes**.

Let us return to the notion of **SWOT** analysis, which we first explored in Chapter One. We might now conclude that marketing consists of the creative process of satisfying customer needs profitably by matching company strengths to marketing opportunities.

Every product or service has what is known as a **life cycle** (Key Concept 7.1). Although this may be prolonged and varied, it remains true that all but a handful of goods and services eventually outgrow their desirability to the customer. Assessing when this point has been reached, and continually making innovations to existing products and services and developing new ones is the key activity which needs to be undertaken to ensure that the organization is producing what the customer requires. In the 1990s, many organizations have decided that the best way to do this is not only to keep close to the customer, but to enlist the customer's aid in the development and monitoring process.

KEY CONCEPT 7.1: THE PRODUCT LIFE CYCLE

In essence, the term 'product life cycle' describes a product's sales history from its introduction to the market to its withdrawal from the market. The graphs which usually accompany discussions of a product life cycle represent sales volume curves. The theory is that products begin their commercial lives with the first sale, sales rise as the life of the product continues until a peak is reached, and then decline until the company considers that their overall contribution to revenue does not justify maintaining their presence in the market.

Clearly, the nature of the cycle varies tremendously from product to product. There are some products, like salt, which have been sold for thousands of years – though, interestingly, the preferred purveyor changes. Thus, before the Second World War, Cerebos was the most popular salt sold in the UK, to the extent that the brand name became accepted as another name for the commodity; in the 1950s and 1960s, Saxa salt took over from Cerebos; while, in the 1990s, the market has become much more fragmented, with supermarkets selling their own brands, and 'healthy' versions such as French sea-salt gradually gaining more and more market share.

Some products – for example, the ill-fated folding bicycle which Sir Clive Sinclair thought was the 1980s solution to urban traffic congestion – fail right at the beginning of their lives. Others have very short lives. Sometimes this is by design – 'cults' and fashions are deliberately pandered to and sometimes engendered by specific products. Skateboards, hula hoops and the many children's toys developed as spin-offs from films and other media all fit into this category. With the increasing sophistication of technology, some products evolve into such sophisticated later versions of themselves that there is little trace left of the original – the computer industry provides many examples of this.

Broadly speaking, however, the product life cycle concept involves an understanding that each product typically flows through several distinct product life cycle stages as sales volume is plotted over time. These stages are introduction, growth, maturity and decline.

Identifying when a product has reached any one of these stages is not always easy. Sometimes, a product can be lifted (backwards or forwards) from one stage to another by specific marketing tactics. The Mars Bar, for example, was invented in 1932, and has enjoyed huge popularity as an item of confectionery ever since. However, by the 1980s, it could be argued that it had reached a stage of maturity; certainly, the competition from other types of confectionery was increasing all the time in a market acknow-ledged to be both tough and fickle. Mars combated this by differ-entiating the product, whilst preserving its distinctive features. Thus, 'fun-size' Mars Bars were introduced, to be followed by a 'King Size' version, the plain chocolate Mars Bar, and, finally, Mars ice-cream. Regular Mars Bars have remained on sale in a variety of packages – buying several is substantially cheaper. By pursuing this strategy, the Mars company has succeeded in taking the product out of the 'mature' stage, and returning it to the 'growth' stage of the product life cycle.

Sometimes, a product is so associated with a company – con-veying an image of quality, reliability, tradition, etc. – that the company may decide to retain it as part of its product portfolio, even though, according to the life cycle theory, it is well into the 'decline' period. An example of this is the 'Kangol' beret. Although Kangol now make all types of hats and other fashion accessories, the beret is the item most closely associated with the brand name, and therefore the company continues to produce them even during periods when they are considered to be unfashionable.

Therefore, all products follow a product life cycle, but the shape of the cycle itself rarely follows the 'textbook' version exactly; there are many variations on the theme.

Companies that make tangible products have also built in a contribu-tion from their suppliers in a similar way, thus enabling a creative three-way relationship to grow to the mutual benefit of all. Such an approach is known as **relationship marketing**.

OPERATIONS

All organizations, whether from manufacturing or service industries, for-profit or not-for-profit, need an effective operations function that maximizes efficiency. 'operations' embraces the idea of the set of actions the organization carries out in order to make the product or service the customer requires. It can therefore refer to an extremely varied range of activities, depending on the nature of the industry.

Despite its essential nature, Operations has often been regarded as the poor man of the traditional organizational functions. It has been seen as an unglamorous but necessary adjunct to marketing. Con-sequently, in traditionally-organized companies there has often been conflict between the operations and the marketing functions. Opera-tions has been seen by marketing as getting in the way of producing what the customer requires by adopting a leaden, procedural approach to the way things are done. Marketing has been criticized by operations for promising customers fast deliveries, or new modifications, which cannot possibly be achieved in the timescale specified.

Clearly, it is important for operations to work as closely with the customer as marketing. New product development and timescales are then decided by mutual agreement, and the customer's input can often push back the boundaries of industrial development faster than might otherwise occur.

In manufacturing industries, operations also needs to work closely with the company's suppliers, in order to achieve maximum efficiency, not only in terms of serving the customer, but also in terms of deploying the organization's resources. Information technology, if intelligently used, can help greatly here. Sophisticated software packages, such as materials requirement planning (MRP and MRPII) can aid the balance sheet by ensuring that the company does not commit more resources than are necessary to building inventory, whilst at the same time guaranteeing that hold-ups do not arise because certain components are missing. Clearly, a close and trusting association with suppliers, following the **Just-in-time philosophy** (Chapter One) is essential. Computer software packages can also help to organize the workflow area (e.g. Computer Aided Manufacturing, or CAM, Computer Integrated Manufacturing, or CIM), and aid in the actual design of the product (e.g., Computer Aided Design, or CAD).

Although the company's or organization's approach to quality, if carried out according to a true TQM philosophy, should be embraced and observed by every employee from the Chief Executive (who should drive and inspire it) to the lowest-paid part-time cleaner, in practice it is the operations function that often acts as the 'quality engine'. This is because formal accreditations of quality, such as ISO 9000, or the implementation of quality-exploring philosophies, such as **benchmarking** (Chapter One), need to be addressed in detail at the nuts-and-bolts, as well as at the strategic, level if they are to work.

FINANCE

Traditionally, the financial function within a company has often been regarded as most important of all. This is because the Financial Director not only holds the key to the purse-strings, and is therefore instrumental in the allocation of cash to projects, but also because he or she (who is often also the Company Secretary) reports to the shareholders on the profit or loss that has been made on their investment in the company. Not-for-profit organizations also have financial directors, whose targets will normally be to operate within budgets, or perhaps to generate some income to offset the organization's costs.

However, there is one major danger (apart from the inherent danger of any *primus inter pares*) of regarding the financial function as of paramount importance: this is the danger of enslaving the organization to the demands of the 'bottom line'. If we accept the 'added value' maxim that what the company is trying to achieve is what the customer requires at a price that he or she is willing to pay, and which results in a profit that will take it successfully into the future, then it will be seen that what is being aimed for is not profit maximization (which is an accountant's approach to strategy), but an optimal profit, i.e., one that will satisfy the requirements of the organization's customers, staff, shareholders and the dictates of its future needs. Therefore, 'enlightened' modern organizations accord the financial function importance equal to but not greater than the other functions.

Nevertheless, sound **investment** and **financing** decisions are crucial to the successful running of the business.

Investment decisions (or capital budgeting decisions)

These involve decisions about acquiring assets. The assets in question will usually be 'real assets' employed within the business to enable it to produce goods or services to satisfy customer demand. These real assets may be tangible – land, buildings, plant, equipment, stocks, etc. – or they may be intangible – patents, trademarks, expertise, etc. Whichever category they fall into, a price can be put on them, and a cost is therefore attached to acquiring them. The main investment decisions which have to be made are:

1 How much should the firm invest?
2 In which projects should the firm invest?

Sometimes, in order to increase its profitability and therefore its attractiveness to shareholders, whilst at the same time maintaining its prices at a level that is attractive to customers, an organization may choose to invest in financial assets outside the business, in the form of short-term securities or deposits. Some supermarket chains – for instance, the Bradford-based William Morrison's Supermarkets – have boosted their financial position very successfully by investing cash gathered at the end of the week until Monday morning in short-term securities. Local authorities sometimes invest 'reserve' cash in longer-term bonds. (This strategy is not without its risks, however. For example, Shetland Council lost more than £2m of ratepayers' money following the collapse of the Bank of Credit and Commerce International in 1992.)

Finance decisions

There are two basic, broad finance decisions that always have to be addressed:

1 How much is needed to fund the firm's operations (including proposed as well as existing projects)?
2 What is the best mix of finance in relation to the overall value of the firm?

The decision regarding the latter depends on a detailed understanding of the external environment and of the structure of the industry within which the organization is operating. All investment and finance decisions are important to the specific company concerned, because they will affect its operating environment and prosperity for the duration of their lives. They are also important to the national and international economy as a whole, because aggregate investment sanctioned in a period is a major factor in determining aggregate demand, and therefore the level of employment. (In the 20 year period 1970–1990, Japan invested, on average, 30 per cent of its GDP; Britain and America, approximately 15 per cent each.)

There is unlikely to be a single agreed view on investment within a company. Stakeholder expectations will probably differ as follows:

- **Shareholders** will be concerned with the payoffs that they can expect both in **dividends** and in **capital growth**. They will also be interested in **risk**, and will expect their returns from a project to reflect the degree of risk that it incurred.
- **Bankers** and other providers of interest-bearing loans will also be concerned about risk, but from a different perspective. On the whole, they are likely to assume that the company knows its own business, but they will want detailed knowledge of its capital structure – particularly the **gearing ratio** (of debt to equity) which indicates how sensitive the solvency of a company is to changes in its profit position.
- **Suppliers** and **employees** will be interested in the liquidity of the company – i.e., its ability to meet short-term commitments to creditors and wages. Cash flow problems – still the major cause of company failure in the UK – are also the concern of bankers, since they may imply additional loans and an increased risk profile.
- **Managers** within a company may be concerned with a number of things other than its performance – for example, increasing their own prestige, or building their own long-term careers. Such hidden agendas may be inevitable, but whatever their other preoccupations, financial analysis is an indispensable tool for competent managers to help them assess the performance of the company, and try to predict the outcome of investments. Ultimately, successful performance is the only way of ensuring the effective co-operation of the other stakeholders over a period of time.

Profitability (or, in the case of not-for-profit organizations, achieving financial targets) has always been the key issue to survival; nevertheless, it must be profitability which is achieved within the firm's value-adding strategy. In other words, the tail should not be allowed to wag the dog. Two very important points follow from this:

1 It is important not to consider financial implications alone, but as part of the firm's overall strategy (and financial directors or managers will often find this difficult to accept).

2 A firm should not take on a project simply to enhance its profitability. Such a strategy is almost certain to rebound if the project does not fit in with its competitive advantage.

Note. With regard to point (2), in some cases, a strict financial policy could be said to constitute the competitive advantage of an organization – e.g., Hanson Trust, which gives the managers of its business units considerable autonomy, provided that they meet agreed financial targets. The question that has to be asked is whether such an approach is sustainable in the long term, and whether it takes sufficient account of the need for investment, the preservation of core competences, and value chain linkages.

It will have become apparent that financial strategy involves some complex considerations and balancing acts. Successful accommodation of all these variations results in the company's being able to add value in the way that the customer desires, and for which he/she is willing to pay in order to maintain the company's health for the future, utilizing capital that has been acquired at the lowest possible cost. The company has then learnt the art of investing in assets (tangible, such as machinery, or intangible, such as skills and reputation) whose worth (by virtue of the business they then generate) exceeds their cost by the amount that will satisfy the stakeholders of the company.

INFORMATION TECHNOLOGY AND PEOPLE

The preceding discussion has been shot through with mention of the contributions made by information technology and people, two vital components of the organization. Now it is time to look at them not individually, but together. They have been taken together, because in today's modern business or not-for-profit organization, they are inextricably interlinked. People will add value better by addressing the challenges of their organization through the utilization of information technology. Information technology, if imaginatively, effectively and economically used, provides people with opportunities of harnessing their creativity in new ways. 'People', of course, refers to the personnel of the organization, but also to its customers, its suppliers and its strategic partners – sometimes even its competitors within an industry. Information technology not only helps the organization to carry out its activities, but provides a vast, potentially non-finite linking mechanism between some or all of these interested groups.

How information technology is used (i.e., the organization's strategic approach towards IT) therefore becomes a key issue (see Case 7.1). IT is emphatically not best applied by automating the manual systems and procedures of the traditional organization. It provides an opportunity for the organization to think about what it does in quite a different way, focusing continually on the fact that it is there to serve the needs of the customer at a price the customer is willing to pay in order for the organization to take itself successfully into the future. Acknowledging and exploring this fact has led to the development of important management philosophies – for example, Total Quality Management and Business Re-engineering (Chapter One).

In the streamlined, competitive and resource-hungry 1990s, correctly addressing the people/information technology issue thus becomes of (literally) vital importance. The organization not only needs to be able to understand itself and therefore work out (perhaps radically different) ways of arranging its activities, but also to understand the value system within which it operates, as well as the external environment at large as it impacts upon it. This is a tall order!

CASE 7.1

'SILLIWOOD'

California is the home of both Hollywood, the glamorous heartland of the film industry, and of Silicon Valley, the nerve centre of high technology. In 1995, the two industries decided to explore the synergy of joining forces in a strategic alliance to create a range of 'new media' ventures known collectively as 'Silliwood'. The anticipated outcome of this alliance was a new generation of multimedia entertainment products, ranging from computer games to on-line services and interactive television shows.

The alliance was developed in response to the realization that traditional entertainment companies were recruiting engineers and programmers from the technology sector, while technology companies were searching for entertainment providers from the film industry. This was because of the way that the products that each made had evolved.

Most of the leading film studios had 'interactive' divisions that had made computer games and other products based on their movies; conversely, the more advanced software companies were producing games that resembled films, and featured real actors rather than computer-generated cartoon characters.

The 'Silliwood' partnership's first projects involved the creation of special effects. Computers were increasingly being used to create illusions that would either be impossible, or prohibitively expensive, using traditional methods. For example, the friendly ghost in *Caspar*, a Steven Spielberg film, was created by computer. *Apollo 13*, a film about the moon-shot directed by Ron Howard and starring Tom Hanks, also made extensive use of digitally-generated images.

In the computer games industry, on the other hand, actors, producers and screenwriters from the film industry were becoming increasingly involved in the development of computer games. Jeffrey Stepakoff, a Hollywood screenwriter who made his name writing feature films and producing television shows, turned his skills to the creation of interactive movie-style games that could be played on a home computer. He believed that the next step in the process would be to create interactive television programmes.

Film studios were also bringing out computer games based on their film properties. Paramount began the concept with Star Trek-based games. The interactive division of Disney released a *Lion King* game for Christmas 1994. Two films released in 1995, *Johnny Mnemonic* and *Caspar*, had on-line games running on the World Wide Web, the multimedia segment of the Internet.

However, the fit between celluloid and silicon was not always a comfortable one. The differing business cultures and expectations of each industry segment sometimes caused communications difficulties. In Silicon Valley, executives had been heard to say that 'Hollywood just doesn't get it.' While film makers had been happy to jump on to the 'interactive bandwagon', they had too often viewed the new technology as a mere adjunct to conventional film making, rather than appreciating that a new medium can be the source of new art forms and types of creativity in its own right. The classical retort from the moguls of Hollywood to such comments had been that 'content is king'. The implication was that technology can fulfil no more exalted purpose than the provision of tools for creative artists.

A further complication to the alliance lay in the geographical location of the two industries. There was a strong rivalry between the north and south of the state of California as to where the new multimedia industry was based. The industry was developing twin nuclei in both Los Angeles and San Francisco – a possible cause for further discord in the future.

One way of 'getting a handle' upon this maze of variables is for the organization to go right back to the building bricks of what it is about, and make sure that it understands its **core competencies** (Chapter One). Some writers, for example, John Kay (Kay, 1993 – see especially Chapter Three), have made a further distinction between competencies and capabilities. A **capability** is a latent competence – i.e., a skill, asset, process or relationship which the organization **could** develop if this would help it to add value.

Kay makes the following observations on capabilities:

'A capability can only be distinctive if it is derived from a characteristic which other firms lack. Yet it is not enough for that characteristic to be distinctive. It is necessary for it also to be **sustainable** (i.e., the firm can keep on maintaining it for a long period of time) and **appropriable** (i.e., the firm can be reasonably certain that it will not be copied by competitors).'

Kay identifies only three types of distinctive capability:

1 **Innovation**. This is difficult to sustain because it invites imitation.
2 **Architecture**. This involves a system of relationships within the firm, or between the firm and its suppliers/customers/competitors, or both.
3 **Reputation**. Kay says that this is easier to maintain than to create, but once created, it meets the essential conditions for sustainability.

Kay says that adding value is the basis of any successful enterprise, but that sustainable value-adding activities can only be achieved by developing a set of relationships which other organizations are unable to make. This is where the concept of architecture comes into its own (see Case 7.2).

CASE 7.2

COMPAQ COMPUTERS

In the period 1991–5, Compaq Computers became the world's largest PC manufacturer. In 1995, annual sales were almost $15bn., and the company enjoyed a reputation for excelling at volume manufacturing and marketing. The company's president and chief executive, Eckhard Pfeiffer, was widely credited with responsibility for its sustained performance after it had seemed to be faltering in the early 1990s. He attributed his success to getting and keeping close to the customer.

In 1995, the PC market was being driven by consumer sales. The consumer market, although still smaller than the commercial market, was growing at about twice the rate of the latter, and was expected to reach the 50–50 ratio by the turn of the century. Eckard Pfeiffer was confident that the PC would be the core element in home entertainment/ information systems in the 21st century, and had no doubt that consumers would continue to spend 'on a highly useful product which is getting more useful with every product cycle'. He predicted that some households would have multiple computers linked together to form home local area networks, using a central PC server and connections to the 'information superhighway'.

Once a company has reached the top of its industry, as Compaq had, the challenge is how to retain this status. The answer, according to Pfeiffer, was both simple and demanding:

'When we analysed what really mattered, we realized that the most important thing is to strive for simple customer satisfaction'. The right product was, of course, important, and this did not mean 'the most stretched, sophisticated product – you just need to have a solid, up-to-date range of products'. Among business customers, loyalty was greater than the customers themselves would usually acknowledge, because large companies who had installed tens of thousands of PCs around the world were looking for consistency, rather than the latest gimmicks.

Compaq had established that customer satisfaction had to be gained and kept in five key areas:

1 **Products**. The PC product line needed to be attractive and not too old. It had to have the features that customers were looking for.
2 **Quality**. Poor quality was bound to jeopardize a business relationship.
3 **Price**. PC prices had to be competitive. By that, Compaq meant, not necessarily cheapest, but in line with the customer's expectations – the customer had to have a feeling that the price was right.
4 **Service**. The service and support provided by the company was very important.
5 **Availability**. It was essential that the product was available when it was required.

Eckard Pfeiffer had set Compaq the new challenge of being the best company at customer satisfaction in 1997. He claimed that achieving this goal would 'not only ensure remaining in the number one position, but probably achieving a significant lead over the nearest competitor'.

In the key consumer market, Compaq believed that its worldwide infrastructure would enable it to take a bigger stake than competitors: the company's ability to customize and localize its products was a key customer requirement, as was the speed it could maintain in responding to developing PC product cyles.

Source: adapted from Taylor, Paul (1995) 'Striving for customer satisfaction (View from the Top)', *Financial Times*, 6 Sept.

How, though, can a robust, effective and uncopiable architecture be put in place? Kay suggests the following:

- The firm may make a new contract or arrangement of contracts – but these are easily replicated. Sustained competitive advantage depends on the ability to protect the innovation – through legal restriction (Chapters Two and Three), or through strategy.
- Customers and/or suppliers may be systematically willing to undertake relationships on terms that they would not make available to others, for example, as a result of reputation. (For instance, airlines enter into strategic alliances with international car hire firms because of their reputation, even though they may charge more and not perform better than smaller, nation-specific car hire companies.)
- Complexity, which depends on a group of contracts. In this scenario, any individual part of the organization can be reproduced, but the complexity of the whole set of relationships defeats imitation. (For

example, Marks and Spencer's enduring 'architecture' of relationships with employees/suppliers/customers.)
- The firm has no distinctive capability, but holds a 'strategic asset'. (For example, a hotel may 'own' a famous waterfall situated in its grounds; a tea manufacturer may own a famous brand name.)

ARCHITECTURE

The concept of 'architecture' is the most sophisticated of these ideas, and the most relevant to adding value in the 1990s. Making it work depends on the acceptance of a number of premises, the most important of which are as follows:

- It is in everyone's interest to do certain things, but in no one's individual interest. A company, a department or an individual can only benefit from a co-operative ethic, or the knowledge and expertise of others, in a working context of reiteration and reciprocation.
- A high but structured degree of informality (but emphatically not disorganization) is necessary to promote the right environment for the necessary creative thinking and development.
- The architecture will be built on a shared expectation of long-term relationships.
- There will be a joint commitment from all parties to the sharing of rewards for collective achievement.

Note. If the structure of relationships that underpins corporate architecture could be formalized, it could also be imitated, and would at that point cease to be a source of competitive advantage.

New Organizational Structures

The philosophy of business re-engineering harmonizes well with the idea of architecture, and, taken to its logical conclusion, facilitates an alternative way of looking at the structure of the organization, which cuts across functional boundaries, and concentrates instead on **core processes** (Chapter Six). For example, an organization may consider it is involved in as few as three core processes – new product development, order fulfilment, and after-sales service – and organize itself accordingly. Some organizations have already taken the radical step of rearranging themselves in this way. Others have kept their traditional 'functional' departments, but overlaid and interlinked them by identifying and working to their core processes.

GROWTH AND THE ORGANIZATION

Although in the 1990s, most organizations are striving to develop more focused, streamlined and targeted strategies, by concentrating on their core competences, cutting out unnecessary layers of management, 're-engineering' how they do things, and outsourcing non-essential activities, it is still the objective of the majority of for-profit organizations to grow, in the sense of increasing market share and shareholder wealth. (Some niche businesses, for example, famous perfume houses, choose to remain small and 'exclusive', whilst, of course, still trying to increase shareholder wealth. Some not-for-profit organizations, which, as we have said, work to budgets, have decided that they are more efficient working in small units, or have had this imposed upon them by some external force – for example, U.K. local authorities in 1996, in the wake of Local Government Reorganization.)

Why has growth consistently been one of the primary business imperatives?

Henry Mintzberg, a famous American business guru (see, for example, Mintzberg, 1983), identifies four goals that 'organizations as systems to themselves' pursue. These are:

1 Growth.
2 Survival.
3 Efficiency.
4 Control of the environment.

The significance and implications of the last three of these goals have formed a large part of the subject matter of this book; the desire for growth by the individual organization is something we now need to consider.

Mintzberg says that businesses want to grow for the following reasons:

- Generally, large organizations are safer than smaller ones: they have more 'slack' to fall back on, and more resources with which to respond to adverse environmental trends. (In view of what we have said about doing more with less, and making the best possible use of resources, we may choose to disagree that this view is valid for the 1990s.)
- Often 'big' means 'powerful' in relation to external stakeholders. Government support is frequently more readily available when there are survival crises in large enterprises, because of the impact of job losses, etc. in terms of the wider environment. Smaller firms are more likely to be left to 'go to the wall'.
- Lower production costs are often achievable through economies of scale and learning curve effects, which are more difficult to realize in small businesses.
- Because growth improves the level of benefits available to the people inside the organization, it becomes a basic system objective of the organization. This especially includes senior management, who, as we have already said, may otherwise choose to work to their own agendas; if these – incorporating such considerations as personal prestige and power – coincide with what is good for the organization, then there is less likelihood of conflict. A growing

organization is likely to be a more fertile place for assimilating the aspirations of its staff at all levels.

Routes to growth

Targeting possible routes to growth is one of the key objectives of corporate strategy. **Organic growth** – where the business grows bigger by doing what it already does, either by increasing its market share, or because it operates in an expanding market, or both – is the slowest way to grow, and difficult in today's climates of static populations in the developed world, market nervousness caused by recession, and mature products. Nevertheless, if the company can afford the luxury of patience, organic growth is often the least risky way of developing a company that is successful in the long term. Many flourishing Japanese organizations have been nurtured in this way. Organic growth enjoys a high success rate, because it is does not involve the fractures in culture, or the leaps into the unknown, which make other types of growth high risk. On the other hand, it may imply a poor return for financial backers over a long period of time, as the company ploughs all its resources into growing. Bankers and shareholders may or may not be prepared to accept this; if they are unsure, then the company may become the subject of a hostile takeover bid. Failure to grow through lack of funds may also mean that the company is overtaken by its competitors. Organic growth therefore works best in relatively stable economic environments, or for cash-rich organizations.

Diversification is the most widely-used route to growth. This usually implies takeover (**acquisition**) of or **merger** with another company. Diversity in organizations is increasing due to two principal related factors:

1 The growth aspirations of organization decision-makers. For example, when asked about his motives for pursuing acquisitions, Lord King of British Airways said: 'It's simple. Like all businesses, we want to grow'. Such a statement takes it for granted that growth is a fundamental modern business goal.
2 The growth aspirations of other environmental players. The growth activities of individual institutions contribute to the macro situation. Richardson explains this as follows:

> 'The nature of the ecosystem [such as innovations within communications systems, new product developments and the global strategies of big corporations] within which modern business operates is now such that, regardless of the organization's own strategic activities, the environment can be expected to bring more, new and wider drawn variables, regularly to the organization'. (Source unknown)

However, the growth imperative is filled with challenges and potential pitfalls, as well as opportunities. **Acquisition** or **joint venture strategies** (where two companies, sometimes competitors, sometimes operating in complementary areas of the value system, unite to work on a big project, or to form a separate business unit) are organizationally more complex than the self-development alternative, and require new and additional operating linkages and relationships within the value system. We have already said that 1990s management philosophy embraces the idea of focus. Therefore, 'scattershot' or undifferentiated marketing approaches towards growth by acquisition are now felt to represent bad strategic decisions. They have been superseded by the 'rifleshot' targeting of newly perceived segments and the design and implementation of differentiated marketing campaigns.

However it is accomplished, growth is always based on innovation – on the ability to design and implement new products, services and processes and to enter new markets. The trick for the organization seeking growth is therefore to

(i) recognize the opportunities that are generated, and,
(ii) match them with its values and resources (or have the courage to reject them if there is not enough 'strategic fit', i.e., **synergy**).

It has become received wisdom that the company which elects not to continually innovate and diversify is in danger of losing ground to other companies whose strategic leaders are more capable and proactive managers of diversity. However, it is too easy to fall into the trap of believing that every 'good idea' represents an opportunity. Michael Porter says:

'To understand how to formulate corporate strategy, it is necessary to specify the conditions under which diversification will truly create shareholder value'. (Porter, 1987)

He offers three essential tests:

1 **The Attractiveness Test**. He says that the industries chosen for diversification must be structurally attractive, or capable of being made attractive.
2 **The Cost of Entry Test**. Porter maintains that the cost of entry must not involve the capitalization of all the future profits.
3 **The Better-Off Test**. This is a 'general well-being' term: either the new unit must gain competitive advantage from its link with the company, or vice versa. (*Core competencies* and *synergy* are again extremely relevant here.)

Many companies in the 1970s and early 1980s failed to apply these tests when diversifying, with the result that the ensuing acquisitions or mergers did not yield the profits hoped for. In those cases where there was a good strategic 'fit', the opportunities it generated were often lost because insufficient attention was paid to accommodating the **culture** of both organizations. Cooper and Cartwright, who made a study of this in 1992, point out that many months are usually devoted to getting the financial aspects of such a deal right, but little time is typically given to addressing the needs of the staff, their insecurities, problems, and diffficulties in adjusting to their new working environment with its new cultural challenges. Thus they are unable to give their undivided and confident attention to building on the opportunities offered by the new organization. Case 7.3 explores the pitfalls of diversification as experienced by the Prudential Insurance Company.

Strategic alliances – i.e., agreements (usually drawn up legally) between two or more organizations to work together on specific projects or in particular markets – have become increasingly popular as a way of spreading cost and risk and managing environmental turbulence in the 1990s. Here, the cultural problems tend to be fewer, because the threat that one organization's culture will 'swallow' the other's does not present itself. (Special projects also tend to be run by 'experts', whose first allegiance is often to the culture of their profession, rather than that of their organization: thus, electronics specialists will find a cultural affinity with other electronics specialists, rather than each with their respective companies. This in itself can, of course, constitute a threat as well as an opportunity to the organization over a period of time.)

Kay is dubious about the value of strategic partnerships; in the long term, he says, one partner is always stronger than the other, and therefore has less to lose by putting less into or even dropping the partnership (Kay, 1993). Porter's earlier writings (Porter, 1985) take a similar view, stating that competitive advantage cannot be gained by such a commitment; however, in his later work (Porter, 1990), he looks more favourably on strategic alliances as a viable way of passing his 'three tests'. The point should be made that in today's world, some projects (e.g., the Channel Tunnel, international telecommunications developments) are so costly that it is impossible for them to proceed except by the mutual co-operation of several organizations.

Strategy and structure

The structure that an organization has adopted as it pursues these alternative strategic options is a crucial determining factor of success or failure. Case 7.3 illustrates how the Prudential Insurance Company's acquisitions strategy foundered at least in part because its corporate structure was 'wrong' for the acquired organizations.

CASE 7.3

DIVERSIFICATION AND THE PRUDENTIAL INSURANCE COMPANY

In 1985, the Prudential Insurance Company, one of the biggest British insurance firms, decided that to diversify into estate agency would release synergistic benefits. It invested £230 million in this exercise, but in 1992 was forced to concede that the whole experiment had gone badly wrong, and that it would have to embark upon an embarrassing and expensive sale. The Prudential would be returning to its core business of insurance: in other words, it was adopting a 'sticking to the knitting' strategy.

What went wrong? Some analysts claimed that the problem lay mainly in timing; since 1990, when the property market 'bubble' exploded, the estate agency business had been very depressed, and was likely to remain so for at least another year. But this was to take a short-term view of what had been intended as a long-term strategic investment. Critics of the Prudential said that it had mishandled the acquisition process, and had in particular tried to over-centralize administration of the various agency networks it had acquired.

More fundamentally, a potential flaw in the Pru's initial strategic logic was pointed to: it may not have made sound strategic sense in the first place to regard estate agency as a promising distribution outlet for insurance and other financial products such as pensions and savings plans. If this analysis was correct, other UK insurers would ultimately learn that they had fallen into the same trap, since this form of diversification for insurance companies was popular in the 1980s.

The logic of the 'synergistic' links and the benefits they would confer was, at best, unproven. From a management discipline point of view, the Prudential also broke one of the basic rules of acquisition.

It is a textbook 'given' that potential acquirers should avoid diversifications that are unrelated to their basic business on more than one of the following dimensions: geography; technology; type of product market; and the sort of head office 'parenting' style that the new business requires (i.e., culture). Experience has proved that unrelatedness on any one of these dimensions is risky, but that to combine two or more is downright dangerous.

This received wisdom notwithstanding, the Prudential's move into estate agency had taken it both into an unrelated type of business and into one which required an unfamiliar type of parenting style: hence its mistake of trying to overcentralize its agencies.

Other service-orientated companies have made similar errors to the Prudential's: for example, Saatchi and Saatchi tried to run its management consultancy acquisitions in the same way as its advertising agencies. This also resulted in failure.

In the manufacturing sector, the track record on parenting is a little better. More companies seem to have learnt (often from the bitter experience of others) that it is important only to take on acquisitions with a parenting style with which they are familiar. However, in other respects, some manufacturers continue to risk unrelatedness in more than one aspect. For example, Northern Telecom's acquisition of STC, the UK telecommunications company, not only took it into Europe for the first time, but also into a new product market (Nortel was basically a switching equipment company, while STC specialized in transmission). It remains to be seen whether this amalgamation will work.

Recession causes otherwise prudent directors of cash rich companies to succumb to the temptation of diversification-through-acquisition at knock-down prices. Remembering the basic rules of acquisition may help them to avoid expensive long-term blunders. But diversification is never easy: and there are many European and US companies who have discovered that the geographical dimension can inject the most risk of all.

Source: adapted from Lorenz, Christopher (1993) 'When diversification is imprudent', *Financial Times*, February.

The degree of planning influence exerted by an organization's central management is the key to the type of corporate governance that is operated within it. This not only influences the strategy that it adopts, but should also be a key consideration before the strategy is formulated. In other words, some organizational structures don't 'work' for some kinds of strategy.

The influence of the centre is a function not only of the **objectives** set, but also of the atmosphere within which the organization's **systems** operate (i.e., its **culture**). Strategy is therefore determined by both 'soft' and 'hard' issues.

Some 20 years ago, the McKinsey Institute identified what it called the '7S framework', which illustrates the links between strategy and structure. Figure 7.1 describes it graphically. Other authors have adapted and modified this framework over the years, but its essential components remain the same. Collectively, they address the many organizational issues which have been raised in this book. The following commentary on them is adapted from Peters, Waterman and Phillips (Peters, Waterman and Phillips, date).

1 **Structure**
   i) The central problem with structure is not how to divide up the tasks; it is one of emphasis and co-ordination: how to make the thing work.
   ii) It is therefore important to develop the ability to focus on those dimensions currently important to the organization's evolution – and be ready to refocus as dimensions shift.
2 **Strategy**
   i) (Quoting Chandler, 1962) Structure follows strategy
      or a strategy of diversity forces a decentralized structure
   ii) Strategy says: 'Here is how we will create unique value'. (See Key Concept 7.2 for a definition of strategy.)
3 **Systems**
   i) Systems demonstrate how the organization really does (or doesn't!) get things done. Therefore, systems is the variable which threatens to dominate all others. (The term does not just mean 'information technology', nor procedures and policies,

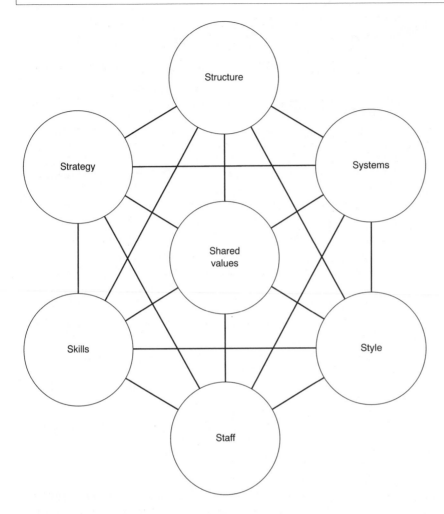

Figure 7.1 The McKinsey 7-S framework

though it includes all these things. It is the muscle and the sinew that allows the structure of the organization to function.)

ii) It is possible to change an organization without disruptive restructuring by changing the systems.

4 **Style**

i) Any organization's problem with style lies not in recognizing it, but in doing something about it.

ii) Organizations may listen to what managers **say**, but they believe what managers **do**. Not words, but patterns of actions are what make decisions, and what people see to be decisive. Therefore, the power of style is that it is essentially manageable.

iii) The skilful management of a manager's inevitably fragmented time is an immensely powerful change lever.

KEY CONCEPT 7.2: WHAT IS STRATEGY?

All students ask for definitions of strategy, but attempts to make them have been notoriously diverse, and sometimes unhelpful. It has therefore been considered more useful to offer the following range of definitions, some from academics, some from key figures in industry, to enable the reader to piece together his or her own idea of what the concept of 'strategy' embraces.

'Strategy is the pattern of objectives, purposes or goals and major policies and plans for achieving these goals stated in such a way as to define what business the company is or is to be in and the kind of company it is or is not to be. A complete statement of strategy will define the product line (in functional, not literal, terms), the markets and market segments for which products are to be designed, the channels through which these markets will be reached, the means by which the operation is to be financed, the profit objective, and the size and kind of organization which is to be the medium of achievement. Strategy can be deduced from behaviour in the absence of conscious planning, for purpose is implied by action. It is easier to work with verifiable statements of purpose'. [*A Concept of Corporate Strategy*, Andrews]

'After the two great expansions of 1908 to 1910 and 1918 to 1920 – perhaps one should say because of them – General Motors was in need not only of a concept of management, but equally of a concept of the automobile business. Every enterprise needs a concept of its industry. There is a logical way of doing business in accordance with the facts and circumstances of an industry, if you can figure it out. If there are different concepts among the enterprises involved, these concepts are likely to express competitive forces in their most vigorous and decisive form'. [*My Years with General Motors*, Sloan]

'Strategy can be defined as the determination of the basic long-term goals and objectives of an enterprise, and the adoption of courses of action and the allocation of resources necessary for carrying out these goals'. [*Strategy and Structure*, Chandler]

'A strategy is a unified, comprehensive and integrated plan that relates the strategic advantages of the firm to the challenges of the environment and that is designed to ensure that the basic objectives of the enterprise are achieved through proper execution by the organization'. [*Business Policy and Strategic Management*, Jauch and Glueck]

'But the important decisions, the decisions that really matter, are strategic. They involve either finding out what the situation is, or changing it, either finding out what the resources are or what they should be. These are the specifically managerial decisions'. [*The Practice of Management*, Drucker]

'Strategic decisions are primarily concerned with external rather than internal problems of the firm and specifically with selection of the product mix which the firm will produce and the markets to which it will sell. To use an engineering term, the strategic problem is concerned with establishing an 'impedance match' between the firm and its environment or, in more usual terms, it is the problem of deciding what business the firm is in and what kinds of businesses it will seek to enter. Specific questions addressed in the strategic problem are: what are the firm's objectives and goals; should the firm seek to diversify, in what areas, how vigorously; and how should the firm develop and exploit its product market position'. [*Corporate Strategy*, Ansoff]

'Most of our beliefs about complex organizations follow from one or the other of two distinct strategies. The closed-system strategy seeks certainty by incorporating only those variables positively associated with goal achievement and subjecting them to a monolithic control network. The open-system strategy shifts attention from goal achievement to survival, and incorporates uncertainty by recognizing organizational interdependence with environment. We suggest that technologies and environments are major sources of uncertainty for organizations, and that differences in those dimensions will result in differences in organization'. [*Organisations in Action*, Thompson]

'Perhaps there are ways of improving the logic of business strategy, or policy making. But the big work behind business judgment is in finding and acknowledging the facts and circumstances concerning the technology, the market and the like in their continuously changing forms. The rapidity of modern technological change makes the search for facts a permanently necessary feature of the industry'. [Sloan]

'That activity which specifies for a business a course of action that is designed to achieve desired long-term objectives in the light of all major external and internal factors, present and future'. [General Electric Company]

iv) Symbolic behaviour is important – for example, having people on the board who understand the business, or are emotionally or professionally committed to its key competence.

5 **Staff (i.e., people)**
   i) Staffing considerations include both the 'hard' end of staff management – appraisal, pay and training – and the 'soft' attributes – attitude motivation and behaviour.
   ii) In recent times, it has been considered more effective to broaden and redefine the nature of the staffing issue, so that the job becomes not only a way of life, with the company as an 'extended family'; but also, the person views his or her career as a continuum, in which he or she is continually building up skills to serve either this company or another in a lifetime career plan.
   iii) Superbly performing companies therefore take immense care over managing the 'socialization' process.
   iv) It would be a mistake either to fall into the trap of saying, 'Get the structure right and the people will fit', or, 'The right people can make any organization work'; but it is vital to recognize that the staff are the organization's most significant variable.

6 **Skills**
   i) These characterize a company's crucial attributes as no other concept can.
   ii) The dominating capability needs to be kept in focus as the company addresses new markets (strtaegy shift) or 'decentralizes to give managers autonomy' (structure shift).
   iii) Perhaps the most difficult problem for those trying to make the organization work effectively is how to tackle the weeding out of old skills – and their supporting systems, structures, etc. – to ensure that important new skills can take root and grow.

7 **Superordinate goals (Culture) (Chapter One)**
   i) These are values and statements which go beyond conventional formal statements and corporate objectives; they are broad notions of the future direction the top management team wants to infuse throughout the organization.
   ii) They resemble the basic postulates in a mathematical system, in that they are the starting-points on which the system is logically built, but are not in themselves derived from logic.
   iii) They are not present in an articulated or jointly understood form in all or even most organizations; but there is a heightened awareness of them amongst all superior performers, because, if they are well-articulated, they make meanings for people within the organization.

At its most powerful, the '7S Framework' forces business leaders to concentrate on interactions and fit (i.e., synergies) within their organization and within their industry. At its most basic level, it still provides what Peters, Waterman and Phillips call 'a deeper bag in which to collect our experiences' (Peters, Waterman and Phillips, 1992) – i.e., an informed and thorough approach towards examining the strategy of the organization.

Henry Mintzberg has written subtly and at length on the complexity and importance of organizational structure (Mintzberg, 1983). He points out that long-range strategic planning systems or organizational development programmes are good for some organizations, but not for others. Therefore, there is no 'one best way' approach. The 'all depends' approach of contingency theory is necessary. The organization's structure should reflect its situation – its age, size, type of production system and the complexity and dynamism of its environment. (As we discussed at length in the preceding chapters, at the end of the 20th century, the environment of almost all organizations is likely to be turbulent, if not volatile.)

Mintzberg (1983) therefore says that more formalized planning is needed by:

- large organizations
- those in stable environments (some organizations, e.g., monopolies, could be said still to enjoy relative stability)
- those in mass production.

On the other hand, he says that greater decentralization is needed by:

- organizations in complex environments (i.e., those that, in today's world, constitute the vast majority)
- those diversified in many markets (i.e., the multinational or 'global' giants that, in today's world, wield the most economic 'clout' internationally.

Box 7.1 explains the fundamentals of Mintzberg's analysis of structure and its relevance to strategy in greater detail.

Box 7.1: Mintzberg's definition of organizational structure

1 **Parts**

Mintzberg identifies six key parts to an organization:

i) **Operating core**: where the basic work of producing the organization's products and services gets done.

ii) **Strategic apex**: the home of top management.

iii) **Middle line.**

iv) **Technostructure**: staff analysts who design systems by which work processes and outputs of others in the organization are formally designed and controlled.

v) **Support staff**: everyone who contributes to the organization outside its operating workflow.

vi) **Ideology**: a 'halo of beliefs and traditions'.

2 **Mechanisms**

He says that six mechanisms are needed to make the organization work:

i) **Mutual adjustment**: achieves co-ordination of work by the simple process of informal communication.

ii) **Direct supervision**: one person co-ordinates by giving orders to others. Also achievable by standardization.

iii) **Standardization of work processes**: specification, of content of work directly.

iv) **Standardization of skills**: worker rather than work or outputs is standardized.

v) **Standardization of norms**: workers share a common set of beliefs, and can achieve co-ordination based on them.

3 **The essential parameters of design**

Mintzberg identifies four basic groups:

i) Design of **individual positions** in the organization.

ii) Design of **'superstructure'** or skeleton of the organization.

iii) Design of **lateral linkages** to flesh out the superstructure. These include planning and control systems and liaison devices.

iv) Design of the **decision-making system**.

4 **Basic configurations**

Mintzberg says that there are six basic configurations that organizational structure can take:

i) **Simple structure**. The organization consists of one large unit, with one or a few managers. Little of the behaviour is formalized, and the absence of standardization means that the organization is organic; it has few middle managers, minimal support staff'and is 'lean' and flexible. It is usually young, and may eventually change its style of configuration. Only very clever leaders can keep control of a simple organization while it grows large – although sometimes, in crisis conditions, large organizations revert to simple structures to allow forceful leaders to try to save them. e.g., any new business set up principally by one leader.

ii) **Machine bureaucracy**. This organizational type is the offspring of the Industrial Revolution. The jobs are highly specialized and standardized, with an elaborate administration. There is a large technostructure to design and maintain the systems of standardization, which therefore gains informal power. A large hierarchy of middle line managers emerges to control the highly specialized work of the operating core, but usually structured on a functional basis all the way up to the top. To enable managers to maintain centralized control, both the environment and the production system of a machine bureaucracy must be fairly simple, and the type fits most naturally with mass production. e.g., a car plant.

iii) **Professional bureaucracy**. Relies on standardization of skills rather than work processes or outputs for its co-ordination; concept of 'professional' dominates: therefore, the organization surrenders a good deal of its power not only to the professionals themselves, but also to the institutions which train them. Therefore, power flows all the way down the hierarchy; there is little need for a technostructure because training takes place outside the organization. Because professionals work independently, the size of the operating units can be very large, typically also with a large support staff. Suitable for an organization operating in a stable yet complex environment, such as an advertising agency or a legal practice.

iv) **Divisionalized form**. This is not so much an integrated organization as a set of independent entities – a conglomerate – coupled together by a loose administrative structure. It differs from other configurations in one central respect: it is not a complete structure, but a partial one superimposed on others. The main reason for divisionalization is diversification of products; HQ uses some direct supervision, but relies most on performance control systems, i.e., standardization of outputs. There is a small central support staff. e.g. one of the giant food corporations or entertainment industries

v) **Adhocracy**. This configuration is for organizations that need to innovate in very complex ways: aerospace, petrochemicals, film-making. They require 'project structures' which can fuse experts from different specialities into smoothly functioning teams. It is an organic structure that relies for co-ordination on mutual adjustment among its highly trained and specialist experts. Typically, experts are grouped in functional units for housekeeping purposes, but deployed in small market-based project teams to do their work. Power is delegated to these teams; therefore, all distinctions of conventional structure disappear. Adhocracies are found in complex, dynamic environments.

vi) **Missionary**. The organization is dominated by the pull to 'evangelize': members are encouraged to pull together, therefore, it tends to be a loose division of labour, with little job specialization. It is held together by the 'standardization of norms' – the sharing of values and beliefs among its members. It makes minimal use of planning and control systems, and has virtually no technostructure. Beyond a certain size, it tends to divide itself into smaller units – 'enclaves' – with perhaps a nominal HQ which serves as a loose strategic apex to act as the depository of the official manifestations of the ideology. The environment is typically stable; an example is a kibbutz.

Obviously, some organizations are hybrids of the six basic types which Mintzberg identifies, but his work is valuable in aiding managers to clarify the nature of their organization, and whether it achieves 'environmental fit'. The central conundrum at the heart of the debate on strategy and structure generated by Mintzberg is which comes first, the structure or the strategy? Mintzberg ultimately says it does not matter, as long as organizations are aware of the possibilities and limitations that their structures offer. To quote him: 'Organizations can select their situations in accordance with their structural designs just as much as they can select their designs in accordance with their situations'.

Study of Mintzberg's work is indispensable to students interested in strategy. Students are referred to the 'References and further reading' section at the end of this chapter.

Innovation and mastering change

The ability to innovate in a creative, intelligent and resource-conscious way in order to reinvent the organization continually so that it can match its activities relevantly and competitively to the needs of its environment is the key to handling the complexity presented by all the environmental variables and strategic options discussed in this chapter, and in this book.

Successful **innovation** can mean revolutionary change, or simply imply the incremental approach of building small change upon small change regularly over a period of time. It can address itself to **what** the organization does (i.e., its core activities, the *raison d'être* of its bid to add value) or to **how** it carries them out (i.e., the processes, procedures and structure that make it operate).

Whatever the decision arrived at by the strategic leader and his/her managers and employees concerning what types of change have taken place in the environment and how they should be addressed, two factors remain constant in a world of perpetual challenge and uncertainty:

1 That environmental change and the corresponding need for organizational change is taking place all the time. Therefore, the organization can never afford to 'rest on its laurels', or lull itself into the false belief that its activities are not affected by time.

2 That corporate change must be mutually decided by, communicated to, and 'bought into' by all the members of the organization. They must understand why the change is needed, and feel a positive belief (preferably by having contributed to the change process) that they and all their colleagues are addressing it in the right way.

An organization in which the members are divided against themselves, and therefore wasting valuable energy on activities that make no contribution towards the adding of value, is unlikely to be able to survive in the long term. Every aspect of the environment and of the organizations we have considered in this book is ultimately governed by the truism that **people are the key to success**. It is easily overlooked, and even more frequently the subject of a lip-service that fails to consider the issues raised. It is hoped that this book will go some way towards helping managers of the present and the future to be aware of such issues, as well as how to evaluate the myriad of threats and opportunities with which they will be bombarded in the business environment.

Case 7.4 (Ettrick Trout Farms) is a full-length case study, of the type which appears in the *Lecturer's Resource Manual*, the companion to this book, which illustrates how some of the important challenges presented by adding value in the business environment have been successfully dealt with by one company.

CASE 7.4

THE ETTRICK TROUT COMPANY

Willy Baxter is a successful entrepreneur. Now in his 50s, he is a multi-millionaire. He has made his money by pursuing his first schoolboy love, which was fishing, and becoming a pioneer developer of salmon farming. In the process, he has achieved national and international stature. However, there is much more to it than this: his story is the story of a man who watched the markets, saw the opportunities, was imaginative enough to see how they could be exploited, and had the courage to do it. In addition to all these things, he is, not so much a workaholic, as someone whose personal and professional lives are interlinked so that they form one continuum.

The early days

Willy Baxter was born into a hard-working Dumfriesshire family in 1942. A bright child, he attended the local academy, and originally intended to go to university to study oil prospecting – an enterprising and promising choice in post-war Scotland. However, as he entered his teens, he became 'hooked' on fishing, and would play truant from school in order to indulge this passion. He still has vivid memories of catching his first fish in an old treacle tin.

By the time he was 15, school had ceased to interest him, and he was not making much headway academically. He therefore decided to leave as soon as possible, working on the farm, and then operating a digger for an earth-moving company. He spent a total of 11 years in this employment.

In 1966, the earth-moving company was asked to build a fish-farm (for trout) at New Galloway. Trout were still netted in the sea at this period, using the ancient practice of trapping them in haaf-nets. A Danish expert came to advise the company on how to set about the task. The Dane was 24 years old, the same age as Willy was at the time, and they got on well together. He did not forget the information that he had gleaned about fish-farming.

In 1971, when he was 29, he decided that it was time that he set up in business on his own. He had not been paid well by the earth-moving company, but he gained an inestimable benefit from having worked for it: its excellent reputation. As a well-known former employee, he was able to take this with him to his own enterprise. He bought two earth-moving machines for £1,500, £1,000 of which he had to borrow from the bank. Within four months, he had paid back his loan. Times were difficult, however, and he realized that it was extremely hard to make good money in the industry. Whatever money he did make was ploughed straight back into the company; better equipment was purchased whenever possible, so that his reputation for reliability and excellence continued to increase.

The first trout farm

In 1973, Willy Baxter bought some land near the village of Ae (about six miles from Dumfries) and built his own trout farm there. This was to be the first of nine fish-farming enterprises. He did not abandon the earth-moving business, however, because by now he was a recognized constructor of fish farms, and by building them for other people, he was able to command a steady income to finance his own trout-farming venture during the first crucial years of its development.

In 1978, he had the opportunity to buy an old woollen mill at Selkirk. He was attracted to this property because it had a good water supply – essential for trout farming – and he immediately set about changing it into his second trout farm. In the years since he had established the farm at Ae, his reputation as a fish-farm builder had grown, and he had also been commissioned to do work abroad. (One of the projects was in the Somme region of France, on the site of a famous First World War battlefield, and during his excavations he recovered 28 unexploded shells.)

Meanwhile, in the financial year 1973/4, he started selling farmed trout. There was a strong market for trout at that period, and demand exceeded supply. After the austere and commonplace foods which formed the staple of British meals during the 1950s and 1960s, people had begun to look for more appetizing and unusual products. They could also afford to buy more 'luxury' food items than had been the case in the past.

Early in his fish-farming career, Mr. Baxter decided that he would deal direct with wholesalers, rather than build up a complex customer base of individual retailers and restaurants. By the time his first farm was half-complete, he had received an offer from one wholesaler to buy all he could produce. Trout, perceived as a 'luxury' food, was rapidly becoming a very fashionable food item.

By 1979, the supply of trout was climbing rapidly to meet the demand, which had reached a peak and then evened out. Competition within the industry was increasing fast. The inevitable happened: the price which the Ettrick Trout Company could command for its product went down. Prices were not uniformly low, however. There was a greater scarcity of 'good' trout in the winter-producing months of January, February, March and April, and therefore the best prices could be negotiated during this period. In 1979, trout fetched 40p per lb from May to December, but up to 70p per lb from January to April. Willy Baxter observed carefully the trout that he was 'growing' at Selkirk, and realized that, although they continued to thrive, they just stopped growing in the winter. The water was so cold that it neutralized their capacity to gain in size or weight.

Experiments with temperature

Tests and experiments suggested that 10 degrees Fahrenheit provided a reasonable 'growing' temperature for the fish. Clearly, this was not going to be achievable by continuing to operate only in the South-West of Scotland. He found the ideal site that he was looking for near Southampton, in the South of England. The land which he acquired was in a chalk basin, which provided sufficient insulation to be able to maintain a constant water temperature of 10 degrees, and thus ensure a reasonable growth rate. He decided that, in order to focus his efforts on this new farm, it would be necessary for him to live in the south, and moved to Hampshire in 1981. Some time after moving, he acquired another site at Fordingbridge, on the River Avon, 20 miles away from the Southampton site, and built his fourth farm there.

Production for the English trout farms was targeted specifically to concentrate on the months of January, February, March and April. During these months, Ettrick Trout Farms was responsible for as much as 70 per cent of the U.K. trout supply. Willy Baxter travelled to South Utah and California, both in the United States, to buy off-season eggs.

Trout farms are not labour-intensive; each of the Ettrick trout farms employs between three and six staff. In 1996, when there were nine farms altogether, only two of them had on-site managers. The whole enterprise was still very much held together by Willy Baxter himself, who had a keen understanding, because of his own expertise, of what kind of staff and managers he was looking for.

Fish farming: an industry in its infancy

In the 30 years or so which followed the Second World War, farmers knew little of markets and the forces of supply and demand. They simply grew things. They knew that they would always be able to sell what they grew. In the 1950s and 1960s, the U.K. imported two-thirds of its total food supply; therefore, there was no need for agriculture to be market-led, because imported food was always more expensive than home-produced food.

Willy Baxter's genius as an entrepreneur consisted of recognizing at exactly the right time that this situation would not continue indefinitely, and he did what was necessary to organize his farming activities in anticipation of a more discerning public and hence more market-led industry. One consequence of this was bound to be a demand for 'luxury' fish which could not be supplied by solely catching them 'in the wild'. He was not interested, however, in cashing in on a good idea on a short-term basis. He sought to provide excellent quality, and to set up close long-term relationships with his key buyers. He used the fact that he could satisfy their demand for the relatively scarce winter produce to ensure their loyalty during the springtime and summer, when there was a glut of produce on the market, and the price dropped. Therefore, he did not stick out for the highest possible price he could get in the winter, but went for a fair and stable price with which both he and his customers were satisfied. He established a fast, reliable transport network of lorries to deliver the trout anywhere in the country. Mostly, the lorries travelled by night, and belonged to carriers that he had tried and could trust – though he did some driving himself.

He rapidly realized that supermarkets stocked and restocked in a matter of days, not weeks. Most of his produce went to supermarkets, each group or chain having stringent quality control measures for every batch of fish, which he set himself the target of beating, and always of meeting. These measures included filling in check-sheets for when each batch was treated with antibiotics or chemicals, and when the drugs were withdrawn. Carrefour, the French supermarket group, operated the most stringent checks of all. In the UK, Marks and Spencer maintained very high standards, only falling slightly behind Carrefour because they could not obtain sufficient volume of produce if they raised their specification any further, and Sainsbury's came a close second.

One feature of his trading relationship with the big supermarket chains and wholesalers is that there is rarely a written agreement. Actual contracts are virtually non-existent in the industry. There may occasionally be a verbal contract for three months' supply of fish, but even this is unusual. This is partly because of the quality control aspect, and partly because of the price fluctuations, a fact of life in the fish industry. The bottom may fall out of the market overnight if, for example, the Norwegian fish farmers decide to flood the marketplace with surplus produce (though Norwegian trout appeals more to Germans than English or French customers, because it has a higher fat content).

The move into salmon farming

In 1987, salmon was overtaking trout as a 'fashionable' fish. Willy Baxter thought that it would be a good time to extend the range of his business into salmon farming, applying the same principles of aiming for high quality and reliable service, and growing out of season, that had proved successful with trout farming.

He knew that there was an underground supply of water at Treegles, near Dumfries, where his grandmother had lived. He checked the temperature of this spring, and found that it maintained a constant heat of ten degrees centigrade summer and winter. The water was coming from quite deep within the earth, and therefore was not affected by ambient temperatures. (When springs flow from shallow sources, their temperature fluctuates from six degrees to 10/12 degrees centigrade, something he had discovered by observing the conditions at trout farms and hatcheries in southern England and Perthshire.)

Mr. Baxter drilled at Treegles, and found more water. His discovery convinced him that he would be able to start a hatchery, and grow salmon out of season in this place. Salmon farming is more complex than trout farming, because the salmon, described by Willy Baxter as a 'mysterious creature', needs to migrate to the sea. The smaltings, or strong, healthy young salmon, have as part of their development to adapt to salt water.

Salmon lay eggs in November, December and January. They hatch, and when the river warms up they spend a short period in April and May feeding. The following April or May, the best growers will undergo a physiological change from par to smalt. Their skin takes on a silvery hue. They travel down the river to the sea, from which most swim to Greenland to the feeding grounds there.

In order to ensure a continuous supply of salmon and less risk of gluts, therefore, what Willy Baxter had to try to do was to persuade them to transfer to the sea at any month of the year, and not just in April or May. He thought that this could be achieved by growing them inside buildings, so that they became accustomed to 'false' seasons. The technique he developed was called 'photoperiod'. Again, the philosophy behind it was that of responding to the market. He developed whole year production successfully, which meant that his theory that the key to it was to overcome temperature and water supply problems was correct. Unfortunately, he failed to patent 'photoperiod', and the technique is now used by a number of other salmon farmers, both nationally and internationally.

The business expands again

As had always been his policy, Mr. Baxter ploughed most of the money he made from his latest venture back into the company. His fifth site was a saltwater salmon farm at Ullapool, in the Western Isles. Then he developed a second hatchery at Dumfries, which became his sixth site, and he acquired an ailing company in Shetland as Number Seven, and turned it round. A further development at Orkney was his eighth venture, and two or three sites which together constituted 'Sea Farms' the ninth, and, in 1996, latest enterprise. The parent company of all these different firms was the Ettrick Trout Company; all of the others were run as subsidiaries. Of the 8,000 shares, Willy Baxter owns 7,999, with just one share being held by someone else, to comply with legal requirements.

The question of succession

Willy Baxter has not given much thought to the question of his successor as the Chief Executive of Ettrick Trout Farms. He almost shies away from the idea of anybody taking over from him. He says that, because it is such a specialized business, it is impossible for anyone to run it unless they love it. Therefore, he might have to be succeeded by some kind of directorial team incorporating Sales, Marketing and Farming. At present, he has three other directors, respectively in charge of Sales, Finance, and Operations. His daughter, who is 27, works for the company, and has been very successful in sales, particularly in tele-sales, but although he praises her for being excellent at what she does, he wouldn't be prepared to hand over to her, because she doesn't understand the farming aspects.

He has himself built up an impressive international reputation as an expert. He has been used as a consultant for existing and prospective fish farmers in America, Greece and Monaco, and has turned down consultancy work in Chile (for practical reasons).

Competition

Competition in the salmon industry takes two main forms: the threat presented to the individual company by other companies operating in the same market, and the threat presented to the industry by the rivalry between salmon and other products in the protein/ luxury food market. Early in 1996, Willy Baxter saw beef as the main threat to his industry, though at the time of writing (Summer 1996), the BSE ('mad cow disease') scare about beef has probably given the salmon industry a huge boost. Salmon is not without its own health scares, however, particularly as some unscrupulous salmon farmers have farmed it so intensively in recent years that their product is not grown in hygienic conditions, and the fish become subject to bacterial disease. The bad reputation that such farmers draw upon themselves is then to some degree reflected throughout the industry.

Major direct competitors of the Ettrick Trout Company include the Booker McConnell food group, and Norsk Hidro, the biggest Norwegian salmon farming company. The latter's main export customers are France and Germany, where consumers do not discriminate against the higher fat content in the Norwegian product. However, periodically, when they have a glut of fish, the Norwegian companies collectively set out to flood the British market with their fish by lowering prices dramatically. In 1995, for example, the Norwegians succeeded in increasing their exports to the UK from 180 tonnes to 280 tonnes by pursuing this strategy. The result for British companies is not only fewer sales, but fewer sales at a lower price.

Other threats and problems

Environmental hazards also pose a threat to the salmon industry generally. Salmon need to be reared in clean, clear water. Willy Baxter's salmon farm on Shetland was polluted by oil from the *Braer* tanker disaster in 1991, and in 1996 he still had not succeeded in negotiating a satisfactory compensation settlement for the damage done and loss of earnings. The government and the *Braer*'s own insurers had made some reparations, but he was still fighting for an outstanding claim of £2.5 million plus interest. One problem was that it was hard to prove the extent of his losses, since his own calculations were based on the rapid expansion achieved in the previous ten years. The *Braer* losses certainly impeded considerably his plans for expansion in the five-year period following the disaster.

Other problems to be tackled by the farmed fish industry include gaining the maximum possible efficiency from the fish feeds. The industry is unusual in that the labour costs are far outweighed by the feeding costs. Willy Baxter achieves a £10 million turnover by operating with just 36 staff: that means that he pays £200 labour per tonne of salmon at 1996 rates. By contrast, feeding costs vary between £750 and £780 per tonne. Despite this, however, salmon is relatively cost efficient when compared with other forms of first-grade farmed protein. Ettrick Farms is able to achieve a one for one conversion rate – i.e., one tonne of feed will produce one tonne of salmon. Chickens are twice as expensive to rear, achieving on average a two for one conversion rate, while beef is even more costly at four for one conversion. The salmon industry also has the advantage that its product is still perceived as a luxury, and can therefore command a premium price. Basically, says Willy Baxter, what he is doing is taking what for humans is an unpalateable but nutritious source of protein, and converting it into an equally nutritious but highly palateable product with social cachet.

Quality

The quality of the fish food itself is extremely important. The type used by Ettrick Farms is of Danish origin, and consists of a food mixture originally developed for trout farmers. It is made at Grangemouth, in Scotland. In 1996, Ettrick Farms was working closely with the feed company to attempt to raise the Omega 3 (unsaturated fat) level in its salmon. Some fish feeds have cheap oil introduced into them, which raises the saturated fat levels in salmon. Willy Baxter believes that if the quality of the feed could be improved, even if it cost £100 per tonne more, there would be a more than corresponding benefit in the marketplace, since it would increase the consistency of the quality of salmon produced, and simultaneously give the company competitive advantage (other companies being unlikely to take on the higher feed costs).

Looking to the future

Ever an innovator, and someone who has throughout his life maintained a keen interest in scientific and technological progress, Willy Baxter is now also investigating the possibilities of genetic engineering as a means of producing the 'ideal' salmon in the most cost-efficient way. He is thinking, as well, of other types of sought-after fish which might respond well to the fish-farming techniques which he has perfected with trout and salmon. If he can farm successfully some of the deep-sea fish which have become 'overfished' in the oceans in recent years, he will be both maintaining the position of Ettrick Trout Farms as an industry leader, and practising the sustainable exploitation of natural resources which environmentalists now consider to be essential if the planet is to survive. He believes that halibut might be a suitable fish for such a project.

The causes of success

When asked why Ettrick Trout Farms has been so successful, Willy Baxter immediately identifies the following factors:
- Right from the outset, he recognized his market and what it wanted, and produced for that market.
- He recognized how and when the market was changing. While maintaining strong relationships with the 'old' network of wholesalers in Billingsgate, Manchester, Birmingham, Nottingham and Glasgow, plus other, smaller, places, he developed new relationships with the buyers of the big supermarket chains, both at home and abroad.
- When he branched into salmon farming, he aimed to keep the production costs very low right from the start.
- He was the first to recognize that investing in 'out of season' production would pay dividends.

Now, he says, it is his major objective to establish a brand name for Ettrick Trout Farms, so that members of the public are familiar with his products and identify them with quality.

To recapitulate very briefly:

- Organizations are about **adding value** at a price which the customer is prepared to pay, and which will provide sufficient income to sustain the organization in the future.
- Added value is created by the **people** of the organization; they achieve it through being close to customers.
- Added value is created by the commitment of the people of the organization to **quality** and **service**.
- The members of the organization are empowered and encouraged by their internal structure, systems, processes and procedures to monitor the external environment effectively, and to deal quickly with the **opportunities** and **threats** that it presents.
- **Managing the business environment** is about adapting added value continually to the needs of the future by means of successful **innovation**.

SUMMARY

Now that you have read this chapter, you are able to do the following:

- Realize the importance of developing a successful strategy (i.e., one that adds value for the customer at a price which he or she is willing to pay, sufficient to take the organization into the future) for every organization.
- Appreciate the roles of, and interrelationships between, the traditional functions of the organization, and how they can be developed or modified by new approaches to strategy.
- Understand the key strategic options available to the organization.
- Recognize the importance of People as they relate to the organization – as customers, as employees, as suppliers – and understand that innovation, which is the lifeblood of all organizations, is always generated by People.

You have now prepared yourself to study a specific course in Strategic Management. Good luck!

REFERENCES AND FURTHER READING

Chandler, A.D. (1962) *Strategy and Structure: Chapters in the History of the American Industrial Enterprise*, MIT Press, Massachusetts.

Kanter, R. (1992) *The Change Masters*, International Thomson Business Press, London.

Kay, J. (1993) *Foundations of Corporate Success*, Oxford.

Mintzberg, H. (1983) *Power in and around organisations*, Prentice Hall, London.

Porter, M.E. (1980) *Competitive Strategy: Techniques for Analysing Industries and Competitors*, Free Press.

Porter, M.E. (1985) *Competitive Advantage: Creating and Sustaining Superior Performance*, Free Press.

Porter, M.E. (1987) 'The state of strategic thinking', *The Economist*.

Daellenbach, H.G. (1994) *Systems and Decision Making: A Management Science Approach*, J. Wiley, Chichester.

Deresky, H. (1994) *International Management: Managing Across Borders and Cultures*, HarperCollins, New York.

Hendry, J. and Johnson, G. (eds.) (1993) *Strategic Thinking: Leadership and the Management of Change*, J. Wiley, Chichester.

Harrison, M. (1993) *Operations Management Strategy*, Pitman, London.

Johnson, G. and Scholes, K. (1993) *Exploring Corporate Strategy* (3rd Edn.), Prentice Hall, London.

Ohmae, K. (1982) *The Mind of the Strategist*, McGraw Hill, New York.

Thompson, J.L. (1994) *Strategic Management: Awareness and Change* (2nd edn.), Chapman & Hall, London.

Students should also familiarize themselves with a good strategic marketing text. There are so many available, it is difficult to single one out as particularly appropriate. However, any of the several works by Philip Kotler is both accessible in approach and 'classic' in content.

Index